Mastering QlikView Data Visualization

Take your QlikView skills to the next level and master the art of creating visual data analysis for real business needs

Karl Pover

BIRMINGHAM - MUMBAI

Mastering QlikView Data Visualization

First published: April 2016

Production reference: 1200416

Published by Packt Publishing Ltd.
Livery Place
35 Livery Street
Birmingham B3 2PB, UK.

ISBN 978-1-78217-325-0

www.packtpub.com

Credits

Author
Karl Pover

Reviewers
Ralf Becher

Miguel Ángel García

Michael Tarallo

Commissioning Editor
Kartikey Pandey

Acquisition Editor
Tushar Gupta

Content Development Editor
Rohit Singh

Technical Editor
Siddhesh Patil

Copy Editor
Priyanka Ravi

Project Coordinator
Izzat Contractor

Proofreader
Safis Editing

Indexer
Monica Ajmera Mehta

Graphics
Kirk D'Penha

Disha Haria

Production Coordinator
Conidon Miranda

Cover Work
Conidon Miranda

About the Author

Karl Pover is the owner and principal consultant of Evolution Consulting, which provides QlikView consulting services throughout Mexico. Since 2006, he has been dedicated to providing QlikView presales, implementation, and training for more than 50 customers. He is the author of *Learning QlikView Data Visualization*, and he has also been a Qlik Luminary since 2014. You can follow Karl on Twitter (`@karlpover`) or on LinkedIn (`https://mx.linkedin.com/in/karlpover`). He also blogs at `http://poverconsulting.com/`.

First and foremost, I would like to thank my wife, Pamela. I owe you several long weekends.

Thanks to the team at Evolution Consulting, especially Julian Villafuerte, Carlos Reyes, and Jaime Aguilar, for taking on more responsibility. A special thanks to Julian for taking the time to review the final version of this book, and Alejandro Morales for helping me develop a few extensions.

As always, thanks to my parents, Judy and Bill, for their love and support throughout my life.

I am grateful to all the technical reviewers, and especially Ralf Becher, who contributed material to this book. I also appreciate the work done by Rohit Kumar Singh and the rest of the Packt team, who gave me a little extra time to make this a great book.

Last, but not least, thanks to all the customers, past and present, who have always asked for the impossible.

About the Reviewers

Ralf Becher has worked as an IT system architect and as an IT consultant since 1989 in the areas of banking, insurance, logistics, automotive, and retail. He founded TIQ Solutions in 2004 with partners. Based in Leipzig, his company specializes in modern, quality-assured data management. Since 2004, his company has been helping its customers process, evaluate, and maintain the quality of company data, helping them introduce, implement, and improve complex solutions in the fields of data architecture, data integration, data migration, master data management, metadata management, data warehousing, and business intelligence.

Ralf is an internationally-recognized Qlik expert with a strong position in the Qlik community. He started working with QlikView in 2006, and he has contributed to QlikView and Qlik Sense extensions. He has also contributed add-on solutions for data quality and data integration, especially for connectivity in the Java and Big Data realm. He runs his blog at `http://irregular.bi/`.

Miguel Ángel García is a business intelligence consultant and QlikView solutions architect. Having worked through many successful QlikView implementations from inception to implementation and performed across a wide variety of roles on each project, his experience and skills range from presales to application development and design, technical architecture, and system administration, as well as functional analysis and overall project execution.

Miguel is the coauthor of the book *QlikView 11 for Developers*, published in November 2012, and its corresponding translation to Spanish, *QlikView 11 para Desarrolladores*, published in December 2013. He has also participated as a technical reviewer in several other QlikView books.

Miguel runs a QlikView consultancy, AfterSync (`http://aftersync.com/`), through which he helps customers discover the power of the Qlik platform. He currently has the QlikView Designer, QlikView Developer, and QlikView System Administrator certifications, issued by Qlik, for versions 9, 10, and 11.

Michael Tarallo is a senior product marketing manager at Qlik. He has more than 17 years of experience in the Data Integration and Business Intelligence space from both open source and proprietary BI companies. Currently at Qlik, he is responsible for a broad spectrum of Marketing and Sales enablement activities for QlikView and Qlik Sense. He is best known for working with the Qlik Community and providing its members with valuable information to get them started with Qlik Sense, which includes the creation of high-quality video content. He has produced numerous videos ranging from promotional to instructional. Prior to Qlik, Mike worked for UPS, Information Builders, Pentaho, and Expressor. His career has spanned from data analysis, customer support, and account management to a solution architect and leader, crafting customer solutions, and painting visions of the "art of the possible" with the companies' software. He humbly admits that he is "a confident jack of all trades but a master of many."

www.PacktPub.com

eBooks, discount offers, and more

Did you know that Packt offers eBook versions of every book published, with PDF and ePub files available? You can upgrade to the eBook version at www.PacktPub.com and as a print book customer, you are entitled to a discount on the eBook copy. Get in touch with us at customercare@packtpub.com for more details.

At www.PacktPub.com, you can also read a collection of free technical articles, sign up for a range of free newsletters and receive exclusive discounts and offers on Packt books and eBooks.

https://www2.packtpub.com/books/subscription/packtlib

Do you need instant solutions to your IT questions? PacktLib is Packt's online digital book library. Here, you can search, access, and read Packt's entire library of books.

Why subscribe?

- Fully searchable across every book published by Packt
- Copy and paste, print, and bookmark content
- On demand and accessible via a web browser

Instant updates on new Packt books

Get notified! Find out when new books are published by following @PacktEnterprise on Twitter or the *Packt Enterprise* Facebook page.

Table of Contents

Preface   **vii**

Chapter 1: Data Visualization Strategy   **1**

    Data exploration, visualization, and discovery   2

    Data teams and roles   **4**

    Data research and development   5

    Data governance team   8

    Agile development   **10**

    User story   11

    Minimum Viable Product   11

    QlikView Deployment Framework   **14**

    Exercise 1   15

    Summary   **15**

Chapter 2: Sales Perspective   **17**

    Sales perspective data model   **18**

    Exercise 2.1   19

    Data quality issues   22

      Missing dimension values   22

      Missing fact values   24

    Data formatting and standardization   26

    Case   26

    Unwanted characters   27

    Dates and time   27

    Master calendar   28

    Customer stratification.   **30**

    Pareto analysis   30

    Exercise 2.2   31

    Exercise 2.3   34

Customer churn	**36**
Exercise 2.4	38
Exercise 2.5	41
QlikView extensions and the cycle plot	**42**
Exercise 2.6	43
Governance – design template	**44**
Summary	**46**
Chapter 3: Financial Perspective	**47**
Financial perspective data model	**48**
Exercise 3.1	48
Financial report metadata	51
AsOfCalendar	**53**
Income statement	**54**
Exercise 3.2	56
Custom format cell	61
Exercise 3.3	65
Balance sheet	**66**
Exercise 3.4	67
Exercise 3.5	69
Cash flow statement	**70**
Exercise 3.6	71
Summary	**73**
Chapter 4: Marketing Perspective	**75**
Marketing data model	**76**
Customer profiling	**79**
Parallel coordinates	79
Exercise 4.1	80
Exercise 4.2	83
Sankey	84
Exercise 4.3	85
Exercise 4.4	86
Market size analysis	86
Exercise 4.5	88
Exercise 4.6	89
Exercise 4.7	91
Social media analysis	92
Sales opportunity analysis	97
Exercise 4.11	98
Summary	**99**

Chapter 5: Working Capital Perspective   **101**

Working capital data model   **102**
Rotation and average days   **106**
Days Sales of Inventory   106
Exercise 5.1   107
Days Sales Outstanding   108
Exercise 5.2   108
Days Payable Outstanding   109
Exercise 5.3   110
Exercise 5.4   111
Working capital breakdown   **111**
Exercise 5.5   112
Inventory stock levels   114
Exercise 5.6   116
Aging report   117
Exercise 5.7   118
Customer stratification   **119**
Stratification by distribution   120
Exercise 5.8   120
Exercise 5.9   122
Visualizing stratification   125
Exercise 5.10   126
Summary   **129**

Chapter 6: Operations Perspective   **131**

Operations data model   **131**
Handling multiple date fields   135
On-Time and In-Full   **136**
Exercise 6.1   137
OTIF breakdown   139
Exercise 6.2   139
Exercise 6.3   140
Predicting lead time   142
Exercise 6.4   143
Exercise 6.5   144
Supplier and On-Time delivery correlation   148
Exercise 6.5   149
Planning in QlikView with KliqPlan   **151**
Planning tool extensions   151
Sales forecasts and purchase planning   152
Other applications   154
Summary   **154**

Chapter 7: Human Resources — 155

Human resources data model — **156**
  Slowing changing dimensions attributes — 158
Personnel productivity — **160**
  Exercise 7.1 — 160
  Exercise 7.2 — 162
Personnel productivity breakdown — **163**
  Age distribution — 164
    Exercise 7.3 — 164
  Salary distribution — 167
    Exercise 7.4 — 167
  Employee retention rate — 170
    Exercise 7.5 — 171
  Employee vacation and sick days — 172
    Exercise 7.6 — 172
  Employee training and performance — 174
    Exercise 7.7 — 175
Personal behavior analysis — **176**
  Exercise 7.8 — 178
Summary — **179**

Chapter 8: Fact Sheets — 181

Customer fact sheet consolidated data model — **182**
Customer Fact sheet Agile design — **186**
  Creating user stories — 187
  User story flow — 188
  Converting user stories into visualizations — 189
  Going beyond the first visualization — 191
Customer Fact sheet advanced components — **192**
  Bullet graph — 192
    Exercise 8.1 — 193
    Exercise 8.2 — 195
  Sparklines — 196
    Exercise 8.3 — 196
Customizing the QlikView User Experience — **198**
  Quick access to supplementary information — 198
    Exercise 8.4 — 199
  Dynamic data visualization — 200
    Exercise 8.5 — 201

Regional settings	205
Currency	205
Language	205
Date and number formats	206
Customer Fact sheet n QlikView	206
Summary	**207**
Chapter 9: Balanced Scorecard	**209**
The Balanced Scorecard method	**210**
The financial perspective	212
The customer perspective	212
The internal business process perspective	213
The learning and growth perspective	214
The Balanced Scorecard consolidated data model	**214**
The Balanced Scorecard information dashboard design	**218**
The Gestalt principles of perceptual organization	218
Proximity	219
Enclosure	220
Closure	221
Connection	222
Continuity	223
Similarity	224
Creating the filter pane bubble	**225**
Exercise 9.1	226
Creating an interactive tutorial	228
Exercise 9.2	228
Measuring success with XmR charts	**231**
Exercise 9.3	233
Summary	**238**
Chapter 10: Troubleshooting Analysis	**239**
Troubleshooting preparation and resources	**239**
Positive mindset	240
General debugging skills	240
Reproduce	240
Diagnose	241
Fix	242
Reflect	242
Resources	242
QlikView Help	242
Local knowledge base	243
Qlik Community	243
Qlik Support	244

Reporting issues   **245**

Common QlikView application issues   **247**

Common QlikView data model issues   247

All expression values are exactly the same   248

The expression total is not equal to the sum of the rows   249

Duplicate values in a list box   250

Data doesn't match user expectation   252

Common QlikView expression issues   255

The expression does not calculate every row   255

The amounts in the table are not accumulating   256

Summary   **258**

Chapter 11: Mastering Qlik Sense Data Visualization   **259**

Qlik Sense and QlikView developers   **259**

Visualization extension examples for cross-selling   **261**

Plan to master Qlik Sense data visualization   **266**

Summary   **268**

Index   **269**

Preface

This may be a horrible way to start a book, but in all honesty my first real-world QlikView experience was a failure. I was assigned to do a proof-of-concept with a prospective client's IT department, and they insisted that I share every mouse click and keystroke on a large projection screen with them. I had taken a QlikView designer and developer course and was developing a QlikView template in my spare time, but this hadn't prepared me for the live development of a real application.

I fumbled around the screen as I developed their first data model and charts. They must have doubted my competence, and I was embarrassed. However, I was surprised to hear that they were impressed with how little time it had taken me to convert raw data to interactive data visualization and analysis. I had created the required indicators and finished their first application within three days.

The goal of the proof-of-concept was to demonstrate the value that QlikView could provide to the prospective client's company, and it all seemed to have gone well. After all, I had created an attractive, functional QlikView application that was filled with the indicators that the IT department had requested. However, I failed to demonstrate QlikView's value directly to the business users; in the end, the prospective client never purchased QlikView.

All was not lost because I ultimately learned that, although it is important to understand all of QlikView's technical features, we can't display its value by only memorizing the reference manual. If we really want to master QlikView, we have to go beyond the technical functionality and learn what business value QlikView enables us to deliver. Moreover, we must bring about a data discovery initiative that changes a company's culture.

This first experience occurred ten years ago and these first failures have given way to success. I am lucky to have the opportunity to work as a QlikView consultant and participate in projects that encompass multiple organizations and various functional areas. All of their difficult challenges and excellent ideas have helped me to constantly learn from our mutual successes and failures.

During the last ten years that I've implemented QlikView projects, I've found that many businesses share much of the same advanced data analysis goals. For example, most sales departments in every company dream about having an easy way to visualize and predict customer churn. We will go over these common, but complicated, business requirements that you can apply to your own company.

As a QlikView master, you have to be just as comfortable discussing the most appropriate performance indicator with a business user, as you are with scripting out a data model that calculates it. For this reason, at one end, we will explain the business reasons for a particular visualization or analysis and, at the other end, we will explain the data model that is necessary to create it.

We will then develop different types of data visualization and analysis that look to push the boundaries of what is possible in QlikView. We will not focus on QlikView syntax or function definitions. Instead, we will see how to apply advanced functions and set analysis to real business problems. Our focus on the business problem will also lead us to look beyond QlikView and see what other tools we can integrate with it.

Practice leads to mastery, so I've included sample data models and exercises throughout this book. If they apply to your business, I recommend that you copy and paste these exercises over your own data to see what feedback you get from your business users. This extra step of adjusting the exercise's code to make it work with a different dataset will confirm your understanding of the concept and cement it in your memory.

Ultimately, I hope that, by sharing my experience, I will help you succeed where I first failed. In doing so, when you finally fail, it will be because you are attempting to do something beyond what I have done. Then, when you finally overcome your failure and succeed, I can learn from you, the master.

What this book covers

Chapter 1, Data Visualization Strategy, begins our journey to create a data-driven organization using QlikView.

Chapter 2, Sales Perspective, explains the data model's importance to data visualization, and shows us how to create advanced analyses, such as customer stratification, churn prediction, and seasonal trends.

Chapter 3, Financial Perspective, illustrates the usage of metadata to format an income statement, a balance sheet, and a cash flow statement.

Chapter 4, Marketing Perspective, walks us through various types of visualization that reveal customer profiles, potential markets, social media sentiment, and the sales pipeline.

Chapter 5, Working Capital Perspective, describes how to analyze days sales of inventory, days sales outstanding, and days payable outstanding, at both a high and a detailed level. It also explains how they are important in order to determine customer stratification.

Chapter 6, Operations Perspective, shows us how to analyze our service levels, predict supplier lead times, and investigate whether on-time deliveries depend on the supplier.

Chapter 7, Human Resources, reveals how to visualize personnel productivity and personal behavior analysis.

Chapter 8, Fact Sheets, demonstrates an ad hoc design method to create a customer fact sheet that includes bullet graphs, sparklines, and a customized UX.

Chapter 9, Balanced Scorecard, details a more formal design method to build an information dashboard containing balanced scorecard metrics.

Chapter 10, Troubleshooting Analysis, takes a look at resources and methods to debug problems in our QlikView applications.

Chapter 11, Mastering Qlik Sense Data Visualization, explains what Qlik Sense means to a QlikView developer and proposes a plan to master Qlik Sense data visualization.

What you need for this book

To complete the exercises in this book, you will need to download and install QlikView Desktop from Qlik (http://www.qlik.com) and the exercise files from the Packt website (https://www.packtpub.com/).

Who this book is for

This book is for those who have some QlikView experience and want to take their skills to the next level. If you are just beginning with QlikView, please read *QlikView 11 for Developers*, by *Miguel Garcia and Barry Harmsen*, before reading this book.

Conventions

In this book, you will find a number of text styles that distinguish between different kinds of information. Here are some examples of these styles and an explanation of their meaning.

Code words in text, database table names, folder names, filenames, file extensions, pathnames, dummy URLs, user input, and Twitter handles are shown as follows: "We can include other contexts through the use of the `include` directive."

A block of code is set as follows:

```
[Customer Purchase Frequency Tmp]:
Load distinct _KEY_Date as [Customer Purchase Date],
     _KEY_Customer
Resident Facts
Where _ActualFlag = 1
  and [Net Sales LC] > 0;
```

Any command-line input or output is written as follows:

```
C:\Qlik\SourceData\99.Shared_Folders\9.Misc\3.Images\ Bubble_UpperLeft_
Arrow.png
```

New terms and **important words** are shown in bold. Words that you see on the screen, for example, in menus or dialog boxes, appear in the text like this: "In the last step, select the option to **Set as default theme** for this document."

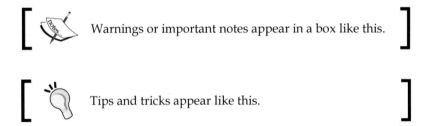

Warnings or important notes appear in a box like this.

Tips and tricks appear like this.

Reader feedback

Feedback from our readers is always welcome. Let us know what you think about this book—what you liked or disliked. Reader feedback is important for us as it helps us develop titles that you will really get the most out of.

To send us general feedback, simply e-mail `feedback@packtpub.com`, and mention the book's title in the subject of your message.

If there is a topic that you have expertise in and you are interested in either writing or contributing to a book, see our author guide at www.packtpub.com/authors.

Customer support

Now that you are the proud owner of a Packt book, we have a number of things to help you to get the most from your purchase.

Downloading the example code

You can download the example code files for this book from your account at http://www.packtpub.com. If you purchased this book elsewhere, you can visit http://www.packtpub.com/support and register to have the files e-mailed directly to you.

You can download the code files by following these steps:

1. Log in or register to our website using your e-mail address and password.
2. Hover the mouse pointer on the **SUPPORT** tab at the top.
3. Click on **Code Downloads & Errata**.
4. Enter the name of the book in the **Search** box.
5. Select the book for which you're looking to download the code files.
6. Choose from the drop-down menu where you purchased this book from.
7. Click on **Code Download**.

You can also download the code files by clicking on the Code Files button on the book's webpage at the Packt Publishing website. This page can be accessed by entering the book's name in the Search box. Please note that you need to be logged in to your Packt account.

Once the file is downloaded, please make sure that you unzip or extract the folder using the latest version of:

* WinRAR / 7-Zip for Windows
* Zipeg / iZip / UnRarX for Mac
* 7-Zip / PeaZip for Linux

Downloading the color images of this book

We also provide you with a PDF file that has color images of the screenshots/ diagrams used in this book. The color images will help you better understand the changes in the output. You can download this file from `https://www.packtpub. com/sites/default/files/downloads/MasteringQlikviewDataVisualization_ ColorImages.pdf`.

Errata

Although we have taken every care to ensure the accuracy of our content, mistakes do happen. If you find a mistake in one of our books—maybe a mistake in the text or the code—we would be grateful if you could report this to us. By doing so, you can save other readers from frustration and help us improve subsequent versions of this book. If you find any errata, please report them by visiting `http://www.packtpub. com/submit-errata`, selecting your book, clicking on the **Errata Submission Form** link, and entering the details of your errata. Once your errata are verified, your submission will be accepted and the errata will be uploaded to our website or added to any list of existing errata under the Errata section of that title.

To view the previously submitted errata, go to `https://www.packtpub.com/books/ content/support` and enter the name of the book in the search field. The required information will appear under the **Errata** section.

Piracy

Piracy of copyrighted material on the Internet is an ongoing problem across all media. At Packt, we take the protection of our copyright and licenses very seriously. If you come across any illegal copies of our works in any form on the Internet, please provide us with the location address or website name immediately so that we can pursue a remedy.

Please contact us at `copyright@packtpub.com` with a link to the suspected pirated material.

We appreciate your help in protecting our authors and our ability to bring you valuable content.

Questions

If you have a problem with any aspect of this book, you can contact us at `questions@packtpub.com`, and we will do our best to address the problem.

1
Data Visualization Strategy

What is the difference between graphic design and data visualization? What distinguishes our actions when we design a website from when we design an executive dashboard? What separates somebody who creates a meaningful icon from another who creates an insightful bar chart?

While both graphic design and data visualization aim to create effective visual communication, data visualization is principally concerned with data analysis. Even though we, who design dashboards and charts, are motivated to create something aesthetically pleasing, we are more passionate about what the data can tell us about our world. This desire to explore our universe via data, and then, communicate our discoveries is the reason that we dedicate our time to learning how best to visualize it.

In this is book, our mission is to create a data-driven business. We start our journey by defining a series of strategies to create and share knowledge using data visualization. In parallel, we propose how we can effectively organize ourselves, our projects, and the applications we develop so that our whole business starts to use insightful visual analysis as quickly as possible. Also, as we survey the entire perspective of our data visualization strategy, we review how we are going to implement it using, arguably, the best data exploration and discovery tool — QlikView.

Let's take a look at the following topics in this chapter:

- Data exploration, visualization, and discovery
- Data teams and roles
- Agile development
- QlikView Deployment Framework

Data exploration, visualization, and discovery

Data visualization is not something that is done at the end of a long, costly **Business Intelligence (BI)** project. It is not the cute dashboard that we create to justify the investment in a new data warehouse and several **Online Analytical Processing (OLAP)** cubes. Data visualization is an integral part of a data exploration process that begins on the first day that we start extracting raw data.

The importance and effectiveness of using data visualization when we are exploring data is highlighted using Anscombe's quartet. Each of the following scatterplots analyzes the correlation between two variables. Correlation can also be explained numerically by means of *R-squared*. If we were to summarize the correlations of each of the following scatterplots using R-squared, we would discover that the number is be the same for each scatterplot, *.816*. It is only by visualizing the data in a two-dimensional space do we notice how different each correlation behaves:

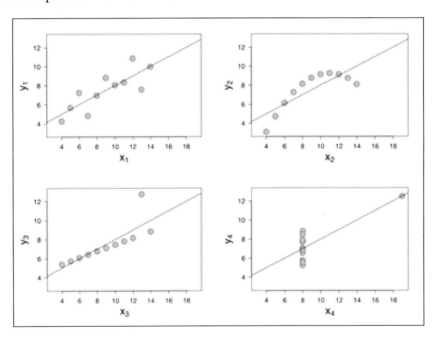

Some tools make it cumbersome to visualize data as soon as it is extracted. Most traditional BI solutions have separate tools for each phase of their implementation process. They have one tool that extracts data, another that creates the OLAP cubes, and yet another that constructs visualizations.

QlikView is a tool that allows us to extract, transform, model, and visualize data within the same tool. Since we can visualize data from the moment it is extracted and throughout the rest of the **extraction, transformation, and load (ETL)** process, we are more likely to discover data anomalies at an earlier stage in the development process. We can also share our discoveries more quickly with business users, and they in turn can give us important feedback before we invest too much time developing analytical applications that don't provide them with real value. Although QlikView is considered a BI software, it stands out amongst its peers due to its extraordinary ability to explore, visualize, and discover data.

In contrast, the implementation of a traditional BI tool first focuses on organizing data into data warehouses and cubes that are based on business requirements created at the beginning of the project. Once we organize the data and distribute the first reports defined by the business requirements, we start, for the first time, to explore the data using data visualization. However, the first time business users see their new reports, the most important discovery that they make is that we've spent a great amount of time and resources developing something that doesn't fulfill their real requirements.

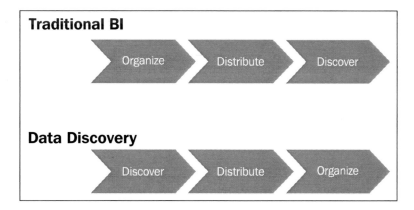

We can blame the business user or the business requirements process for this failure, but nobody can exactly know what they need if they have nothing tangible to start from. In a data discovery tool like QlikView, we can easily create prototypes, or what we later explain as **Minimally Viable Products (MVPs)**, to allow business users to visualize the data within a matter of days. They use the MVP to better describe their needs, discover data inadequacies, and among other things, confirm the business value of the analysis with their executive sponsors. Only after making and sharing these first discoveries do we invest more of our resources into organizing an iteratively more mature data analysis and visualization.

Data Visualization Strategy 1: Use data visualization as an integral part of data exploration and discovery from the very beginning, and all throughout our project.

We've established a general data visualization strategy to support our data exploration and discovery. Now, let's review the strategies that we assign to the teams who are tasked with not only exploring the data directly, but also making sure everyone else in the business can perform their own data exploration.

I often come across customers who have data quality issues. They often battle with whether to hold off investing in QlikView until they've cleaned the data or invest in QlikView regardless of the poor data quality. Those who implement QlikView over poor-quality data data quality and make the problem transparent tend to clean their data more quickly and more effectively.

Data teams and roles

The exact composition of the teams whose principal job is to enable their coworkers to make data-driven decisions will vary as a business's entire data strategy matures. However, many misinterpret what it means to run a mature data-driven business. They believe that at some point all data will and should be governed, and that the team that develops the first QlikView data exploration and discovery projects with will be that governing body.

While a mature data-driven business does count with a large set of governed data and a talented data governance team, it should never be without new, unknown datasets, or without ideas about how to exploit existing datasets in new ways. It is also unrealistic that the same team enforce conformity at the same time that they must strive to innovate. It is for that reason that every mature data-driven business should have both a data research and development (R&D) team, and a data governance team. Each team will have a different data visualization strategy.

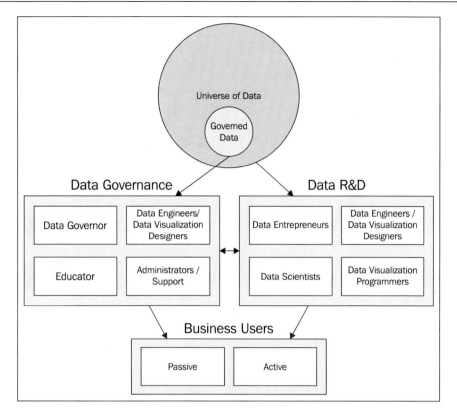

Data research and development

The data R&D team is constantly investigating and creating new solutions to our business problems. When we implement our first data exploration and discovery projects using QlikView, it is common to find out that we are part of a cross-functional, investigative, and proactive team. This team can be the keystone of a more formal data R&D team.

At a minimum, the team should consist of data engineers, data visualization designers, and data entrepreneurs. Data scientists and data visualization programmers may be optional in the beginning, but they become important elements to add as we continue to revolutionize how our business uses data.

It is worth repeating that even though this team will start the data exploration and discovery process, it will not evolve into the data governance team. Instead, this team will continue to look for ever more innovative ways to create business value from data. Once the team develops a stable solution with a long life expectancy, they will migrate that solution and transfer their knowledge to the data governance team.

Our data R&D teams will range in size and capacity, but in general, we aim to cover the following roles within a team that uses QlikView as its primary data exploration tool.

 The list of roles is not all-inclusive, and our business may have particular necessities or other tools for which we need to add other roles.

- **Data entrepreneurs**: We look to fill this role with a business analyst who has knowledge of the company, the available datasets, and the business user requirements. We also look for our data entrepreneur to be an early adopter and a cornucopia of ideas to solve the most important problems. They work with all the other team members to develop solutions as the product owner.

- **Data engineers/data visualization designers**: Although this role can be split between two people, QlikView has revolutionized this role. We can now realistically expect that the same person who extracts, transforms, and models data, can also formulate metrics and design insightful data visualization with the data entrepreneur's guidance.

- **Data visualization programmers**: Although this profile is likely not necessary in the beginning, we will eventually need somebody proficient in web development technologies who can create custom data visualizations. For example, we would need this role to create charts that are not native to QlikView like the following cycle plot chart we use for our sales perspective in *Chapter 2, Sales Perspective*. This role can also be outsourced depending on its importance.

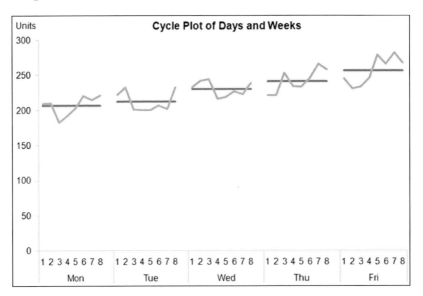

- **Data scientists**: Data science is an ambiguous term. Like many of us who work with data, data scientists are ultimately concerned with extracting knowledge from data. However, they are more focused on using statistics, data mining, and predictive analysis to do so. If they aren't part of the team from the beginning, we should add them later to ensure that the data R&D team continues to innovate.

As far as data visualization is concerned, every member of the data R&D team uses it to make sense of the data and communicate their discoveries with their peers. As such, they should be given space to experiment with advanced data visualization techniques, even when those techniques may appear obscure, or even esoteric. For example, the following scatterplot matrix may not be suitable for most business users, but may help a data scientist create a predictive model:

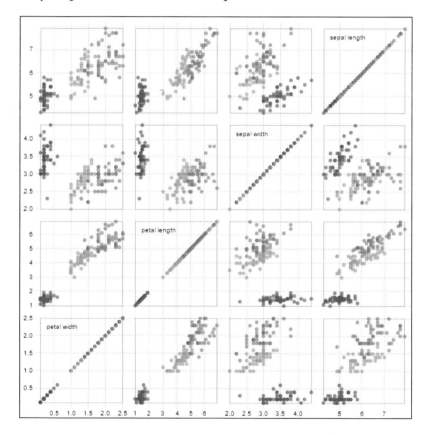

 Data Visualization Strategy 2: Encourage the data R&D team to experiment with new data visualization techniques.

When the data R&D team creates a stable, long-term analytical solution that is going to be used by business users to make their own discoveries, then they should migrate that solution to the data governance team. At this point, both teams should work together to make the data visualization as clear and simple as possible for the business user. While we may be able to train them to use some new data visualization techniques, we will also have to translate other advanced data visualizations into the more commonly used sort.

Data governance team

Data governance is a fundamental part of enabling our entire business to be data driven. The data that is used across the whole company to support common business activities, such as employee performance reviews, financial investments, and new product launches, should be held to a set of standards that ensures its trustworthiness. Among the standards that the data governance team defines and enforces are business rules, data accuracy, data security, and data definitions. The data governance team's job is no less challenging than that of the data R&D team, not the least being because they are the face of the data for most of the business users.

Data governance has a responsibility to make sure data is visualized in a way that is accessible to all business users. Data visualizations should use proper colors, adequate labeling, and approved metrics. The data governance team is also responsible for helping the business users understand data visualization standards, and support those who are going to actively use data to create their own analyses.

Just like our data R&D team, the exact size and makeup of the data governance team will vary. The following list contains the roles that we wish to fill in a team that uses QlikView as its primary data exploration tool:

- **Data governor**: We look for somebody with a similar background as the data entrepreneur in the data R&D team to fill this role. However, the data governor's responsibility is to ensure data quality, uniform business rules, security, and accessible data visualization. They can also be referred to as data stewards. Similar to data entrepreneurs, they help the other team members prioritize pending tasks.

- **Data engineer/data visualization designer**: We create this role to receive solutions from the R&D team and bring them up to the data governance's standards. In addition, they develop QlikView applications for internal control. Even though they don't belong to the R&D team, we expect them to develop innovative ways to visualize the data so that they can enforce the company's data standards more effectively. For example, the following process control chart is an example of the visual analysis that would help them detect data anomalies:

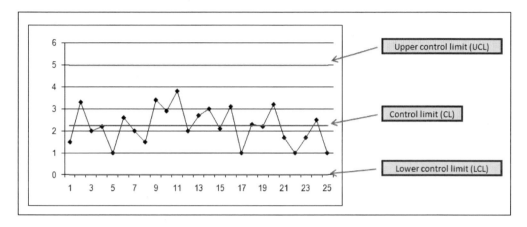

- **Administrator/Support**: This role helps us reduce the distractions our data engineers and data visualization designers face when dealing with daily administration and support issues. Since common QlikView support issues include users unable to access their applications and automatic reload failures, we can often assign the same person to both administrator and support.

- **Educator**: This role performs the never-ending and pivotal job of making business users feel comfortable using the analytical solutions that we develop. Along with teaching business users to use QlikView, they also review the application's content. It is important to note that understanding data visualization is not innate. Therefore, our educators have the responsibility to teach business users how to interpret both simple and advanced data visualizations.

The data governance team may experiment with some data visualization techniques to best analyze , for example, data accuracy or QlikView Server log data. However, for the most part, the data governance team is responsible for establishing and enforcing data visualization standards that create trustworthiness, increase accessibility, facilitate maintenance, reduce training time, and promote clear enterprise communication.

[**Data Visualization Strategy 3:** Enable the data governance team to establish and enforce data visualization standards. **]**

Each team has a separate set of tasks and priorities. However, all data teams should take advantage of agile project management. The data governance team should be especially careful not to confuse data governance with the creation of bureaucratic project management methods. Otherwise, any competitive advantage gained by using QlikView for fast, flexible data exploration and discovery will be wasted.

Agile development

QlikView is software that is best implemented using agile project management methods. This is especially true when we work closely with the business user to deliver data visualization and analysis that provide real value.

The exact agile project management method that we use is not important. The most popular methods are Scrum, *Lean*, and **Extreme Programming (XP)**. We can find plenty of books and other material that help us decide which method best fits our situation. However, we do take time in this book to review the overall principles that define agile project management:

> "*Manifesto for Agile Software Development*
>
> *We are uncovering better ways of developing software by doing it and helping others do it. Through this work we have come to value:*
>
> *Individuals and interactions over processes and tools*
>
> *Working software over comprehensive documentation*
>
> *Customer collaboration over contract negotiation*
>
> *Responding to change over following a plan*
>
> *That is, while there is value in the items on the right, we value the items on the left more.*
>
> *Kent Beck, Mike Beedle, Arie van Bennekum, Alistair Cockburn, Ward Cunningham, Martin Fowler, James Grenning, Jim Highsmith, Andrew Hunt, Ron Jeffries, Jon Kern, Brian Marick, Robert C. Martin, Steve Mellor, Ken Schwaber, Jeff Sutherland, Dave Thomas*
>
> *© 2001, the above authors, this declaration may be freely copied in any form, but only in its entirety through this notice.*"

We take the liberty to mix a few key words from the different agile methods throughout the rest of the book. The following is a list of the most important terms that we will use, and the context in which we will use them. We also reference the specific method that uses the term.

User story

In each chapter we will describe a series of business user requirements using user stories. A *user story* is common to all agile methods, and describes the business user requirements from the user's perspective in their own words. The following is an example user story from the sales department:

> *"As a salesperson, I would like know who my most important customers are so that I can focus my attention on them."*

An *epic* is a collection of multiple user stories with a common theme.

User stories have a way of helping us look through the eyes of the business users as we develop the best ways to visualize data. This user empathy is important when we create a Minimum Viable Product.

Minimum Viable Product

Henry Ford famously said, "If I had asked people what they wanted they would have said faster horses." If we always ask the business users what they want, they are likely to say prettier Excel tables. We often have to depend on our data entrepreneur, or ourselves as data visualization designers, to develop new ways of analyzing data in QlikView. Then, we have to sell the idea to the business user. In these cases, we are new product developers more than we are software developers.

In his book *Lean Startup,* Eric Ries explains how startups use agile methods for new product development. He recommends building a Minimum Viable Product (MVP), measuring how a customer uses the MVP, and then learning how to improve it.

A QlikView prototype might, for example, only show that it is possible to create a bar chart. A QlikView MVP is a working application that may have only a bar chart, but it displays pertinent information to the user. We can then learn from the user's interaction with the MVP and listen to his or her feedback. We go through the following iterative process each time we decide whether or not to build additional functionality into the MVP. We usually continue this loop pictured here until the value we can add to the MVP is less than the cost to develop it:

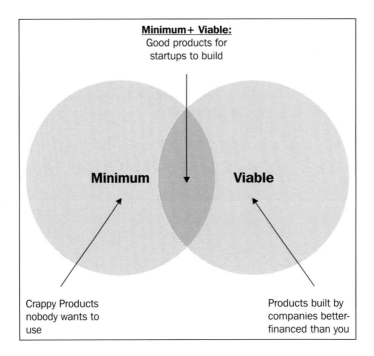

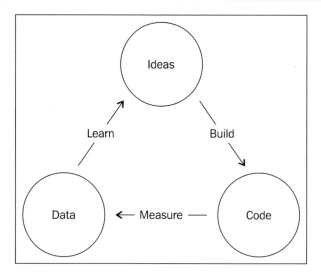

 Even if we have already developed a QlikView application for a department, we should continue to use the MVPs to introduce new functionality.

Whether we realize it or not, we may already follow a process similar to the one in the previous diagram when we develop data visualization and analysis in QlikView. As we begin to master QlikView, we should continue to follow the same iteration, or use a more well-established agile method like Scrum. However, we should avoid using waterfall project management methodologies that don't take advantage of QlikView's flexibility.

In each chapter, we will teach you to create several different visualizations that you can use to create a QlikView MVP using your own business data. Then, you can listen to your business users' feedback and learn how to incrementally improve it based on your business's unique necessities. In this way, we will help you avoid the trap of replicating Excel, or whatever other tool you had previously used, in QlikView.

Data Visualization Strategy 4: Collaborate closely with the business user using agile project management methods.

Data Visualization Strategy 5: Propose our own solutions to business problems using new technologies like QlikView, and avoid only reproducing legacy reporting methods.

Along with collaborating closely with the business users and their needs, we also have to be concerned with the overall technical architecture of our solution. Our first technical architecture requirement is to establish a common framework that will make developing QlikView throughout our whole business easier.

QlikView Deployment Framework

The **QlikView Deployment Framework (QDF)** allows us to easily reuse resources and separate tasks between different teams and people. A common folder structure, data, color schemes, and expressions are among the resources that we can share between the data governance team, the R&D team, and active business users.

The QDF is built using a resource container architecture. In the same way that a shipping container on board a ship or stacked in a port can easily be moved from one place to another, QDF containers are independent capsules that can easily be moved and stored in different computers and servers.

When we install QDF, we assign it to a folder where we are going to store these containers. How we define a container depends on how we want to organize the QlikView applications in our business. A container may be a project, it may be a department, or it may define a phase in the **Extraction, Transform, and Load** (ETL) process.

The QDF has two special containers: `0.Administration` and `99.Shared_Folders`. The `0.Administration` container keeps track of the containers that are in the QDF folder. It also contains templates that we can use to create our own containers and a few QlikView applications that monitor QlikView usage and governance. The `99.Shared_Folders` container stores all the resources that we want all containers to share.

We can find out more information about the latest version of the QDF in the QDF group in the Qlik Community (`http://community.qlik.com/groups/qlikview-deployment-framework`). Magnus Berg and Michael Tarallo have created an excellent repository of written documentation and step-by-step videos to help us implement the QDF in our business.

We will need to install QDF on our computers before we can perform the advanced analysis exercises in *Chapter 2, Sales Perspective*.

Exercise 1

In order to install the QlikView Deployment Framework, we carry out the following steps:

1. Go to the QlikView Deployment Framework group in Qlik Community (`http://community.qlik.com/groups/qlikview-deployment-framework`).

2. Follow the instructions on the group's home page to install the latest version of QDF and learn more about how to use QDF.

Summary

Our mission is to create a data-driven business, and data visualization plays a key role in accomplishing can perform the advanced analysis exercises. The data visualization strategies that we defined in this chapter are the following:

Data Visualization Strategy 1: Use data visualization as an integral part of data exploration and discovery from the very beginning and all throughout our project.

Data Visualization Strategy 2: Encourage the data R&D team to experiment with new data visualization techniques.

Data Visualization Strategy 3: Enable the data governance team to establish and enforce data visualization standards.

Data Visualization Strategy 4: Collaborate closely with the business user using agile project management methods.

Data Visualization Strategy 5: Propose our own solutions to business problems using new technologies like QlikView and avoid only reproducing legacy reporting methods.

Now, let's begin to apply these strategies and create advanced data analysis in our sales department's QlikView application.

2
Sales Perspective

The success of all businesses is at some point determined by how well they can sell their products and/or services. The large amount of time and money that companies spend on software that facilitates the sales process is testament to its importance. **Enterprise Resource Planning (ERP)**, **Customer Relationship Management (CRM)**, and **Point of Sales (PoS)** software not only ease the sales process, but also gather a large amount of sales-related data. Therefore, it is not uncommon that a company's first QlikView application is designed to explore and discover sales data.

Before we begin to create data visualization and analysis for our sales perspective, let's review the data model that supports it. In the process, we will resolve data quality issues that can either distract users' attention away from a visualization's data or distort how they interpret it. Next, we'll introduce two common sales department user stories and build solutions to stratify customers and analyze customer churn. Finally, let's take our first look at QlikView extensions and overall application design.

In this chapter, let's review the following topics:

- The data model for the sales perspective
- Common data quality issues
- Customer stratification and churn analysis
- QlikView extensions and the cycle plot chart
- QlikView design templates

Let's get started and review the data model that we will use to create our sales perspective in QlikView.

Sales perspective data model

Our company sells gadgets to customers throughout the United States and our sales perspective data model is based on data from an ERP system. The following figure shows the data model that we are going to work with throughout this chapter:

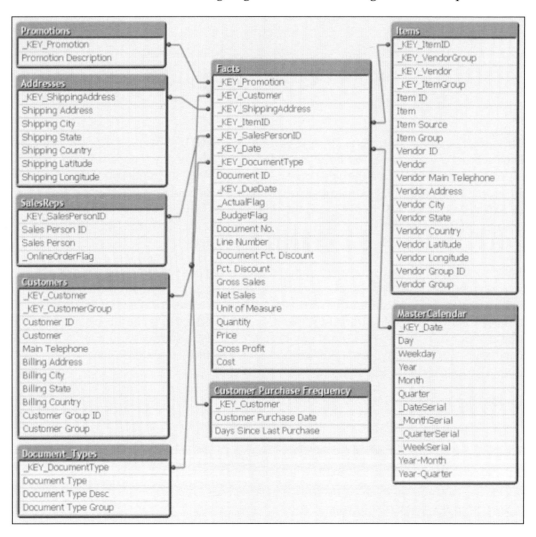

Exercise 2.1

With the following steps, let's migrate the sales perspective container from the book's exercise files to where we've installed QDF on our computers and start to explore the data together:

1. In the Ch. 2 folder of the book's exercise files, copy the container called 1001.Sales_Perspective to the QDF folder that is located on your computer. By default, the QDF folder will be C:\Qlik\SourceDate.

2. In the QDF folder, open the VariableEditor Shortcut in the 0.Administration container.

3. Click Container Map Editor. If the button hangs, then enable the **Open Databases in Read and Write** mode in the **Setting** tab of the **Edit Script** window and try again.

4. In the container map table, go to the empty line after 99.Shared_Folders, and under the Container Folder Name column, click the black arrow indicating that it is an input field.

5. Enter the name of the new container that we just copied, 1001.Sales_ Perspective, into the input field.

6. Continue along the row and enter the Variable Prefix as Sales and the Container Comments as Container for Sales Perspective.

7. Click the **Update Map and create Containers** button that is located in the top-left of the container map table, and when prompted, click **Update Container Map**.

8. Save the QlikView file.

Now that we've finished migrating the container to our local QDF, let's open Sales_Perspective_Sandbox.qvw in the 1.Application folder of the 1001.Sales_ Perspective container and explore the sales data in more detail.

The data model that we are using is a star schema and it includes a set of events common to many companies. In the fact table at the center of the model, we store the following events:

• Sales invoices
• Sales credit memos
• Sales budget

 The sales budget may not come from our ERP. It may exist in Excel or in the database of a specific-planning software.

Sales invoices are the principal event of the data model. We don't use the general journal entries that the sales invoices often generate in an ERP system because it does not have the level of detail that a sales invoice does. For example, product details are often not included in the general journal entry.

However, it is important that the total sales amount from our sales invoices matches the total sales that we have in our financial reports. For that reason, it is important to consider any sales cancelation or other sales adjustment. In this data model, sales credit memos properly adjust our total sales amount to match the financial reports that we will see in *Chapter 3, Financial Perspective*.

Finally, we cannot analyze or judge our sales performance without comparing it with something. Basic sales analysis involves comparing current sales with either historical or planned sales. Therefore, we should aim to have at least two years of sales data or the sales budget in our data model. In this data model, we have both historical sales and planned sales data.

 Planned sales can be either a sales budget, a sales forecast, or both.

All of these events are discrete events. In other words, they only exist at a discrete point in time. The fact table that stores discrete events is called a transactional fact table. The date dimension in a transactional fact table holds the date when the event occurred.

Along with the date dimension, we use the 7Ws (who, what, where, when, how many, why, and how) in the following table to describe an example set of metrics and dimensions that we expect to find in a sales perspective data model:

Dimensions		
7Ws	**Fields**	**Comments**
Who	Customer	Sometimes, customers are only identifiable by the sales ticket number from a POS system. Otherwise, we hope to have a rich set of attributes that describe our customers as in the case of our data model.
Who	Sales Person	In our data model, the sales person is defined at the invoice level. This might also be an attribute of a customer, a product, or an office. We also should include any sales structure hierarchy if it exists.
What	Item	Whether it be a product or a service, we should describe what we sell to a customer in a detailed dimension table.

Dimensions		
7Ws	**Fields**	**Comments**
Where	`Billing Address,` `Shipping Address`	The location can either be related to the customer, the sales office, or the store where the sale took place.
When	`Date`	Here, we record the exact date of the sales invoices and credit memos. We don't usually make daily sales budgets, so we assign our monthly budget to the first day of the month.
Why	`Promotion` `Description`	Giving a possible reason for sales variation versus historical or planned sales is a part of the analytical process. Therefore, we should include any element that is intended to cause variation, such as sales offers and promotions, into the data model.
How	`_OnlineOrderFlag`	We should also include whether we sell our products face to face, online, telephonically, or through any other sales channel.
Metrics		
7Ws	**Fields**	**Comments**
How many	`Net Sales`	The net sales field records an invoice's sales dollar amount after discount. It also stores the net sales budget so we use `_ActualFlag` or `_BudgetFlag` fields to determine whether the amount is actual or budget.
How many	`Quantity`	Sales quantity helps us understand sales in a manner that is independent of any change to the sales price. Quantity can be based on different units of measurement. For example, we can measure hours, kilograms, or pieces.
How many	`Gross Profit`	Although gross profit is not always easy to calculate and might not be available, it is vital to understand the effectiveness of our sales. Like net sales. The amount can also be actual or budget.

For more information on data modeling, read *Data Warehouse Toolkit* by Ralph Kimball, and *Agile Data Warehouse Design* by Lawrence Corr.

Data quality issues

Great data visualization and analysis starts with having a well-built data model that contains high-quality data. If this is our first data exploration and discovery project, one of the most important discoveries that we are going to make is that our data contains a great deal of garbage. One of the most noticeable data-quality issues is the absence of a value in a field.

For example, in Sales_Perspective_Sandbox.qvw, the `Vendor` attribute in the `Items` table does not always have a value. The absence of a value in a field is referred to as a null value. In QlikView, a user can't select a null value. However, we often want to select null values to know which items have missing attributes and send that list of items to whomever is responsible for the catalog's data quality.

In order to select item's with missing vendor information, we replace all the null values in the `Vendor` field with the string `N/A`, by inserting the following code before we load the `Items` table in order to replace all null value in the load script:

```
MappingNULL_NA:
Mapping
LOAD NULL() as NULL,
   'N/A' as Mapped_Value
AutoGenerate (1);
MAP Vendor USING MappingNULL_NA;
```

> Although we have the option to suppress null values in the **Dimensions** tab of a QlikView object, we never use this option unless we understand why the dimension values are null. These null values may indicate a larger problem with our data or the data model.

Missing dimension values

The previous mapping will not get rid of all the null values that we see in our charts because what we perceive in QlikView to be a null value may in fact be a missing value. Unlike missing values, null values can be observed the in the table where they reside. For example, can go to the **Table Viewer**, preview the `Items` table, and see the null values in the `Vendor` field.

However, what if the fact table contains an item key that refers to an item that does not exist in the `Items` table? Or, what if the fact table is missing the item key for some transactions? Despite running our previous null value mapping, we will still see `Vendor` as null in QlikView because the item key that the fact table refers to does exist in the `Items` table. It is a missing value.

The way to give users the ability to select missing items values to replace incorrect and null item keys in the fact table with a key to a fictitious item. The key to the fictitious item is defined as negative one (-1). Our first step to replace incorrect and null item keys is to create a mapping table using the Items table where we map all the existing item keys with their own values:

```
MappingMissingIncorrectItemsKeys:
Mapping
LOAD _KEY_ItemID,
  _KEY_ItemID
FROM
$(vG.QVDPath)\2.Transform\Items.qvd
(qvd);
```

The second step is to save the original value stored in _Key_ItemID in another field and apply this map to the _Key_ItemID field when we load the Facts table:

```
Facts:
LOAD [Document ID],
_KEY_ItemID as Original_ItemID,
     applymap('MappingMissingIncorrectItemsKeys',_KEY_ItemID,-1) as
     _KEY_ItemID,
     _KEY_Date,
     ...
FROM
$(vG.QVDPath)\2.Transform\Facts.qvd
(qvd);
```

Our final step is to create a fictitious item called 'Missing' with an item key of negative one (-1) in the Items table:

```
Concatenate (Items)
LOAD -1 as _KEY_ItemID,
     'Missing' as [Item ID],
     'Missing' as Item,
     'Missing' as [Item Source],
     'Missing' as [Item Group],
     ...
AutoGenerate (1);
```

Missing fact values

After the previous two adjustments, we will still encounter some missing values in QlikView. For example, do you notice anything missing from the following chart that shows the monthly net sales for the item *Bamdax 126* in `Sales_Perspective_Sandbox.qvw.`?

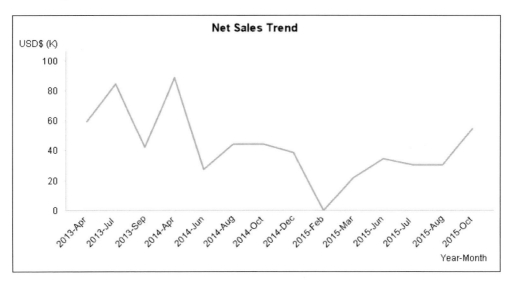

If you noticed that various months do not appear on the horizontal axis, then you are correct. As Bamdax 126 is not sold during every month, there is no relation between Bamdax 126 and the months when the item was not sold. The values are missing, and these missing values distort the line chart.

In order to completely resolve this issue, we would have to complement the fact table with the Cartesian product of any or all dimension key sets, and in effect, measure *nil events*. However, we should take into account that this may cause a severe degradation of our QlikView application's performance. Therefore, we should apply this solution pragmatically to solve specific analytical needs.

In this case, we specifically want to see a more accurate net sales trend for Bamdax 126 that includes the months that we did not sell the item. We do this by adding the following code to our load script after loading the `Facts` table. The code creates a Cartesian product of the `Product` and `Date` dimension key sets and adds it to our `Facts` table:

```
Missing_Facts_Tmp:
Load distinct makedate(Year(_KEY_Date),Month(_KEY_Date)) as _KEY_Date,
   1 as _ActualFlag
Resident Facts;
```

```
Left Join (Missing_Facts_Tmp)
Load distinct _KEY_ItemID
FROM
$(vG.QVDPath)\2.Transform\Items.qvd
(qvd);

Concatenate (Facts)
Load *
Resident Missing_Facts_Tmp;

DROP Table Missing_Facts_Tmp;
```

> In order to reduce the number of rows in the Cartesian product we only use the month and year of the date. We could have optimized it further using the exists() function to concatenate the dimension combinations that don't already exist in the Facts.

Finally, we untick the **Suppress Zero-Values** checkbox in the **Presentation** tab of the line chart in order to see the correct net sales trend for Bamdax 126. You will notice that the following line chart shows that Bamdax 126 is purchased almost every two months. It is difficult to make this observation in the previous chart.

> Again, be very careful when creating a Cartesian product in QlikView. We create a Cartesian product by joining two or more tables that do not have a field in common. If the tables are large, then this may cause QlikView to use all the available RAM memory and freeze the computer.

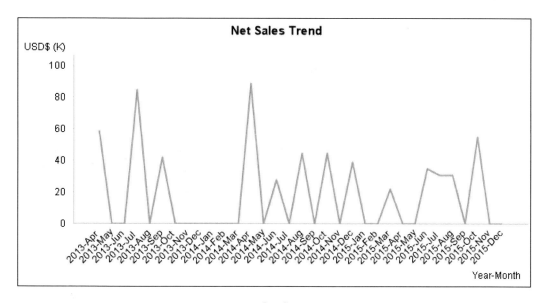

These steps to eliminate null and missing values in the data model will help improve our data analysis and visualization. However, we will most likely not use all the fields in the data model, so we shouldn't waste time to clean every field or create every missing value until they've proven their business value.

Data formatting and standardization

While QlikView is not data-cleansing software, it does allow us to implement some formatting and standardization that makes it easier to visualize data. We perform these actions in the data model load script as best practice. However, we can also use the same QlikView functions directly in any QlikView object.

Case

We read by identifying the overall shape of words. If we use text values with all uppercase letters, then all the words have the same block shape. Which makes words harder to identify and reduces readability. Also, all uppercase text values tend to be less aesthetically appealing.

A quick search in Google reveals that some people have begun to challenge this belief. Hopefully, future scientific studies will soon allow us to make the best decision and confirm how to optimize text readability.

An even worse scenario is when a field has some text values in all uppercase and others in lowercase. This is common when we integrate two data sources, and it is an unnecessary distraction when we visualize data.

First, we use the `capitalize()` function when the field is a proper noun, such as customer name, employee name, or city. The function will return a mixed-case text value with the first letter of every word being a capital letter. Secondly, we use the `upper()` function to standardize text fields that are abbreviations, such as state or units of measurement. Lastly, we use the `lower()` function to standardize all other text fields.

This solution is not perfect for some text values, such as a street address that contains both proper nouns and abbreviations. For example, Cedar St. NW requires a more nuanced approach. However, a street address is rarely used for analysis, and any extra effort to standardize this or any other field should be weighed against its business value.

Unwanted characters

Text values with strange characters can also be an unnecessary distraction. Characters, such as a number sign (#), an exclamation mark (!), a vertical bar (|), and so on, can sometimes find their way into text descriptions where they don't belong. We can eliminate them with the `purgechar()` function or the `replace()` function.

Also, extra spaces between words in a dimension value can make our charts look sloppy. QlikView tends to eliminate leading and trailing spaces, but it doesn't eliminate extra spaces between words. We can accomplish this using the following expression, preferably in our `load` script:

```
replace(replace(replace(FieldName,' ','<>'),'><',''),'<>',' ')
```

Hopefully, in the future, regular expressions will be native to QlikView, and we will have a greater ability to clean and standardize data. Barry Harmsen has created custom script functions that allow us to use regular expressions in the load script (http://www.qlikfix.com/2010/10/18/regular-expressions-in-the-load-script/). A third-party tool called QVSource also allows us to use regular expressions in the load script (http://wiki.qvsource.com/Using-Regular-Expressions-In-QlikView.ashx).

Dates and time

Finally, we make sure that all date fields have the same format. This is especially the case when we extract data from different data sources. We use the `date()` or `time()` function to change the format to the default date format that we define in the list of system variables at the beginning of the script.

When we create analysis that is intended for an international audience where some users use the MM/DD/YYYY format and others use the DD/MM/YYYY format, we should consider using the YYYY/MM/DD format. This format won't leave users guessing whether 11/1/2016 refers to November 1, 2016 or January 11, 2016.

Master calendar

Along with formatting field values, we also standardize the use of whole dimension in order to facilitate analysis of tables. Those that we reuse between different data models are called conformed dimensions. The date dimension is ubiquitous and serves as a great example to create the first conformed dimension.

The range of dates that we use in each data model may change, so instead of using the exact same table for each data model, we create a master calendar reusing the same script. We call these reusable scripts subroutines, and in QDF we store script subroutines in the following file path:

```
C:\Qlik\SourceData\99.Shared_Folders\3.Include\4.Sub
```

Although QDF has a master calendar subroutine, we will use the master calendar subroutine that is available from QlikView Components (`http://qlikviewcomponents.org`). Qlikview Components is a library of script subroutines and functions that were developed by Rob Wunderlich and Matt Fryer. We prefer this mastercalendar subroutine because it automatically creates several calendar-based set-analysis variables that we can use in our charts.

 QDF is not the end but rather the means. It is designed to be flexible so that we can adapt it to our needs. We can create, import, and modify any reusable component that best fits our business requirements.

We can download the latest release of QlikView Components from GitHub (`https://github.com/RobWunderlich/Qlikview-Components/releases`). We then integrate it with our QDF by copying the `Qvc.qvs` file that is found under the `Qvc_Runtime` folder to `C:\Qlik\SourceData\99.Shared_Folders\3.Include\4.Sub`. We choose to save it to `99.Shared_Folders` so that we can use these subroutines and functions in every container that we create.

In our `load` script, we add the following code after initializing QDF:

```
$(Include=$(vG.SharedSubPath)\Qvc.qvs);
```

We then add the following code to create the master calendar and the calendar-based set-analysis variables:

```
SET Qvc.Calendar.v.CreateSetVariables = 1;
call Qvc.CalendarFromField('_KEY_Date');
```

Every QlikView Components release contains working examples of all its subroutines. We can use these examples to learn the possible parameters and results of each subroutine.

We finish the load script by running a subroutine that eliminates any temporary variables that were used to create the master calendar:

```
CALL Qvc.Cleanup;
```

After running our `load` script, we now have the following master calendar:

_KEY_Date	Day	Weekday	Year	Month	Quarter	_DateSerial	_MonthSerial	_QuarterSerial	_WeekSerial	Year-Month	Year-Quarter
41365	1	Mon	2013	Apr	Q2	41365	1	1	1	2013-Apr	2013-Q2
41382	18	Thu	2013	Apr	Q2	41382	1	1	3	2013-Apr	2013-Q2
41395	1	Wed	2013	May	Q2	41395	2	1	5	2013-May	2013-Q2
41426	1	Sat	2013	Jun	Q2	41426	3	1	9	2013-Jun	2013-Q2
41456	1	Mon	2013	Jul	Q3	41456	4	2	14	2013-Jul	2013-Q3
41463	8	Mon	2013	Jul	Q3	41463	4	2	15	2013-Jul	2013-Q3
41487	1	Thu	2013	Aug	Q3	41487	5	2	18	2013-Aug	2013-Q3

Most of these columns look familiar. However, the columns that end with `Serial` may be new to you. To those of us who have battled with defining date ranges with set analysis, the `Serial` columns help make this an easier task.

For example, we can calculate **year-to-date (YTD)** sales easily with the following expression:

```
sum({$<Year={$(=max(Year))},Month=,_DateSerial={"<=$(=max(
_DateSerial))"},_ActualFlag={1}>}[Net Sales])
```

However, instead of repeating this set analysis in every chart, we can use the calendar-based set-analysis variables to calculate YTD sales. We can improve the preceding expression using the set-analysis variable called `vSetYTDModifier`:

```
sum({$<$(vSetYTDModifier),_ActualFlag={1}>} [Net Sales])
```

We can review all of the available calendar-based set-analysis variables in **Settings | Variable Overview**.

Now that we've reviewed the sales perspective data model and methods in the load script make it support cleaner data visualization and analysis, let's look at our first user story.

Customer stratification.

Many of the user stories that we take into account when we start to use more advanced data analysis and visualization techniques are not new. For example, we have probably already used basic QlikView methods to resolve the following user story.

 As a sales representative, I want to see who my most important customers are so that I can focus my time and effort on them.

The simplest way to define customer importance is to base it on how much they've purchased or how much profit they've generated. In its simplest form, we can resolve this user story with a bar chart that ranks customers by sales or gross profit.

However, given our increasing experience with QlikView, we'll take another look at this user story and use a more advanced analysis technique called customer stratification. This method groups customers according to their importance into bins. The number of bins can vary, but for this exercise we will use four bins: A, B, C, and D. We use two techniques to stratify customers. The first technique involves using the Pareto principal, and the second involves using fractiles. We will review the first technique in this chapter, and then in *Chapter 5, Working Capital Perspective*, we will review the second technique.

Pareto analysis

Pareto analysis is based on the principle that most of the effects come from a few causes. For example, most sales come from a few customers, most complaints come from a few users and most gross profit come from a few products. Another name for this analysis is the 80-20 rule, which refers to the rule of thumb that, for example, 80% of sales come from 20% of customers. However, it is important to note that the exact percentages may vary.

We can visualize this phenomena using the following visualization. Each bar represents the twelve-month rolling net sales of one customer. The customers are sorted from greatest to least and their names appear along a line that represents the accumulation of their sales. The customers whose names appear below the horizontal reference line called 80% total sales line make up 80% of the total company's twelve-month rolling net sales. These are the customers in which we want to dedicate more of our time to provide great service:

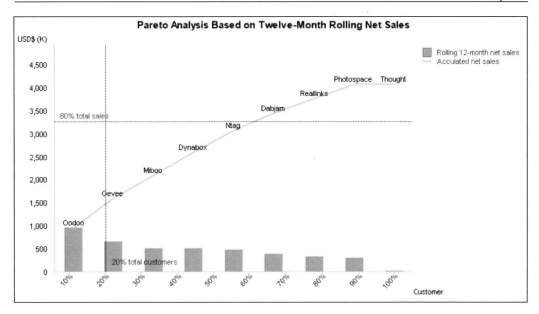

We also confirm that we don't depend on too few customers by including a reference line that represents 20% of the total number of active customers. While the exact percentage depends on the business, we usually hope to have 20% or more of our customers make up 80% of our sales. The preceding chart clearly shows whether this is true by verifying that the accumulated sales line crosses the **80% total sales** reference line to the right of where the **20% total customers** reference line does.

Exercise 2.2

Let's construct this chart in `Sales_Perspective_Sandbox.qvw` using the following chart properties. These are only the principal chart properties that are necessary to create the chart. Adjust the color, number format, font, and text size as you like:

Chart Properties	Value
General / Chart Type	Choose to create a combo chart.

Dimensions / Used Dimensions	Use the following code to create a calculated dimension labeled Customers:
	
	`=aggr(rank(sum({$<$(vSetRolling12Modifier),`
	`_ActualFlag={1}>} [Net Sales]),4)/count({$<$(v`
	`SetRolling12Modifier),_ActualFlag={1}>} Total`
	`Customer),Customer)`

Chart Properties	Value
| Expressions | Use the following code to create an expression labeled Rolling 12-Month Net Sales:<br><br>```
sum({$<$(vSetRolling12Modifier),
_ActualFlag={1}>} [Net Sales])
```<br>Choose to display the expression as a bar: |
| Expressions | Use the following code to create an expression labeled Accumulated Net Sales:<br><br>```
sum({$<$(vSetRolling12Modifier),
_ActualFlag={1}>} [Net Sales])
```<br>Choose to display the expression as a line and enable the Full Accumulation option. |
| Expressions | Use the following code to create an expression labeled Customer:<br><br>```
if(
   sum({$<$(vSetRolling12Modifier),
_ActualFlag={1}>} [Net Sales])
    /
   sum({$<$(vSetRolling12Modifier),
_ActualFlag={1}>} Total [Net Sales])

   >=.05,

   Customer,
   ' '
   )
```<br>Choose to display the expression as Values on Data Points. |
| Axes / Dimension Axis | Choose to Continuous option in the Dimension Axis section. |
| Presentation / Reference Lines | Use the following code to create a reference line labeled 80% Total Sales:<br><br>```
=sum({$<$(vSetRolling12Modifier),_ActualFlag
={1}>} [Net Sales])*.8
```<br>Choose the option to Show Label in Chart and the option to locate it on the Primary Y axis. |
| Presentation / Reference Lines | Use the following code to create a reference line labeled 20% Total Customers:<br><br>```
=.2
```<br>Choose the option to Show Label in Chart and the option to locate it on the Continuous X axis. |
```

We avoid overlapping labels on the data points by adding some intelligence into the expression called *Customer* and only show the label when the customer's sales participation is greater than 5%.

While this is a powerful visualization, we simplify customer stratification for our sales representatives and assign each customer a particular letter according to how they are ranked as per the Pareto analysis. Those that are assigned the letter A are our most important customers, while those that are assigned the letter D are our least important customers. The following table details how we assign each letter to our customers:

Assigned Letter	Accumulated Sales Percentage
A	0-50%
B	50-80%
C	80-95%
D	95-100%

If we use the chart accumulation options like in the previous exercise or other methods like inter-row chart functions to determine which group each customer belongs to, we are forced to always show every customer. If we select any customer or apply any other filter then we lose how that customer is classified. In order to assign a letter to each customer and view their classification in any context, we use a method that uses alternate states. Let's perform the following tasks to classify our customers based on rolling twelve-month net sales.

This method was first introduced by Christof Schwarz in the Qlik Community (https://community.qlik.com/docs/DOC-6088).

Exercise 2.3

Perform the following steps for this exercise:

1. Create an **Input Box** that contains three new variables: vPctSalesA, vPctSalesB, and vPctSalesC. Assign the values 50%, 80%, and 95% to each variable, respectively.

2. In **Settings -> Document Properties**, click **Alternate States...** in the **General** tab. Add three new alternate states: A_CustomerSales, AB_CustomerSales, and ABC_CustomerSales.

3. Create a button named Calculate Stratification with the following actions:

Actions	Values
Copy State Contents	We leave the Source State empty and use the following Target State: A_CustomerSales
Pareto Select	We will use the following field: Customer We will use the following expression: sum({$<$(vSetRolling12Modifier),_ActualFlag={1}>} [Net Sales]) We will use the following percentage: =vPctSalesA We will use the following alternate state: A_CustomerSales
Copy State Contents	We leave the Source State empty and use the following Target State: AB_CustomerSales
Pareto Select	We will use the following field: Customer We will use the following expression: sum({$<$(vSetRolling12Modifier),_ActualFlag={1}>} [Net Sales]) We will use the following percentage: =vPctSalesB We will use the following alternate state: AB_CustomerSales

Actions	Values
Copy State Contents	We leave the Source State empty and use the following Target State: `ABC_CustomerSales`

Pareto Select	We will use the following field:
	
	`Customer`
	
	We will use the following expression:
	
	`sum({$<$(vSetRolling12Modifier),_ActualFlag={1}>} [Net Sales])`
	
	We will use the following percentage:
	
	`=vPctSalesC`
	
	We will use the following alternate state:
	
	`ABC_CustomerSales`

4. Finally, create a straight table with Customer as the dimension and the following two expressions:

Label	Expression
Rolling 12-month net sales	`=sum({$<$(vSetRolling12Modifier),_ActualFlag={1}>} [Net Sales USD])`

`Classif.`	`aggr(if(len(only({A_CustomerSales} Customer)) <> 0,`
	`'A',`
	`  if(len(only({AB_CustomerSales} Customer)) <> 0, 'B',`
	`   if(len(only({ABC_CustomerSales} Customer)) <> 0,`
	`'C',`
	`if(len(only(Customer)) <> 0,'D'))))`
	`,Customer)`

5. Optionally, add a background color that corresponds to each letter with the following expression:

```
if(len(only({A_CustomerSales} Customer)) <> 0, blue(100),
  if(len(only({AB_CustomerSales} Customer)) <> 0, blue(75),
   if(len(only({ABC_CustomerSales} Customer)) <> 0,
blue(50),blue(25)))))
```

After some final adjustments to each object's presentation, we should have something similar to the following figure:

vPctSalesA	= 50%		
vPctSalesB	= 80%		
vPctSalesC	= 95%		

Calculate Stratification

🖳 XI _ 🗖

Customer	Rolling 12-month net sales	Clasif.
	4,070,549	
Oodoo	954,122	A
Gevee	642,405	A
Miboo	500,666	A
Dynabox	495,883	B
Ntag	470,080	B
Dabjam	382,969	B
Reallinks	324,256	C
Photospace	300,051	C
Thoughtworks	118	D

Using this method we can select any customer and still observe how it is classified. We can perform this same stratification technique using other additive metrics, such as gross profit. Also, instead of customers, we can also stratify items or sales representatives.

The second part of stratification involves using nonadditive metrics. For example, we cannot use the Pareto principal to classify customers based on the average number of days they their invoices. In *Chapter 5, Working Capital Perspective* we will review how we can classify customers using fractiles and create a visualization that gives us a general overview of how they are stratified.

Sales representatives can now easily see which customers have the most impact on sales and dedicate more time to provide them with better service. At the same time, they need to avoid losing these customers. So let's take a look at how we can help them anticipate customer churn.

Customer churn

Customer churn is a measure of the company's tendency to lose customers. Our user story speaks of the need to detect at-risk customers and prevent them from becoming a lost customer.

As a sales representative, I want to see which customers I'm at risk of losing so that I can take action today to prevent their leaving.

Surely, there are many variables that we may use to predict customer churn. In this case we expect customers to consistently make a purchase every so many days, so we will use a variable called customer purchase frequency to detect those that we are at risk of losing.

We could calculate the average number of days between purchases and warn sales representatives when the number of days since a customer's last purchase exceeds that average.

However, a simple average may not always be an accurate measure of a customer's true purchasing behavior. If we assume that their purchase frequency is normally distributed then we use the t-test to determine within what range the average is likely to fall. Moreover, we prefer the t-test because it can be used for customers that have made less than thirty or so purchases.

If we want our model to be sensitive to customer inactivity then we send an alert when the days since their last purchase exceeds the average's lower limit. Otherwise, if we don't want to overwhelm the sales representatives with alerts then we use the average's upper limit to determine whether we are at risk of losing a customer. We'll apply the later case in the following example.

Before we calculate the upper limit of a t-distribution, we need to add a table to the data model that contains the number of days that elapse between field the purchases each customer makes. We add the Customer Purchase Frequency with the following code that we add to the load script after having loaded the Facts table:

```
[Customer Purchase Frequency Tmp]:
Load distinct _KEY_Date as [Customer Purchase Date],
     _KEY_Customer
Resident Facts
Where _ActualFlag = 1
  and [Net Sales] > 0;

[Customer Purchase Frequency]:
Load [Customer Purchase Date],
   _KEY_Customer,
     if(_KEY_Customer <> peek(_KEY_Customer),0,[Customer Purchase
Date] - Peek([Customer Purchase Date])) as [Days Since Last Purchase]
Resident [Customer Purchase Frequency Tmp]
Order by _KEY_Customer,[Customer Purchase Date];
DROP Table [Customer Purchase Frequency Tmp];
```

The previous script will produce the following table:

_KEY_Customer ⊙	Customer Purchase Date	Days Since Last Purchase
1	4/18/2013	-
1	6/23/2013	66
1	8/16/2013	54
1	9/23/2013	38
1	11/11/2013	49
1	12/19/2013	38

This is a great opportunity to use a histogram to understand the distribution of a customer's purchasing frequency. We can also compare the distribution to a normal or a t-distributions in the same chart. Let's use the following properties to create our histogram:

Exercise 2.4

Chart Properties	Value
General / Chart Type	Choose to create a combo chart.
Dimensions / Used Dimensions	Use the following code to create a calculated dimension called Days Since Last Purchase: `=ValueLoop($(=min([Days Since Last Purchase])),$(=max([Days Since Last Purchase])),1)`

Expressions	Use the following code to create a expression called Number of Purchases:
	
	`sum(if([Days Since Last Purchase]=ValueLoop($(=min([Days Since Last Purchase])),$(=max([Days Since Last Purchase])),1),1))`
	`/`
	`count([Days Since Last Purchase])`
	
	Choose to display the expression as a bar.

Chart Properties	Value
Expressions	Use the following code to create a expression called Normal Distribution: ``` NORMDIST(ValueLoop($(=min([Days Since Last Purchase]))),$(=max([Days Since Last Purchase]))),1) ,avg([Days Since Last Purchase]),stdev([Days Since Last Purchase]),0) ``` Choose to display the expression as a line.
Expressions	Use the following code to create a expression called t-Distribution: ``` TDIST((fabs(ValueLoop($(=min([Days Since Last Purchase]))),$(=max([Days Since Last Purchase]))),1) -avg([Days Since Last Purchase]))) / (Stdev([Days Since Last Purchase]) / sqrt(count([Days Since Last Purchase]))) ,count([Days Since Last Purchase]),1) ``` Choose to display the expression as a smooth line.
Axes / Dimension Axis	Choose to Continuous option in the Dimension Axis section.
Presentation / Reference Lines	Use the following code to create a reference line called Mean Days Since Last Purchase: ``` =Avg([Days Since Last Purchase]) ``` We set the following location: Choose the option to Show Label in Chart and the option to locate it on the Continuous X axis.
Presentation / Reference Lines	Use the following code to create a reference line called Upper Limit (95%): ``` =TTest1_Upper([Days Since Last Purchase]-0,(1-(95)/100)/2) ``` Choose the option to locate it on the Continuous X axis.
Presentation / Reference Lines	Use the following code to create a reference line called Lower Limit (95%): ``` =TTest1_Lower([Days Since Last Purchase]-0,(1-(95)/100)/2) ``` Choose the option to locate it on the Continuous X axis.

After additional adjustments to the presentation, we have the following chart. This particular chart compares the actual purchasing frequency distribution for customer *Gevee.* with both a normal and a t-distribution curve:

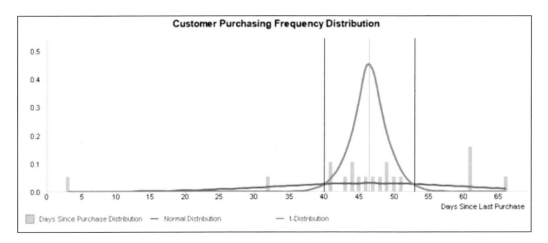

If we alert the sales representatives any time that a customer waits more than the mean number of days, then we could be sending too many false alarms, or in other words false positives. However, if we define at-risk customers as those who wait longer than the upper limit of the 95% confidence level, we have a higher probability of alerting the sales representative about customers that are really at-risk, or true positives.

Let's also keep in mind that not all lost customers have the same effect on the company, so let's combine the stratification that we performed earlier in the chapter with our churn-prediction analysis. In this way, sales representatives know to focus their attention on **A** customers that are at-risk, and not invest too much time to follow-up on **D** customers. The following table shows what this analysis may look like:

Customer	Rolling 12-month net sales	Clasif.	At-risk
	4,070,549		
Oodoo	954,122	A	
Gevee	642,405	A	
Miboo	500,666	A	
Dynabox	495,883	B	
Ntag	470,080	B	
Dabjam	382,969	B	
Reallinks	324,256	C	
Photospace	300,051	C	
Thoughtworks	118	D	

We add the following expression to the customer-stratification table that we created in a previous exercise. The background color expression calculates the days since the last purchase and compares it with the upper limit of the 95% confidence level. Refer the following table for a clear view:

Exercise 2.5

Expressions	Expression for an at-risk customer
	`= ' '`
	We set the **Background Color** as follows:
| | ```
if(max({$<_ActualFlag={1},Year=,Month=,_
DateSerial={"<=$(=max(_DateSerial))"}>} Total _KEY_
Date)
 - max({$<_ActualFlag={1},Year=,Month=,_
DateSerial={"<=$(=max(_DateSerial))"}>} _KEY_Date)
 >
 TTest1_Upper({$<_ActualFlag={1},Year=,Month=,_
DateSerial={"<=$(=max(_DateSerial))"}>} [Days Since
Last Purchase]-0,(1-(95)/100)/2), red(100))
``` |

Customer stratification together with customer-churn prediction is a very powerful business tool. Now, let's take our first look at QlikView extensions and introduce the cycle plot.
```

QlikView extensions and the cycle plot

If we are going to work with advanced data visualization in QlikView, we have to get used to working with extensions. We can either develop the QlikView extension ourselves or use open source extensions that are available in Qlik Branch (http://branch.qlik.com).

For example, we are presented with the challenge to find a better way to visualize **year-over-year (YoY)**, **week-over-week (WoW),** or any other period-over-period analysis. The following line chart demonstrates how difficult it can be to compare a large number of periods:

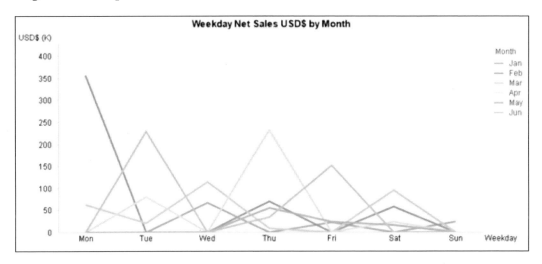

A cycle plot (*Cleveland, Dunn, and Terpenning, 1978*) offers a alternate way to compare a large number of periods. The following cycle plot is a QlikView extension that displays the average sales by weekday in each month and compares it to the total average sales represented by a flat horizontal line:

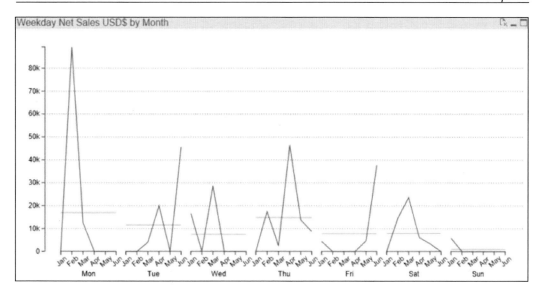

Exercise 2.6

Let's create this cycle plot in `Sales_Perspective_Sandbox.qvw` using the following steps:

1. In the `Ch. 2` folder of the book's exercise files, double-click the `CyclePlot.qar` file. QlikView will automatically open and notify you that the extension has been installed successfully.

2. In `Sales_Perspective_Sandbox.qvw`, activate **WebView**.

3. Right-click over an empty space and select **New Sheet Object**.

4. Click **Extensions Objects** and drag the extension called **Cycle Plot** to a empty place in the sheet.

5. Define the following properties to the cycle plot. The expression is

```
sum({$<_ActualFlag={1}>} [Net Sales])
/
count(distinct _KEY_Date)
```

The properties of an extension are unique to that extension. We should review the extension's documentation for more information about each option.

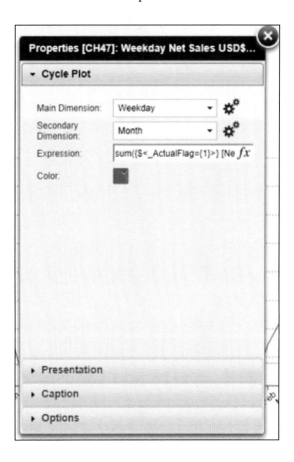

We should now see the cycle plot similar to the one previously shown. We will continue to explore more QlikView extensions in later chapters.

Governance – design template

Although we may think that we should create a design template before creating the first application, it is often better to do so once we've created the first application. After we've made the design adjustments that the business user requests then we can use that application as a template for future ones.

We convert the first QlikView application into a design template by first leaving only the sheets with unique layouts. A layout may include a background, a logo, a sheet title, and lines that separate sections. We may also leave a few example objects, such as list boxes and charts, that serve as references when we create the actual objects that are specific to the each perspective. We save this template into a new QVW file and use a copy of it every time we create a new QlikView application. The following image shows an example layout that we use as a design template:

When we create the actual objects for a QlikView application, we can either use the **Format Painter Tool** to transfer the property options of the existing reference objects to the new ones, or we can create a simple QlikView theme based on an existing chart. The key to making an effective theme is to not over fit the design. We should only be concerned with simple properties, such as borders and captions. Let's create a simple theme and enable it to be used to create all new objects from this point on:

1. In the **Properties** dialog of the pareto analysis we created in Exercise 2.2, let's click **Theme Maker...** in the **Layout** tab.

2. We select **New Theme** and save our theme as `Basic_Theme.qvt` in `C:\Qlik\SourceData\99.Shared_Folders\9.Misc.`

3. We select **Object Type Specific** and **Caption Border**.

4. In the **Object Type Specific** properties, we select only **Axis Thickness**, **Axis Font**, **Axis Color**, and **Chart Title Settings**.

5. In the **Caption and border** settings, we leave the default selections.

6. In the last step, select the option to **Set as default theme** for this document. We can also change this setting in the **Presentation** tab of the **Document Properties**.

We will now save a few seconds every time we create a new chart object. We should repeat the same procedure for any other objects we frequently create. Also, if we notice any other repetitive design changes that we are making to new objects, we can update the theme using the same **Theme Maker** wizard.

Summary

Our QlikView sales perspective is a great place to start to use more advanced data visualization and analysis techniques. Sales departments traditionally have both the resources and the data available to continue to improve their QlikView applications.

Apart from the sales data model that we reviewed, we should continue to include additional data. Adding cross-functional data from finance, marketing, and operations gives sales representatives the information that they need to succeed. We can also add external data sources, such as census data or any other government data. When we add this additional data, we should keep in mind the cleaning and standardization tips that we learned in this chapter.

Like customer stratification and customer churn, we can often create minimally viable solutions using basic QlikView. However, we can develop a better solution by understanding and applying more advanced techniques like Pareto analysis and statistical distributions.

We can also add more powerful visualizations and analysis if we use extensions. The cycle plot is an excellent example of a useful visualization that is not available as a native QlikView object. In the next chapter, let's review the data model, user stories, analytical methods and visualization techniques for the financial perspective.

3
Financial Perspective

The financial perspective includes arguably the most important measures of a business. We judge the actions and metrics of all other perspectives based on the effect that they have on the financial situation. Financial reports, such as the balance sheet, the income statement, and the cash flow statement, are universal measures of a company. These reports are used by outside investors, creditors, and the government, and there is a standard way that they are presented.

Accountants use standardized bookkeeping practices to record the financial data. Although we don't have to learn everything that they know about bookkeeping, we do have to understand the basic idea of what it means. For example, we have to understand how to interpret debits and credits in the data that originates from the accounting software. We also have to understand whether a measure is calculated over a certain period or based on an accumulated total. We review a financial data model that will consider these points and makes it easier to calculate financial metrics.

When we develop a QlikView financial perspective, we have to be ready for a challenge. The task is made even more arduous due to the static nature of the reports to which the business users are accustomed. QlikView is a data discovery tool and not a static report builder. Therefore, we need to add metadata to the data model that helps us to format these reports. We also review a few areas where we can take advantage of QlikView to visualize otherwise simple tables.

In this chapter, we will review the following topics:

- The data model for the financial perspective
- Metadata to format reports
- Standard financial reports
- Expenses and other financial indicators

Let's get started and review the data model that we use to create our financial perspective in QlikView.

Financial perspective data model

The data model for our financial perspective is similar to our sales data model. Let's load the data model and review it.

Exercise 3.1

For this exercise, you need to perform the following steps:

1. In the Ch. 3 folder of the book's exercise files, copy the container called 1002.Financial_Perspective to the QDF folder located on your computer. By default, the QDF folder will be C:\Qlik\SourceData.

2. In the QDF folder, open the VariableEditor shortcut in the 0.Administration container.

3. Click **Container Map Editor**.

4. In the container map table, go to first empty line, and under the Container Folder Name column, enter the name of the new container that we just copied, 1002.Financial_Perspective, into the input field.

5. Continue along the row and enter the Variable Prefix as Financial and the Container Comments as Container for Financial Perspective.

6. Click the **Update Map and create Containers** button located at the top-left of the container map table, and when prompted, click **Update Container Map**.

7. Save the QlikView file.

If we open 1.Application\Financial_Analysis_Sandbox.qvw and look at the data model then we can review the following data model.

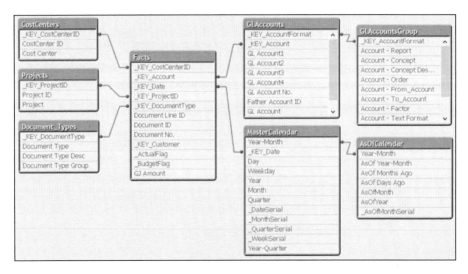

Similar to the data model for the sales perspective, the one that we use for the financial perspective contains a fact table surrounded by dimension tables. In the fact table at the center of the model, we store the following events:

- General journal entries
- Financial budget

General Journal (GJ) entries record all financial information. For example, different GJ entries are created to reflect the financial effects of a sales invoice, a purchase invoice, or a bank deposit. We can also create journal entry directly, without any supporting document.

A GJ entry consists of two types of numeric values: debit, and credit. Each entry assigns a debit or credit amount to two or more **General Ledger (GL)** accounts in such a way that the total debit amount always equals the total credit amount. The following diagram shows a general journal entry for a sales invoice:

GL Account Name	GL Account Number	Debit	Credit
Customer	1-10-1000	114.99	
Value Added Tax (VAT)	2-10-1000		15.00
Sales	4-10-1000		99.99
Total		114.99	114.99

Whether an account is debited or credited depends on the normal balance of the account. For example, GL accounts that measure sales have a normal credit balance. So, if we want to increase the value of sales, then we would credit the account. Inversely, if the customer cancels a sale, we decrease the value of sales by debiting the account.

As keeping track of debits and credits can become confusing, we simplify the handling of debits and credits in the data model and calculate a third field called [GJ Amount] ::

    [GJ Amount] = Debit - Credit

The following table shows the [GJ Amount] values for the previous GJ entry. At first it may seem counterintuitive that we increase sales with a negative amount, but we will talk about how to handle the sign of the **Amount** field when we talk about the data model's dimensions tables.

GLAccount	GLAccoutName	Debit	Credit	Amount
1-10-1000	Customer	114.99	0.00	114.99
2-10-1000	Value Added Tax (VAT)	0.00	15.00	-15.00
4-10-1000	Sales	0.00	99.99	-99.99

Similar to the sales data model, a GJ entry is a discrete event. Other than the date dimension, the financial data model does not have many dimensions. Let's take a look at the few dimensions that regularly describe GJ entries in the following table.

 We can also encounter a financial data model that is based on a recurring event that measures the balance of each GL account on a monthly basis. We will look at this type of data model in *Chapter 5, Working Capital Perspective*.

Dimensions		
7Ws	**Fields**	**Comments**
What	GL Account	This is the most important dimension that describes the GL accounts that correspond to the GJ entry amounts. We use it to identify the GL account type and how we should handle the amount in the reports. Great financial analysis is made easier when accountants precisely define and use a list of GL accounts called a chart of accounts (COA).
Who / Where	Cost Center	This is a field that usually defines the business department or unit to which a certain cost or expense can be assigned. The cost centers can be based on segmented numbers that, for example, define the company with the first two numbers, the branch with the next three numbers, and the department with the last three numbers. Revenue is described by a similar dimension called a profit center.
What	Project	Project accounting is important to determine the cost and possible income of any business endeavor. Like this field, there may also exist other high-level groupings that are important to the company.
When	Date	We record the exact date of the GJ entries. Our financial budgets are defined on a monthly basis, so we assign a budget to the first day of the month.
Metrics		
7Ws	**Fields**	**Comments**
How many	GJ Amount	This field is the result of subtracting the credit amount from the debit amount.

The data model for our financial perspective is a slight variation of the *star schema*. As the `AsOfCalendar` dimension table is not directly linked to the `Facts` table, but rather, they are linked to other dimension tables; this data model is called a *snowflake schema*. We prefer to use the star schema, but we've kept two dimensions separate so that we can explain their purpose better in the next two sections. Even though we create an additional link in the data model, the small size of both dimension tables means that there will be no perceivable change to the application's performance.

Financial report metadata

The `GLAccountsGroup` table contains information on how to organize and format the financial reports. The field called `Account - Factor` is of particular importance because it helps determine how to handle the sign of the GJ Amount for the reports. For example, if we sum the sales amount directly from the `GJ Amount` field, we will get a negative number because the GL account for sales has a normal credit balance. However, when we look at this number in a report, we want to see it as a positive number. So, we multiply the sum by the number in `Account - Factor` in order to change the sign of sales.

In general, the first digit of a GL account number indicates the account type and whether we need to change the sign of the amounts assigned to it. The following diagram shows the normal balance of the principal account types according to a common numbering scheme and the value we will store in `Account - Factor`:

Example chart of accounts			
GL Account Group	First digit in GL Account Number	Debit or Credit Balance	Factor
Asset	1	Debit	1
Liability	2	Credit	-1
Equity or Capital	3	Credit	-1
Revenue	4	Credit	-1
Costs of Sales	5	Debit	1
Expenses	6, 7, 8, or 9	Debit	1

Along with `Account - Factor`, we also store information about how each financial report groups the GL accounts differently. Unlike customer and product groups in the sales perspective, GL account groups are not only informative, but they are also an essential part of financial analysis. We must take care to verify each account's grouping with an accountant, or else we risk creating erroneous analysis.

Finally, we also include information about how we want to format our financial reports in the same table. We assign a particular format to each group and calculation. By defining that information in this table, we maintain the report's format much easier than if we defined the format directly in the QlikView object:

①	②	③	④		⑤	⑥	⑦	⑧	⑨
Report	Concept	Order	From_Account	To_Account	Factor	Format	Indentation	Color	Background Color
Profit_Loss	Income	100	4000	4999	-1	<b>	0	RGB(0,0,0)	RGB(256,256,256)
Profit_Loss	Costs	200	5000	5999	1	<i>	5	RGB(128,128,128)	RGB(256,256,256)
Profit_Loss	Gross Profit	300	4000	5999	-1	<b>	0	RGB(0,0,0)	RGB(256,256,256)
Profit_Loss	Expenses	400	6000	6999	1	<i>	5	RGB(128,128,128)	RGB(256,256,256)
Profit_Loss	EBIT	500	4000	6999	-1	<b>	0	RGB(0,0,0)	RGB(256,256,256)
Profit_Loss	Financial Costs	600	7000	7999	1	<i>	5	RGB(128,128,128)	RGB(256,256,256)
Profit_Loss	Other Income y Expenses	700	8000	8999	1	<i>	5	RGB(128,128,128)	RGB(256,256,256)
Profit_Loss	Net Profit	800	4000	8999	-1	<b>	0	RGB(0,0,0)	RGB(256,256,256)
Balance_Sheet	Assets	100	1000	1999	1	<i>	5	RGB(128,128,128)	RGB(256,256,256)
Balance_Sheet	Total Assets	199	1000	1999	1	<b>	0	RGB(0,0,0)	RGB(256,256,256)
Balance_Sheet	Liabilities	200	2000	2999	-1	<i>	5	RGB(128,128,128)	RGB(256,256,256)
Balance_Sheet	Capital	300	3000	3999	-1	<i>	5	RGB(128,128,128)	RGB(256,256,256)
Balance_Sheet	Net Profit	400	4000	9999	-1	<i>	5	RGB(128,128,128)	RGB(256,256,256)
Balance_Sheet	Total Capital and Liabilities	500	2000	9999	-1	<b>	0	RGB(0,0,0)	RGB(256,256,256)

Let's review the data that we store in our GLAccountsGroup table in more detail. Each of the following numbers corresponds to one or more columns in the previous diagram:

1. The first column defines the report that corresponds to the grouping or calculation that define in this row. In this case, we have three reports: an income statement, a balance sheet, and a cash flow statement.

2. In the next column, we include the text description of the account grouping or calculation.

3. Here, we define the order in which each concept must be displayed. We choose numbers in increments of a hundred so that we have room to insert new concepts in between two others without having to reassign the value of every other concept.

4. Account groupings are usually defined by a range of GL accounts. We use intervalmatch() in the script to link this table with our GLAccounts table. For more information on intervalmatch() review the QlikView help documentation where you can find a great example of how it works.

5. We define factor to be negative one (**-1**) for all accounts with a normal credit balance. We also apply a factor of negative one (**-1**) to every calculated group that includes a credit account. For example, we use negative one (**-1**) as a factor for gross profit because it is the sum of income (a normal credit balance) and costs (a normal debit balance). In doing so, we obtain the following results:

     ∘   If income is greater than costs, we have a profit. As income is a normal credit balance, we first see this as a negative number. As we want to see profit as a positive number, we multiply it by a factor of negative one (**-1**).

     ∘   Otherwise, if costs are greater than income, we have a loss. As costs are a normal debit balance, we first see this as a positive number. As we want to see loss as a negative number, we multiply it by a factor of negative one (**-1**).

6. We decide whether we want the account group's description and to appear in bold (`<b>`), italic (`<i>`), or bold italic (`<b><i>`) . If we want the text to be normal, we leave the cell blank.

7. We use indentation to help users recognize any group hierarchies. The number represents the amount of spaces that we will use to indent the group's text description.

8. We can color normal text dark grey and important text black. A good dark grey to use is `rgb(128,128,128)` or `DarkGray()`.

9. Finally, we leave the option to highlight certain rows with a background color.

Once we define the financial report metadata in the data model, we can then easily format our financial reports. We can also use this technique to maintain the format of any other legacy report in QlikView. Before we create our first financial report, let's look at one other element in the data model that facilitates financial analysis.

AsOfCalendar

When we perform financial analysis, we have to be able to easily adjust over which period we are going calculate each metric. For example, return on assets is net income divided by total assets. Net income is calculated over the past twelve months while total assets is an accumulated amount calculated over all previous months.

We can use set analysis to calculate these metrics at any one moment in time; however, we also would like to visualize the trend of these metrics. The best way to calculate that trend is to combine set analysis with an `AsOfCalendar`.

An `AsOfCalendar` contains the same months and years as a regular calendar. However, when we select a date in the `AsOfCalendar`, we see everything that is prior to this data in the `Facts` table. For example, in the following diagram if we select **2013-Jun** in the **AsOf Year-Month** field, then we see all months prior to it in the data model as possible values in the **Year-Month** field:

AsOf Year-Month	Year-Month
2013-Jun	2013-Apr
2013-Apr	2013-May
2013-May	2013-Jun
2013-Jul	2013-Jul
2013-Aug	2013-Aug
2013-Sep	2013-Sep
2013-Oct	2013-Oct
2013-Nov	2013-Nov

We use a subroutine, `Qvc.AsOfTable` in QV Components, to create the `AsOfCalendar` and insert the following script after creating the `MasterCalendar` table. We also add the `AsOf Year` and `AsOf Month` fields manually to make the table more useful. The table also contains a field called `AsOf Months Ago` that tells us how many months difference there is between the `AsOf Year-Month` and the `Year-Month`. This field can be quite useful when we need to calculate rolling periods:

```
CALL Qvc.AsOfTable('Year-Month');
AsOfCalendar:
Load *,
  Month([AsOf Year-Month]) as AsOfMonth,
  Year([AsOf Year-Month]) as AsOfYear
Resident [AsOfTable_Year-Month];
Drop table [AsOfTable_Year-Month];
```

In order to take advantage of this calendar, we also need to replace the usual year and month filters with ones that use `AsOf Year` and `AsOf Month`. The filters will look exactly the same as the year and month filters in the sales perspective that uses the master calendar table. However, in the following sections, we see what changes we have to make to accurately calculate the expressions.

Let's start visualizing the financial perspective with the three most important reports.

Income statement

An income statement is an essential report for all the business's stakeholders. We'll take an executive's perspective for our user story.

As an executive, I want to know whether the business made or lost money over a certain period of time. I also want to know the possible reasons for this result so that I can measure the results of the strategic actions that I took during that period.

Financial statements have been around for so long that most business users are going to want to see them in the format that they are accustomed to. As legacy reporting in QlikView involves using advanced methods, let's take the time to create them in their standard format. We will then look at how we can make a report more visual and easier to understand at a glance.

In the following income statement example, we start by calculating the sales that we generated during the course of the year. Proceeding downward through the report, we subtract the costs and expenses that were incurred in these same period. Then at certain moments in the report, we calculate a subtotal. For example, gross profit is sales minus costs, operating profit is gross profit minus expenses, and net profit is operating profit minus other concepts, such as taxes and interest.

Each of these main groups (sales, costs, and expenses) can be divided into further subgroups. These subgroups depend on the business and what the stakeholders want to measure. For example, we want to dissect expenses into various subgroups, such as travel and payroll, and see how each affects whether we make money or not. Let's create an income statement in the following *Exercise 3.2*.

	Jan 2015 Monthly	%	YTD	%
Sales Revenue	1,481,031	100%	1,481,031	100%
Other Revenue	-	-	-	-
Total Revenue	**1,481,031**	**100%**	**1,481,031**	**100%**
COGS - Cost of Goods Sold	1,159,277	78%	1,159,277	78%
Cost Variances	-	-	-	-
Gross Profit	**321,753**	**22%**	**321,753**	**22%**
Travel Expenses	-	-	-	-
Payroll Expenses	-	-	-	-
Bad Debt Expenses	-	-	-	-
Admin Expenses	-	-	-	-
Depreciation and Amorti...	-	-	-	-
Office Expenses	-	-	-	-
Legal Expenses	-	-	-	-
Other Expenses	-	-	-	-
Operating Profit	**321,753**	**22%**	**321,753**	**22%**
Financial Costs	0	0%	0	0%
Other Income y Expenses	-	-	-	-
Net Profit	**321,753**	**22%**	**321,753**	**22%**

Exercise 3.2

In the `Financial_Perspective_Sandbox.qvw` application that is found in the `C:\Qlik\SourceData\1002.Finance_Perspective\1.Application`, let's start by creating a straight table with the following properties:

1. Add the `[Account - Concept]` field as a dimension.

2. Add the following five metrics:

Label	Expression

=' '	`only({1<[Account - Report]`
	`={'Income_Statement'}>}`
	`[Account - Order])`

=monthname(
max(
[AsOf Year-
Month]
))
&
chr(10)
& 'Monthly'
	`sum({$<[Account - Report]={'Income_Statement'},`
	`[Month]=, [Year]=,_MonthSerial={'$(=max`
	`(_AsOfMonthSerial))'}>} [GJ Amount])`
	`* only([Account - Factor])`

%	`sum({$<[Account - Report]={'Income_Statement'},`
	`[Month]=, [Year]=,_MonthSerial={'$(=max`
	`(_AsOfMonthSerial))'}>} [GJ Amount])`
	`* only([Account - Factor])`
	`/`
	`sum({$<[Account - Report]={'Income_`
	`Statement'},[Account - Concept]={'Total  Revenue'},`
	`[Month]=, [Year]=,_MonthSerial={'$(=max`
	`(_AsOfMonthSerial))'}>} Total [GJ Amount]) * -1`

=chr(10) &
'YTD'
	`sum({$<[Account - Report]={'Income_Statement'}, [Mon`
	`th]=, [Year]={$(=max(AsOfYear))},`
	`_MonthSerial={'<=$(=max(_AsOfMonthSerial))'}>} [GJ`
	`Amount])  * only([Account - Factor])`

%	`sum({$<[Account - Report]={'Income_Statement'},`
	`[Month]=, [Year]={$(=max(AsOfYear))},`
	`_MonthSerial={'<=$(=max(_AsOfMonthSerial))'}>} [GJ`
	`Amount])`
	`* only([Account - Factor])`
	`/`
	`sum({$<[Account - Report]={'Income_`
	`Statement'},[Account - Concept]={'Total  Revenue'}`
	`, [Month]=, [Year]={$(=max(AsOfYear))},`
	`_MonthSerial={'<=$(=max(_AsOfMonthSerial))'}>}`
	`Total [GJ Amount])`
	`* -1`

The first expression looks unusual. It doesn't aggregate anything and doesn't even appear in the example income statement. That's because it works as a placeholder for account groups that do not have any GJ entries during the selected period. Unlike QlikView, legacy reports usually show dimensions even when the sum of their corresponding metric is zero. We change the expression's **Text Color** to white() so that it is hidden from the user.

Now that we've added the necessary dimension and expressions let's change a few detailed properties and apply the financial report metadata to the QlikView object:

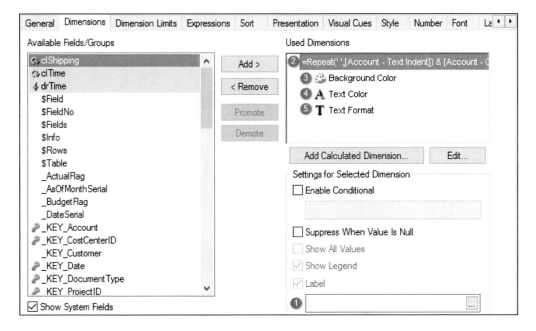

1. In the **Dimensions** tab, select the **Account – Concept** and insert a blank space in the **Label** field.

2. Click **Edit...** and insert the following code to enable the text indentation:

   ```
   =Repeat(' ',[Account - Text Indent]) & [Account - Concept]
   ```

3. Expand the dimension's properties and click **Background Color**. Click **Edit...** and insert the following code:

   ```
   =Only({1} [Account - Background Color])
   ```

4. Click **Text Color** and click **Edit...** and insert the following formula:

   ```
   =Only({1} [Account - Text Color])
   ```

5. Finally, click **Text Format** and then click **Edit...** and insert the following formula:

    ```
    =Only({1} [Account - Text Format])
    ```

6. In the **Dimensions** tab, there is a little-used option that we can use to adjust the row spacing to make the table more readable and aesthetically pleasing. Click **Advanced...** in the **Dimensions** tab and make the two changes that appear in the following diagram:

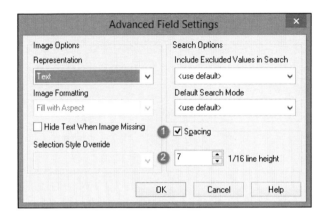

7. Now, let's apply the same formatting changes to the expressions, as follows:

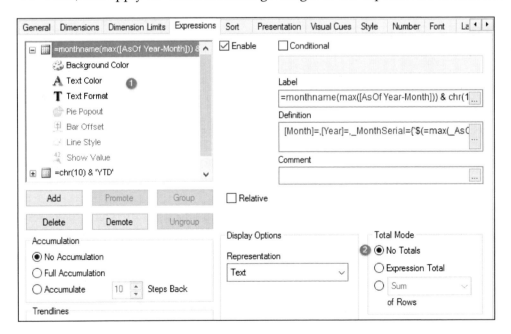

8. In the same way that we defined the properties of the dimension, we define the **Background Color**, **Text Color**, and **Text Format** in the **Definition** field for every expression except for the one we use as a placeholder:

Background Color	`=Only({1} [Account - Background Color])`
Text Color	`=Only({1} [Account - Text Color])`
Text Format	`=Only({1} [Account - Text Format])`

9. Finally, for each expression select the **No Totals** radio button in the **Total Mode** section.

10. Let's move on to the **Sort** tab. Go through the steps in the following diagram to properly sort the report's concepts. The sort expression is `=only({1< [Account - Report]={'Income_Statement'}>} [Account - Order]):`

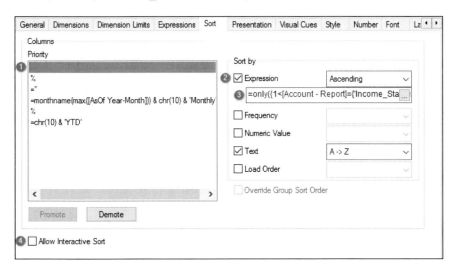

> We can reduce the work in this step if we use the `dual()` function in the script to combine the text description and order number into one field:
>
> `dual([Account - Concept], [Account - Order]) as [Account - Sorted Concept]`
>
> We would then only need to sort `[Account - Sorted Concept]` by **Numeric Value**.

11. Now in the **Presentation** tab, let's copy the options that are seen the following diagram:

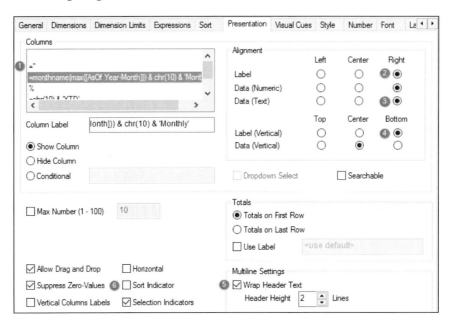

It is good practice to align the column label in the same way that we did to its data. We also keep the label close to the data and vertically align the label on the bottom of a two-line header. Make sure to set these alignments for every expression.

Along with proper formatting, we want to alert users to any negative values. Such values in one of the income statement's calculated groups, such as Gross Profit or Operating Profit, indicate a loss. If found in other groups they may indicate an unusual transaction that affects an account contrary to its normal balance. We enable these alerts in the **Visual Cues** tab.

If we have room enough to only use whitespace to divide columns, let's remove the borders in the **Style** tab in two easy steps:

1. Uncheck **Vertical Dimension Cell Borders**.
2. Uncheck **Vertical Expression Cell Borders**.

Finally, let's perform these last two steps to clean the number format and to hide the caption:

1. In the **Number** tab, define both expressions as integers.
2. In the **Caption** tab, uncheck **Show Caption**.

We should now have a fairly clean income statement, but what if we want to go a little further and change the background of the column header or row borders? We can use a hidden feature called **Custom Format Cell** to make these additional changes.

Custom format cell

Straight tables and pivot tables have an additional properties dialog to further customize a table's style. It is not available by default, so first we go to the **Settings** file menu, and then **User Preference...**.

In the **Design** tab of **User Preferences**, tick the option to **Always Show Design Menu Items**, as shown in the following screenshot:

We now have a new option called **Custom Format Cell** when we right-click over any table:

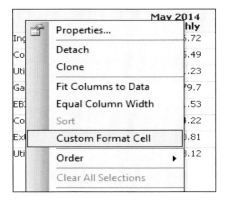

This option opens a window that allows us to define the cell borders, cell backgrounds, text color, text style, and text size of each dimension and expression. Any change that we make to one cell applies to all other cells belonging to the same expression or dimension. In other words, we cannot define a different format for two different cells of the same expression or dimension.

Regardless of this limitation, **Custom Format Cell** does provide us with several options to create a custom table style. Let's go ahead and make our final changes to the format of the income statement as follows:

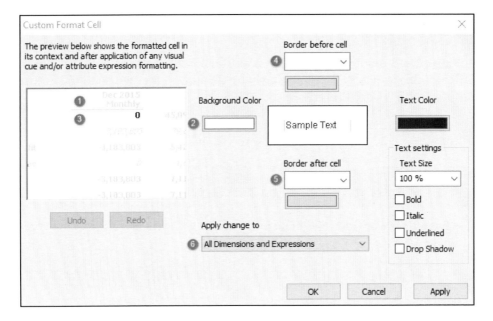

You will notice that on the left-hand side of the window, we can navigate throughout the table and define the style for each dimension and expression without having to close the window and reopen it by right-clicking on a different area of the table. Let's start by clicking on the first expression's column header:

1. Change the **Background Color** to white.
2. Now, click on the first cell with data.
3. Change the **Border before cell** to nothing.
4. Change the **Border after cell** to nothing.
5. Select **All Dimensions and Expression** in the **Apply change to** drop-down box and click OK.

If we add a few more metrics and move the account names to the center of the table, we can achieve a more detailed *winged report* with monthly metrics on one side and year-to-date metrics on the other. You can review the following example in the exercise solution file:

Mar 2015 Monthly	%	LY	%	Var	% Var		YTD	%	LY	%	Var	%Var
3,977,941	100%	2,333,228	100%	1,644,712	70%	Sales Revenue	10,580,068	100%	6,358,645	100%	4,221,424	66%
·	·	·	·	·	·	Other Revenue	·	·	·	·	·	·
3,977,941	100%	2,333,228	100%	1,644,712	70%	Total Revenue	10,580,068	100%	6,358,645	100%	4,221,424	66%
3,310,852	83%	2,117,383	91%	1,193,468	56%	COGS - Cost of Goods Sold	10,894,354	103%	6,037,336	95%	4,356,519	80%
·	·	·	·	·	·	Cost Variances	·	·	·	·	·	·
667,089	17%	215,845	9%	451,244	209%	Gross Profit	-314,286	-3%	320,809	5%	-635,095	-198%
						Travel Expenses						

Now that we have a well-formatted income statement, let's examine how we can use common visualization techniques to make it more effective. We use a slightly modified version of the previous user story to identify the key points that executives look for in an income statement.

> As an executive, I want to quickly see how the income statement has been changing over the course of this year. I also want to see how each period compares to the same period last year so that I can discover whether my strategies are improving our financial results.

Modern accounting has been around for more than 500 years, and we are probably not going to change how accountants visualize data in our lifetime. The accountant's instinct to use numbers and tables to solve this user story may result in something like the following example, which is a common format to analyze how an income statement is trending:

AsOfMonth									Jan		Feb
	Month	Month LY	Var	% Var	YTD	YTD LY	Var	% Var	Month	Month LY	Var
Sales Revenue	1,481,031	321,808	1,159,222	360%	1,481,031	321,808	1,159,222	360%	5,121,097	3,703,608	1,417,48
Total Revenue	1,481,031	321,808	1,159,222	360%	1,481,031	321,808	1,159,222	360%	5,121,097	3,703,608	1,417,48
COGS - Cost of Goods Sold	1,159,277	280,221	879,057	314%	1,159,277	280,221	879,057	314%	6,424,225	3,640,231	2,783,99
Cost Variances	-	-	-	-	-	-	-	- -	-	-	
Gross Profit	321,753	41,588	280,166	674%	321,753	41,588	280,166	674%	-1,303,128	63,376	-1,366,50
Admin Expenses	-	-	-	-	-	-	-	- -	-	-	

Any argument to say that they shouldn't analyze data in this way will cause them to question QlikView's ability to satisfy their reporting needs. Therefore, I recommend that we do it in the way that they are most comfortable with. Luckily, the AsOfCalendar table makes this report possible without reverting to methods, such as island tables and if-statements, that can cause the report's calculation time to grow exponentially. You can review the details on how to make the table in the exercise solution file.

Then, in addition to the table, we should propose more abstract ways to view the data more efficiently. Converting a table full of metrics into an abstract visualization is one of the most difficult challenges that we will ever face as data visualization designers. We have to come to terms with the fact that we cannot fit every metric into one chart without making it as hard to read as the originating table. Regardless of whether we use lines, bars, points, or some purportedly omniscient chart, we cannot fit everything into one visualization.

The best solution is to create a group of charts in which each element highlights a different aspect of the income statement. For example, we can create one bar chart to analyze year-to-date amounts and variations, and another graph to analyze monthly amounts and variations. Then we can add a line chart to view the trend of the most important account groups, and another to view the trend of detailed expense accounts.

Another alternative is to use the same familiar table structure to create a grid chart. Again, if we try to fit everything into one chart, we have to sacrifice a certain level of detail, metrics, or dimensions. At the same time, we can use the following grid chart to start a story that will lead us to look at specific charts and tables as we dive deeper into our story:

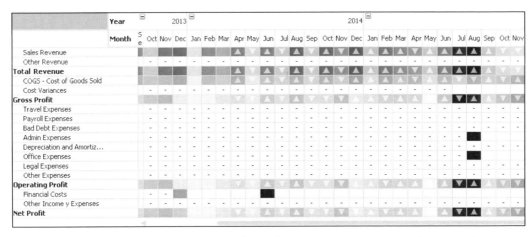

In order to make this chart, we have to sacrifice measuring year-to-date metrics. We've maintained the same number of dimensions, but we've replaced actual numbers with color and year-over-year variation with an arrow.

Even so, we can quickly perceive that we had our highest sales in July and August 2015, while strangely, our cost of goods sold was highest in December 2014. The fact that cost of goods sold is not always correlated to sales is curious. Such an observation may be a great place for a business user to start a story that leads to price and inventory analysis.

Exercise 3.3

In the `Financial_Perspective_Sandbox.qvw` application, let's first create a variable that makes the chart expressions cleaner, as follows:

1. Add the following variables that calculate the GJ amount for the current month and the same month last year:

Name	Definition
vExp_CYMTD_ GJAmount	sum({$<[Account - Report]={'Income_Statement'}, [AsOf Months Ago]={0}>} [GJ Amount])
vExp_LYMTD_ GJAmount	sum({$<[Account - Report]={'Income_Statement'}, [AsOf Months Ago]={12}>} [GJ Amount])

2. Clone the income statement that we created in *Exercise 3.2* and change the chart type to pivot table.

3. Add the dimensions `AsOfYear` and `AsOfMonth` to the cloned table and pivot them so that they become columns as in the previous figure.

4. Replace the existing metric with the following that creates an up arrow, or `chr(9650)` if the current month is greater than the same month last year and a down arrow otherwise, or chr(9660). This expression also serves as a placeholder for inactive accounts:

Label	Expression

Month	```if(
	    $(vExp_CYMTD_GJAmount) * only([Account - Factor])
	    /
	    $(vExp_LYMTD_GJAmount) * only([Account - Factor])
	    -1
	    <0,chr(9660),
	    if(
	        $(vExp_CYMTD_GJAmount) * only([Account - Factor])
	        /
	        $(vExp_LYMTD_GJAmount) * only([Account - Factor])
	        -1
	        >0,chr(9650),
	        if(not isnull(only({1< [Account - Report]={'Income_
	Statement'}>} [Account - Concept]))
	            ,'')
	        )
	    )```

5. Add the following code as a background color of the expression. The `aggr()` function helps define a different range of lightness and darkness for each account. Otherwise, the accounts with the largest numbers like revenue and costs would always be a dark color and every other smaller account a light one:

```
ColorMix2 (
  if($(vExp_CYMTD_GJAmount) * -1  < 0
    ,-Sqrt(($(vExp_CYMTD_GJAmount) * -1)/min(total <[Account
- Concept]> aggr($(vExp_CYMTD_GJAmount)* -1,[Account -
Concept],AsOfMonth,AsOfYear)))
    ,Sqrt(($(vExp_CYMTD_GJAmount) * -1)/max(total <[Account
- Concept]> aggr($(vExp_CYMTD_GJAmount)* -1,[Account -
Concept],AsOfMonth,AsOfYear))))
    , ARGB(255, 255, 128, 0), ARGB(255, 0, 64, 128), ARGB(255, 255,
255, 255))
```

6. Add `white(150)` as the expression's text color. We make the arrow slightly transparent so that it contrasts less with the background, which makes for easier reading and a more refined look.

We now have an income statement grid chart. We can experiment with the options that we learned earlier in this section to add cell borders and any fine-tuning adjustments. After doing so, let's move on to the next important financial report — the balance sheet.

Balance sheet

We use the following user story to understand the needs of the business users that require a balance sheet.

> As an executive, I want to understand the overall financial health of the business so that I can create the necessary strategy to ensure its future.

As an executive, I want to understand the overall financial health of the business so that I can create the necessary strategy to ensure its future.

The balance sheet is a complete analysis of a company's financial situation. It is the sum of all GJ amounts divided into three principal groups: assets, liabilities, and capital. The income statement from the previous section is a small part of the balance sheet that is classified as Retained Earnings in the capital account group. The following is an example balance sheet:

Balance Sheet

	Current Month	%	Last Month	%	Var	%Var
Current Assets	442,873,038	100%	407,692,027	100%	35,181,011	9%
Fixed Assets	-	-	-	-	-	-
Long-term Assets	-	-	-	-	-	-
Total Assets	**442,873,038**	**100%**	**407,692,027**	**100%**	**35,181,011**	**9%**
Current Liabilities	423,008,636	96%	397,324,153	97%	25,684,483	6%
Long-term Liabilities	-	-	-	-	-	-
Total Liabilities	**423,008,636**	**96%**	**397,324,153**	**97%**	**25,684,483**	**6%**
Stock	-	-	-	-	-	-
Past Retained Earning	-	-	-	-	-	-
Current Retained Earning	19,864,402	4%	10,367,873	3%	9,496,529	92%
Total Capital	**19,864,402**	**4%**	**10,367,873**	**3%**	**9,496,529**	**92%**
Total Capital and Liabilities	**442,873,038**	**100%**	**407,692,027**	**100%**	**35,181,011**	**9%**

Unlike an income statement where we only see financial movements over a certain period of time, a balance sheet shows us an accumulated total of all the financial movements that have occurred prior to the selected month. Another requirement is that total assets must always be equal to the sum of liabilities and capital.

Also, we often divide assets, liabilities, and capital into smaller account groups that permit us to perform a deeper financial analysis of the company. For each group we calculate its percentage contribution with reference to total assets or total capital and liabilities. Finally, variation is calculated between consecutive periods. Year-over-year analysis is less common because seasonality is not as important for the balance sheet as it is for the income statement.

We create a balance sheet in the same way that we create an income statement. Let's create one in the next exercise.

Exercise 3.4

We start to create our balance sheet by cloning the income statement that we created in *Exercise 3.2* and then go through the following steps:

1. Change the placeholder expression to the following code:

```
only({1<[Account - Report]={'Balance_Sheet'}>} [Account - Order])
```

2. Change the expression that calculates the current month to the following code:

```
sum({$<[Account - Report]={'Balance_Sheet'}, [Month]=, [Year]=,
_MonthSerial={'<=$(=max(_AsOfMonthSerial))'}>} [GJ Amount]) *
only([Account - Factor])
```

3. Change the expression that calculates the percentage contribution liabilities to the following code:

```
sum({$<[Account - Report]={'Balance_Sheet'},[Month]=,[Year]=,
_MonthSerial={'<=$(=max(_AsOfMonthSerial))'}>} [GJ Amount])
* only([Account - Factor])
/
sum({$<[Account - Report]={'Balance_Sheet'},[Account -
Concept]={'Total Assets'}
,[Month]=,[Year]=,_MonthSerial={'<=$(=max(_AsOfMonthSerial))'}>}
Total [GJ Amount])
```

4. Replace the remaining two expressions in the cloned chart by repeating steps two and three to calculate the previous month's balances. In doing so, we change the set analysis that refers to `_MonthSerial` from `{'<=$(=max(_AsOfMonthSerial))'}` to `{'<=$(=max(_AsOfMonthSerial)-1)'}`.

5. Add variation and percentage variation columns as shown in the example balance sheet.

6. Change the set analysis in the sort expression so that it refers to `[Account -Report]={'Balance_Sheet'}`.

When we create data visualization that supports a balance sheet, we tend to analyze the ratio between amounts. For example, a metric such as return on assets, which is the net income divided by the average total assets, tells us how well a company uses its assets to earn a profit. Another example is the acid test ratio that divides current assets, such as cash, accounts receivable, and short-term investments, by current liabilities, such as accounts payable. This ratio tells us how well the business can cover short-term liabilities. Similar to these there are numerous other ratios that the accounting department may use to evaluate the current financial situation of a company. You can find out what a certain financial ratio means and how to calculate it at `http://www.investopedia.com/`.

The actual visualizations for these ratios are often quite simple. In part, this is true because The balance sheet has relatively few dimensions that pertain to it. Fields related to company and time are usually the only applicable dimensions that are available. Even so, it can be difficult to calculate them in QlikView and we often calculate financial ratios for a selected moment in time using set analysis. However, when we add the `AsOfCalendar` to the data model, we have the ability to analyze how they change over time.

In the next exercise, let's make a simple line chart that shows how return on assets behave over time.

Exercise 3.5

1. Add the following variable that includes two parameters that allow us to see the end-of-month balance of any concept. The first parameter defines the concept, and the second determines whether the balance is from the current month or any previous month. Zero (0) is the current month, one (1) is the previous month, two (2) is the month before that, and so on:

Name	Definition
vExp_EOM_ GJBalance	`sum({$<[Account - Report]={'Balance_ Sheet'},[Account - Concept]={$1},[AsOf Months Ago]={">=$2"}>} [GJ Amount])`

2. Create a bar chart with `[AsOf YearMonth]` as the dimension and with the following expression. The expression divides the last three months of net income by the three-month average of assets:

```
(sum({$<[Account - Report]={'Balance_Sheet'},[Account
- Concept]={'Current Retained Earning'},[AsOf Months
Ago]={">=1<=3"}>} [GJ Amount LC]))*-1
/
(
RangeSum(
$(vExp_EOM_GJBalance('Current Assets',0))
,$(vExp_EOM_GJBalance('Current Assets',1))
,$(vExp_EOM_GJBalance('Current Assets',2))
)/3
)
```

3. Adjust the bar chart's properties to produce a graph that is similar to the following figure:

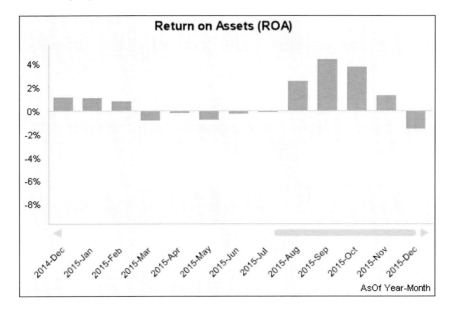

Without the `AsOfCalendar` table, this trend analysis and visualization would be difficult and slow to create. We use the `[AsOf Months Ago]` field in the set analysis to calculate over a rolling period that depends on the value of the `[AsOf YearMonth]` dimension.

Unlike the **Accumulation** option in the **Expression** tab or the `above()` function, we don't have to worry about the first few values of a selected data months being incorrect. Whether the user selects one month or one year, every bar in this chart will show the correct value. Although the final visualization is simple, the data model and calculation that we need to create it is quite elegant.

Cash flow statement

A *cash flow statement* is a report that analyzes the financial movements that affect cash flow.

As an investor, I want to understand how the company receives and spends its cash so that I can understand whether the company is funded by its own operations, investing in the future, and/or borrowing excessively.

Cash flow is classified in the following ways:

- Operations can be calculated using a direct or indirect method that is explained as follows:

    ° The indirect method starts with the net income from the income statement and adjusts it according to the net changes of accounts receivable (A/R), accounts payable (A/P), and inventory

    ° The direct method sums cash transactions between our customers, suppliers, and employees

- Investing includes purchasing and selling assets, such as offices or equipment
- Financing includes receiving or paying a bank loan

Cash Flow Statement	目 XL _ ☐	
	Movement	%
Net Income	903,622	33%
Depreciation and Amortization	0	0%
Inventory Increase (Decrease)	-36,387,104	-1,349%
Accounts Receivable Increase (Decrease)	-6,297,010	-233%
Accounts Payable Increase (Decrease)	44,477,921	1,649%
Cash Flow from Operations	2,697,428	100%
Capital Expenses	0	0%
Cash Flow from Investing	0	0%
Notes Payable	0	0%
Cash Flow from Financing	0	0%
Total Cash Flow	2,697,428	100%

To create a cash flow statement, we have to find every G/L account that affects the accounts that represent cash assets. In order to be successful at this, we have to team up with an accountant who can help us find and classify these accounts. When the total cash flow in this statement equals the net change of all cash assets then we've successfully found all the accounts.

In the next exercise, we will create a high-level cash flow statement using the more popular indirect method.

Exercise 3.6

We start to create our cash flow statement by cloning the balance statement that we created in *Exercise 3.2* and then go through the following steps:

1. Change the placeholder expression to the following code:

```
only({1<[Account - Report]={'CashFlow'}>} [Account - Order])
```

2. Change one of the expressions to calculate net movements across all accounts:

```
sum({$<[Account - Report]={'CashFlow'},[AsOf Months Ago]={0}>} [GJ
Amount] * [Account - Factor])
```

3. Change one of the expressions to calculate the relative percentage between each amount and the total cash flow:

```
sum({$<[Account - Report]={'CashFlow'},[AsOf Months Ago]={0}>} [GJ
Amount] * [Account - Factor])
/
sum({$<[Account - Report]={'CashFlow'},[Account - Concept]={'Total
Cash Flow'},[AsOf Months Ago]={0}>} Total [GJ Amount] * [Account -
Factor])
```

4. Delete all other expressions.

5. Change the set analysis in the sort expression so that it refers to `[Account - Report]={'CashFlow'}`.

The magic we do to create this report is in the financial report metadata that we reviewed earlier in this chapter. We use the **Factor** field the following table to add or subtract amounts as defined by the accountant. This method of report making is not always easy to grasp at first, so we should take our time to explore and experiment with the metadata.

Report	Concept	From_Account	To_Account	Factor
CashFlow	Net Income	40000000	99999999	-1
CashFlow	Depreciation and Amortization	61500000	61599999	1
CashFlow	Inventory Increase (Decrease)	11300000	11399999	-1
CashFlow	Accounts Receivable Increase (Decrease)	11200000	11299999	-1
CashFlow	Accounts Payable Increase (Decrease)	21100000	21199999	-1
CashFlow	Cash Flow from Operations	40000000	61499999	-1
CashFlow	Cash Flow from Operations	61600000	99999999	-1
CashFlow	Cash Flow from Operations	11300000	11399999	-1
CashFlow	Cash Flow from Operations	11200000	11299999	-1
CashFlow	Cash Flow from Operations	21100000	21199999	-1
CashFlow	Capital Expenses	16100000	16199999	-1
CashFlow	Cash Flow from Investing	16100000	16199999	-1
CashFlow	Notes Payable	21440000	21440000	-1
CashFlow	Cash Flow from Financing	21440000	21440000	-1
CashFlow	Total Cash Flow	40000000	61499999	-1
CashFlow	Total Cash Flow	61600000	99999999	-1
CashFlow	Total Cash Flow	11300000	11399999	-1
CashFlow	Total Cash Flow	11200000	11299999	-1
CashFlow	Total Cash Flow	21100000	21199999	-1
CashFlow	Total Cash Flow	16100000	16199999	-1
CashFlow	Total Cash Flow	21440000	21440000	-1

The most important analysis introduced by the user story in the beginning of the section is to see what percentage of cash is received or spent within each group of activities. The cash flow statement looks distinct for different businesses during each stage in their lives. A start-up will not have much cash flow in operations, but it will have a lot of investment and financing activities. A mature company will have a more balanced cash flow with the greater amount classified as operations. A simple bar chart to that compares these three principal activities over time would be the optimal visualization.

Summary

A QlikView financial perspective is a challenge for any master. The creation of clean, clear, traditional financial reports is just as important as any other way to visualize data. However, we shouldn't stop there. We should strive to go beyond these first reports and create charts that allow financial analysts and executives to discover opportunities that are not so easy to find in a table full of numbers.

Be sure to review the use of the financial report metadata and the as-of calendar as tools to help create the income statement, balance sheet, and cash flow statement. They are also vital to create the supporting data visualization.

In the next chapter, we will leave behind traditional reports and experiment with more advanced data visualization in the QlikView marketing perspective.

4
Marketing Perspective

The most successful businesses understand the market that they serve. They understand that talking with a customer about their needs is more effective than babbling about their own product or service. We can use the marketing perspective to analyze actual customers, potential customers, business competitors, and society at large. Although we have a fair amount of internal data about our own customers, we also look for other data resources to examine other market variables.

One of the internal data sources that we can exploit is the **Customer Relationship Management (CRM)** system. This includes data about current customers that isn't necessarily related to actual sales, such as visits, sales opportunities, and service calls. It also stores sales opportunities with potential customers. In addition to a CRM, we can also use the same sales data from *Chapter 2, Sales Perspective*, to better understand our current customers' purchasing behavior.

Depending on the company, we may also find data that is useful from external sources. If the business is actively involved in social networks, then we can gather market data from Facebook, Twitter, or LinkedIn. We can also purchase data from market research companies or download free, public data from several governmental and nongovernmental organizations.

In this chapter, we will review the following topics while we create the QlikView marketing perspective:

- Marketing data model
- Customer profiling
- Market analysis
- Social media analysis
- Sales opportunity flow analysis

Let's get started with a look at how we combine the CRM data with the existing sales data model from *Chapter 2, Sales Perspective*.

Marketing data model

A CRM system serves several functions. Along with keeping track of our sales process and the level of customer service, it also gives us first-hand data about our customers and leads. It contains an evolving event called a sales opportunity that, in itself, contains various discrete events, such as visits, and calls, and sales quotes. All this data is important first-hand information about our market. This is especially true in the case of sales quotes, which are documents that are similar to invoices and give us an idea what customers are interested in buying, how much they plan to purchase, and at what price. An opportunity may also include information about its origins, competing offers, and any reason why we failed to convert it into an actual sale.

A CRM system also tends to add more information to the customer catalog, such as demographic information. If customers are people, then we may gather data about their age, sex, education level, income level, marital status, and so on. Otherwise, if our customers are businesses, then we may gather data about the industry group that they belong to along with the number of employees and annual revenue. We may also add more detailed geographical data, such as latitude and longitude.

We can find the marketing perspective container called `1003.Marketing_Perspective` in the *Chapter 4, Marketing Perspective*, folder of the book's exercises. Let's load this container into the QDF in the same way that we did in *Chapter 2, Sales Perspective*. Once we've transferred the container, let's open the marketing perspective called `Marketing_Perspective_Sandbox.qvw` in the `1.Application` folder and see how sales opportunities and other marketing data combine with the previous sales data model.

As you can see, the following data model is quite similar to that of the sales perspective. We've added some additional fields in the `Facts` table to help us measure the following events:

- Sales opportunities
- Sales quotes
- Customer-related activities, such as visits and calls

Sales quotes and activities are discrete events that occur on a given date. However, sales opportunities are evolving events that go through several stages. Each stage represents a step that we expect to perform in every sales process. For example, going to the first meeting, sending a sales quote, and negotiating the final sales terms are common steps in a sales process.

In our analysis, we want to know how the process is evolving. More specifically, we want to identify its current step along how it progressed through past steps. We use `intervalmatch()` in the load script to link the start and end dates of each step with the corresponding discrete dates in the `MasterCalendar` table. A side effect of using `intervalmatch()` is the existence of a synthetic key table in the data model. A synthetic table is QlikView's way of linking tables that share more than one key field. Usually, we avoid using these tables as they may affect the performance of the data model, but in this case we leave it in the data model. Any attempt to eliminate the synthetic key table created by `intervalmatch()` often nullifies its purpose or causes the related tables to grow too large.

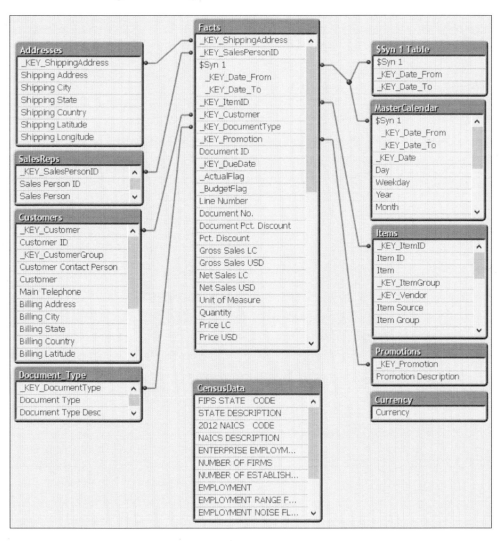

Finally, we add business demographic data and geographical data to the `customer` catalog along with a related table with public census data that helps us look for new markets that share the same attributes as the business's current customers.

 We can download the latest US business census data from `http://www.census.gov/`. The census data that we use in this data model is from `http://www.census.gov/econ/susb/`.

Apart from this additional data, we reuse many of the dimensions and metrics that we saw in *Chapter 2, Sales Perspective*. For example, Customer, Sales Person, and Item also exist in this data model. Let's take a closer look at some of the new dimensions and metrics that pertain to marketing.

Dimensions		
7Ws	**Fields**	**Comments**
Who	Customer NAICS (2-digit)	This customer attribute comes from the **North American Industry Classification System (NAICS)**, which is a hierarchical group of numbers that classify our customers.
Who	Customer Employee Size	This attribute helps us determine the demographics of the customer base.
Who	Competitor	This market information helps us to examine who we are competing against and measure our success rate against them.
Where	Sales Opportunity Stage	This is where we identify both the current and closed steps of an evolving sales process.
Metrics		
7Ws	**Fields**	**Comments**
How Many	Potential Sales	This is where we estimate how much we will be able to sell to a customer or a prospect.
How Many	Sale Opportunity Close %	This is a standard practice to calculate a more accurate potential sales amount, which is is to multiply it by the probability that we will succeed in closing the sale. As we progress through the sales process the probability increases.

Now that we have a marketing data model, let's create current customer profiles and discover where we can find similar businesses according to the census data.

Customer profiling

In the marketing data model, we use each customer's NAICS code, employee size, and average revenue to create profiles. We want to look for profitable customers, so we also cross this data with the the gross profit each customer generates. We use a parallel coordinates chart and a Sankey chart to visualize customer profiles.

 As a market analyst, I want to discover demographic characteristics of our current customers so that I can search for potential customers among companies with similar attributes.

Parallel coordinates

In `Marketing_Perspective_Sandbox.qvw`, we are going to make the following parallel coordinates chart. This chart helps us analyze multivariate data in a two-dimensional space. We often use metrics that result in numbers to create it and we can find such example at `http://poverconsulting.com/2013/10/10/kpi-parallel-coordinates-chart/`.

However, in the following chart, we use descriptive values for **NAICS**, **Size**, and **Average Revenue** that we can see in detail in the text popup. The highlighted line represents construction companies that have **10-19** employees and **$100,000-$250,000** in annual revenue. The width of the line represents the relative number of customers of this type compared to other types.

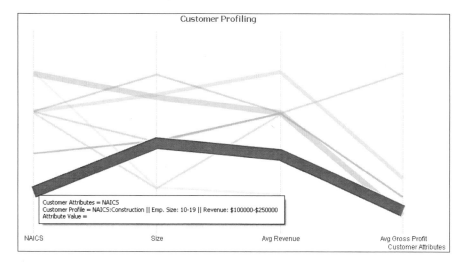

Exercise 4.1

Before we begin to create this chart, let's create the following variable:

Variable	
Label	**Value**
vIgnoreSelectionToHighlight	[Customer NAICS]=,
	[Customer Employment Size]=,
	[Customer Est. Annual Revenue]=

Now, let's create a line chart with the following property options:

Dimensions	
Label	**Value**
Customer Attributes	CustomerProfileAttribute
Customer Profile	='NAICS:' & [Customer NAICS] & ' || Emp. Size:' & [Customer Employment Size] & ' || Revenue:' & [Customer Est. Annual Revenue]
Expressions	
Label	**Value**

Attribute Value	pick(match(only({$<$(vIgnoreSelectionToHighlight)>} CustomerProfileAttribute),'NAICS','Size','Avg Revenue','Avg Gross Profit')
	
	,only({$<$(vIgnoreSelectionToHighlight)>}[Customer NAICS (2digit)])
	    /max({$<$(vIgnoreSelectionToHighlight)>} total
	[Customer NAICS (2digit)])+(Rand()/50-(1/100))
	
	,only({$<$(vIgnoreSelectionToHighlight)>}[Customer Employment Size])
	    /max({$<$(vIgnoreSelectionToHighlight)>} total [Customer Employment Size])+(Rand()/50-(1/100))
	
	,only({$<$(vIgnoreSelectionToHighlight)>}[Customer Est. Annual Revenue])
	    /max({$<$(vIgnoreSelectionToHighlight)>} total [Customer Est. Annual Revenue])+(Rand()/50-(1/100))
	
	,avg({$<$(vIgnoreSelectionToHighlight)>}
	    aggr(sum({$<$(vIgnoreSelectionToHighlight)>}[Gross Profit])
	,Customer,CustomerProfileAttribute,[Customer NAICS],[Customer Employment Size],[Customer Est. Annual Revenue]))
	/max({$<$(vIgnoreSelectionToHighlight)>}
	    total aggr(sum({$<$(vIgnoreSelectionToHighlight)>}[Gross Profit])
	,Customer,CustomerProfileAttribute,[Customer NAICS],[Customer Employment Size],[Customer Est. Annual Revenue]))
	)

Expression Attributes	**Value**
Line Style	='<w' & (count(Customer)/max(total aggr(count(Customer),CustomerProfileAttribute,[Customer NAICS (2digit)],[Customer Employment Size],[Customer Est. Annual Revenue])) * 7.5 + .5) & '>'

The `CustomerProfileAttribute` dimension is an island table in the data model that includes a list of customer attributes for this chart. We use this island table instead of a `valuelist()` function because we are going to use the `aggr()` function in the metric expression. In a chart, the `aggr()` function works properly only when we include every chart dimension as a parameter, and it doesn't accept a `valuelist()` function as a parameter.

The expression is quite long because it includes a different expression for each attribute. If we are not accustomed to the use of `pick()` or `match()`, we should review their functionality in *QlikView Help*. In the script that loads the data model, we assign a number value behind each attribute. For example, we use the `autonumber()` function to assign a number for each NAICS description. This number's only purpose is to define a space for the description along the Y-Axis. Its magnitude is meaningless.

We then normalize the number by dividing each customer attribute value by the maximum value of that particular attribute. The result is a number between 0 and 1. We do this so that we can compare variables that have different scales of magnitude. We also add a random number to the attribute value expression when it is descriptive, so as to reduce overlapping. Although it is not a perfect solution, a random number that moves the line one-hundredth of a decimal above or below the actual value may help us handle a greater number of lines.

We also dynamically define each line's width in the Line Style expression attribute. A line's width is defined as `<Wn>` where n is a number between .5 and 8. We calculate each line's width by first calculating the percentage of customers each represents, which give us a number between 0 and 1. Then, we multiply that number by 7.5 and add .5 so that we use the line width's full range.

Finally, the numbers along the Y-Axis don't add any value, so we hide the axis and we add dimensional grid lines that are characteristic of parallel coordinate charts. It is likely that this chart will contain myriad lines, so we make every color in the color bucket about 50% transparent, which helps us see overlapping lines, and we disable the option to show the chart legend.

Although this chart is already loaded with features, let's add the ability to dynamically highlight and label the profiles that are most interesting to our analysis. When we are done, we should be able to select a line and have it stand out amongst the others and reveal the detailed profile it represents.

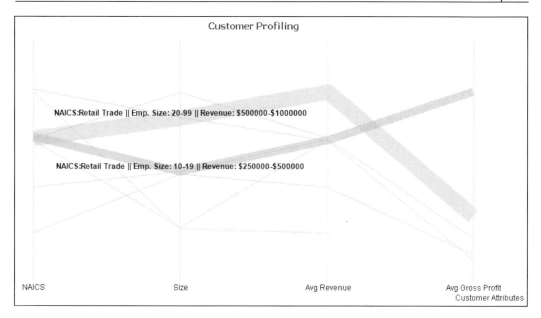

Exercise 4.2

We added the first element of this feature in the previous exercise when we defined
the set analysis of various functions as `{$<$(vIgnoreSelectionToHighlight)>}`
in the chart's expression. This causes the expression to ignore all selections made
to the profile attributes. The final step to enable dynamic highlighting is to add the
following code to the background color expression attribute of the chart expression:

```
if(
not match(only({1} [Customer NAICS (2digit)]&'_'&[Customer Employment
Size]&'_'&[Customer Est. Annual Revenue]),
    Concat(distinct [Customer NAICS (2digit)]&'_'&[Customer Employment
Size]&'_'&[Customer Est. Annual Revenue],','))
,LightGray(200)
)
```

The next step is to reveal the labels of only the highlighted lines. To do so, we use the
`dual()` function to mask the line's number values with text. The general layout of the
Attribute Value metric will be `dual(text,number)`. The number parameter will be
the expression that already exists in **Attribute Value** and the text parameter will be
the following code:

```
if(
   count(total distinct [Customer NAICS (2digit)]&'_'&[Customer
Employment Size]&'_'&[Customer Est. Annual Revenue])
   <>
```

```
    count({1} total distinct [Customer NAICS (2digit)])&'_'&[Customer
Employment Size]&'_'&[Customer Est. Annual Revenue])

    and CustomerProfileAttribute='Size'

    ,'NAICS:' & [Customer NAICS] & ' || Emp. Size:' & [Customer
Employment Size] & ' || Revenue:' & [Customer Est. Annual Revenue]

    ,''
)
```

This code only returns a nonempty text when at least one line is filtered and only appears on the data point where the dimension value is equal to size. We make the text conditional so as to reduce the risk overlapping labels. We also make the label stand out by adding the ='<b>' to the **Text Format** expression attribute. Finally, only when we tick the **Values on Data Points** option for the **Attribute Value** metric will any label appear.

Optionally, we left out the set analysis that contains the vIgnoreSelectionToHighlight variable in the line width expression in the first exercise, so that every line that isn't selected becomes extra thin to let the highlighted lines stand out more. If you want to conserve the line width of the lines that are not highlighted, then we add the set analysis that contains vIgnoreSelectionToHighlight to this expression.

The parallel coordinates chart offers us a native QlikView solution to visualize customer profiles. Let's also look at another powerful visualization that we can add to QlikView by means of an extension.

Sankey

Similar to the parallel coordinates, the Sankey chart is an excellent method to analyze the relationship between dimensional attributes. In the following chart, the width of the bands represents the number of customers that have each attribute value. We can easily see which are the most common at the same time that we see how each attribute value relates to the others.

The order of the attributes is important. For example, we can infer that all construction companies have **10-19** employees using the following chart, but we can't say that all construction companies have 10-19 employees and an annual revenue of $10-25 million. The only thing we can be sure of is that all construction companies have 10-19 employees and an annual revenue of $10-25 million or $25-50 million.

This visual representation may seem inferior to the previous section's parallel coordinates chart where we could follow a continuous line. However, the Sankey is easier to read than a parallel coordinates chart when we are dealing with a large number of customer profiles. In every analytical problem that we encounter, we should respect both the weakness and strengths of type of visualization as we analyze data.

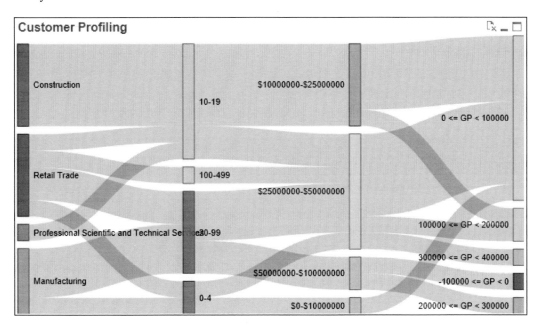

Let's create this chart in our marketing perspective sandbox.

Exercise 4.3

The following steps show you how to create a marketing analysis sandbox:

1. Download and install the Sankey extension created by Brian Munz in Qlik Branch (`http://branch.qlik.com/#/project/56728f52d1e497241 ae69783`).

2. In **Web View**, add the extension to the marketing perspective sandbox and assign the [Customer Profile Path] field to **Path**.

3. Add the following expression to **Frequency**:

    `=count(distinct Customer)`

We should now have a Sankey chart with three attributes: NAICS, Employee Size, and Annual Revenue. The [Customer Profile Path] field contains a comma-delimited list of these predefined attributes. We decide to dynamically calculate the fourth attribute that measures the average yearly gross profit that a customer contributes to the business. This allows us to select certain products and see how much gross profit each profile contributes only to these products. Let's go back to the properties of the Sankey and add this dynamic attribute to the path.

Exercise 4.4

1. Navigate to the edit expression window of **Path** by clicking on the cog button and then the expression button.

2. Add the following expression to the edit expression window:

```
=[Customer Profile Path] & ',' &
  class(
    aggr(avg(
      aggr(sum([Gross Profit])
        ,Customer,Year))
    ,Customer)
  ,100000,'GP')
```

We add the dynamic attribute using the class() function over two aggr() functions that calculate each customer's average annual gross profit contribution. The cross between a customer's contribution and its attributes helps us to not only look for new customers, but profitable new customers. Let's take a look at how we can use the census data to look for a new profitable market.

Market size analysis

Now that we can identify profitable customer profiles, we use the census data to look for companies that fit that profile. We begin our search using a layered geographical map that helps us choose which regions to focus our marketing efforts in.

 As a market analyst, I would like to visualize potential markets geographically so that I can execute a more effective advertising campaign.

Even though we have geographical data, such as states, or countries, it doesn't mean that we should use a map to visualize it. Bar charts are usually enough to analyze the top ranking geographical regions. However, maps can be useful when it is important to see both the physical proximity of each entity along with the magnitude of the associated metrics. For example, in the United States, we can expect California and Texas to rank the highest because they have the largest populations. However, the group of smaller states in the northeast may not rank as high as separate states in a bar chart, but, in a map, we can appreciate the proximity of their populations.

QlikView does not have a native map chart object. However, there are multiple third-party software options that are well-integrated with QlikView. QlikMaps (`http://www.qlikmaps.com`), GeoQlik (`http://www.geoqlik.com`), and Idevio (`http://www.idevio.com`) create popular mapping extensions for QlikView.

In this example, we are going to use Idevio to create geographical analysis. You can request an evaluation license and download the extension from `http://bi.idevio.com/products/idevio-maps-5-for-qlikview`. We install this extension like any other by double-clicking the `.qar` file. Once you've installed it, let's create the following geographic heat map that reveals the number of companies that are similar to our own customers in each state:

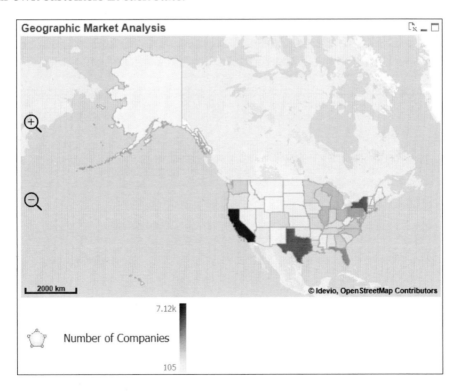

Exercise 4.5

1. In **WebView**, right-click anywhere on the sheet and select **New Sheet Object**.

2. In the **Extension Objects**, add a **Idevio Map 5** object and a **Area Layer** object to the sheet.

3. Open the **Properties** dialog of the **Area Layer** object and set STATE as the **Dimension** and the following expression as the **Color Value**:

    ```
    =sum([NUMBER OF FIRMS])
    ```

4. Click **More…** and go to the **Location** tab.

5. Make sure **Advanced Location** is not enabled and select United States in the **Country** drop-down box.

6. In the **Legend** tab, disable the **Color Legend Auto** option and add an empty space to the first expression field and Number of Companies in the second expression field. This last step will make the legend clean and simple.

We've used states in this example, but geographic maps that have a greater level of detail, such as counties, or zip codes, have greater analytical value. Also, political or administrative boundaries may not always be the best way to divide a population. Imagine if meteorologists used the previous map to show today's weather forecast. Like weather analysis, we may more easily recognize patterns in human behavior if we were to use heat map that can group data beyond artificial boundaries.

Let's create the following geographical analysis that helps us appreciate the market size of the northeast that is made up of smaller states:

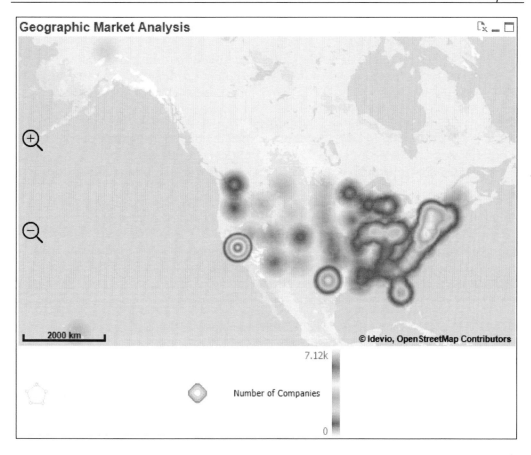

Geographic Market Analysis

2000 km

© Idevio, OpenStreetMap Contributors

7.12k

Number of Companies

0

Exercise 4.6

The following steps help us to create the geographical analysis:

1. In **WebView**, right-click anywhere on the sheet and select **New Sheet Object**.

2. In the **Extension Objects**, add a **Heatmap Layer** object to the sheet.

3. Open the **Properties** dialog of the **Heatmap Layer** object and set STATE as the **Dimension** and the following expression as the **Weight Value**:

   ```
   =sum([NUMBER OF FIRMS])
   ```

4. Click **More...** and go to the **Location** tab.

5. Make sure that **Advanced Location** is not enabled and select United States in the **Country** drop-down box.

6. In the **Legend** tab, disable the **Color Legend Auto** option and add an empty space to the first expression field and Number of Companies in the second expression field.

At first, we'll see both layers together in the same map. Left-click the **Area Layer** legend and disable **Visible**. We can now appreciate how the proximity of each state's populations can create groups outside their political boundaries. Along with counties and zip codes, this type of heat map also works well with latitude and longitude.

As we saw in the previous exercise, we can overlap several analytical layers in the same geographical map. This multilayering effect can provide a data-dense, insightful chart. For example, we can combine a bubble, area, and chart layer to compare market size, market penetration, and customer location in the same map. The following chart uses the same area layer that we created in *Exercise 4.5* along with overlapping bubble and chart layers:

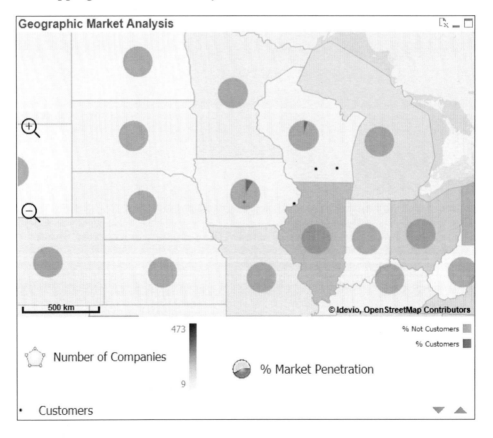

Exercise 4.7

First, let's add the layer of pie charts and then let's add the points that indicate customer locations. Although pie charts are not an ideal data visualization, in this case, they are the best possible solution until we can add other charts, such as bullet graphs:

1. In **WebView**, right-click anywhere on the sheet and select **New Sheet Object**.

2. In the **Extension Objects**, add a **Chart Layer** object to the sheet.

3. Open the **Properties** dialog of the **Chart Layer** object and set STATE as the **ID Dimension**.

4. Define the **Chart Dimension Label** as % Market Penetration and the following expression as the **Chart Dimension**:

   ```
   =ValueList('% Customers','% Not Customers')
   ```

5. Define the **Chart Value Label** as % and the following expression as the **Chart Value**:

   ```
   =round(
   pick(match(ValueList('% Customers','% Not Customers'),'%
   Customers','% Not Customers')

   ,count(DISTINCT if(STATE=[Billing State], Customer)) / sum([NUMBER
   OF FIRMS])*100

   ,(1-count(DISTINCT if(STATE=[Billing State], Customer)) /
   sum([NUMBER OF FIRMS]))*100

   )
   ,.01)
   ```

6. Click **More...** and go to the **Location** tab.

7. Make sure that **Advanced Location** is not enabled and select United States in the **Country** drop-down box.

8. In the **Legend** tab, disable the **Color Legend Auto** option and add an empty space to the first expression field and % Market Penetration in the second expression field.

9. In the **Presentation** tab, adjust the **Radius** to 20.

10. In the **Color** tab, disable the **Auto** option. Select **By Dimension** in **Color Mode** and **Categorized 100** in **Color Scheme**. Adjust **Transparency** to 25.

11. Close the **Properties** dialog of the **Chart Layer** object, and in the **Extension Objects**, add a **Bubble Layer** object to the sheet.

12. Open the **Properties** dialog of the **Bubble Layer** object and set Customer as the **ID Dimension**.

13. Define **Latitude / ID** as = [Billing Latitude] and **Longitude** as = [Billing Longitude].

14. Define **Size Value** as 1.

15. Click **More...** and go to the **Legend** tab, disable the **Size Legend Auto** option, and add Customer in the first expression field.

16. In the **Shape and Size** tab, define **Min Radius** and **Max Radius** as 2.

17. In the **Color** tab, disable the **Auto** option. Select **Single Color** in the **Color Mode** and **Black** in the **Color Scheme**. Adjust **Transparency** to 25.

If we select one of the most common customer profiles (NAICS: Educational Services || Emp. Size: 100-499 || Revenue: $25000000-$50000000) and zoom into the central part of the United States around Iowa and Wisconsin, we can reproduce the chart as shown in the previous figure. After creating the maps and its different layers, we organize the legends next to the map, so that the business user can left-click any of the legends at any time to hide or show a layer as they see fit. We also help the user add as many layers as possible by using visual elements such as transparency, as we did in the previous exercise.

Social media analysis

Once we understand the demographics of our current customers and our potential market, we may want to understand what they are saying about our company, products, and services. Over the last decade, social media sites, such as Twitter, Facebook, and LinkedIn, have become an increasingly important source of data to measure market opinion. They can also exert a large amount of influence on a potential customer's decision to do business with us more than any other marketing campaign that we run.

As a market analyst, I want to analyze what our customers are saying about us through social media sites so that I can take an active role to increase customer satisfaction and convince potential customers to do business with us.

Data from social media sites is often unstructured data. For example, we cannot directly analyze text comments without first using a semantic text analysis tool. Along with several other different types of analysis, these tools apply advanced algorithms over text in order to extract keywords, classify it under certain topics, and determine its sentiment. The last piece of data, text sentiment, is whether the text has a positive, negative, or neutral connotation.

In the following example, we use QlikView's RESTful API to extract tweets containing the hashtag, #qlik, from Twitter. The RESTful API is a free connector from QlikView. You can download the installation file and the documentation that explains how to retrieve data from Twitter at Qlik Market (http://market.qlik. com/rest-connector.html).

After extracting the data, we use the same RESTful API to evaluate each tweet's keywords and sentiment using a semantic text analytical tool called AlchemyAPI (http://www.alchemyapi.com/). AlchemyAPI is free for up to one thousand API calls per day. If you want to evaluate more than one thousand texts, then they offer paid subscription plans. We've stored the result of this process and the example script in Twitter_Analysis_Sandbox.qvw which we can find in the application folder of the marketing perspective container.

In the following exercises, we first use powerful data visualization techniques, such as a histogram and a scatterplot, to analyze text sentiment. Then, we'll use a word cloud to display important keywords extracted from the texts. Although a bar chart is a more effective way to compare keyword occurrence, a word cloud may make for an insightful infographic summary of all the tweets.

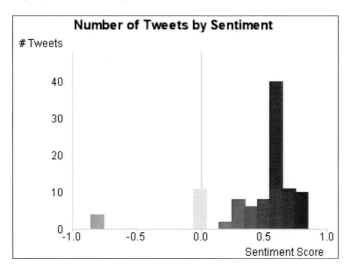

Exercise 4.8

Sentiment is divided into three groups. We represent sentiments that are negative as a negative number, those that are positive as a positive number, and those that are neutral as zero. The closer the number is to -1 or 1, the more negative or positive the sentiment, respectively. Histograms are the best data visualization method to view the distribution of numerical data. In order to create a histogram, we create numerical bins as a calculated dimension and then count how many instances fit into each bin. We also take care to visualize this diverging sequence with a similarly diverging color scheme:

1. Add the following color variables that we will use throughout the next three exercises:

Variable Name	Variable Definition
vCol_Blue_ColorBlindSafePositive	ARGB(255, 0, 64, 128)
vCol_Orange_ColorBlindSafeNegative	ARGB(255, 255, 128, 64)
vCol_Gray_ColorBlindSafeNeutral	ARGB(255, 221, 221, 221)

2. Add a bar chart with the following calculated dimension that creates numerical bins one-tenth of a decimal wide:

   ```
   =class([Sentiment Score],.1)
   ```

3. Add the following expression that counts the number of instances that fit into each bin:

   ```
   =count([Tweet Text])
   ```

4. Open the **Edit Expression** window of the metric's **Background Color** attribute and, in the **File** menu, open the **Colormix Wizard…**.

5. In the wizard, use avg([Sentiment Score]) as the **Value Expression**.

6. Set the **Upper Limit color** to $(vCol_Blue_ColorBlindSafePostive) and the **Lower Limit color** to $(vCol_Orange_ColorBlindSafePositive). Enable the **Intermediate** option, set the value to 0 and the color to $(vCol_Gray_ColorBlindSafeNeutral). Finish the **Colormix Wizard…**.

7. Go to the **Axes** tab and, in the **Dimension Axis** section, enable **Continuous**.

8. In the **Scale** section that is found within **Dimension Axis**, set **Static Min** to -1 and **Static Max** to 1.

After cleaning up this presentation, we should now have a chart that is similar to the one pictured before the exercise, which shows how tweets are distributed by sentiment score. We easily note that most of our tweets with the #qlik hashtag are positive. Now, let's compare a tweet sentiment with the number of times that users like that tweet.

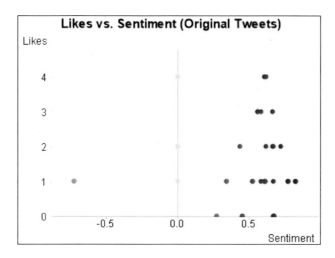

Exercise 4.9

Scatterplots are the best data visualization method to view the relationship between two numerical values. In the previous chart, each dot represents a tweet. Its two-dimensional position depends on its number of likes and its sentiment. We also use the same diverging color scheme as the histogram in order to emphasize the sentiment.

1. Add a scatterplot chart with **Tweet Text** as the dimension and the following two metrics:

Metric Label	Metric Expression
Sentiment	avg({$<Retweet={0}>} [Sentiment Score])
Likes	sum({$<Retweet={0}>} [Like Count])

2. Similarly to the previous exercise, use the **Colormix Wizard** under the Sentiment metric to determine each dot's color.

The scatterplot shows us that most tweets are positive and that those that are moderately positive tweets are the ones that receive the most likes.

The next step in our social media analysis is to visualize the keywords that are used in these tweets by importance. Although we could compare keyword instance using a bar chart more accurately, a word cloud provides an excellent way to present an executive summary of all tweets:

Exercise 4.10

Word clouds can be a great way to visually analyze unstructured data, such as text. The size of each keyword or phrase is related to its importance, which can be determined by the number of times that it appears in a text or a relevance score. In this case, we've used AlchemyAPI to extract keywords or phrases and give them a relevance score between 0 and 1. In the same way an internet search engine ranks search results according to their relevance to a query, AlchemyAPI ranks a keyword's relevance to each tweets. The higher the relevance value, the larger the text size. We also use a diverging color scheme for the text color so as to determine whether they are more common in tweets with negative or positive sentiments:

1. Download and install the Word Cloud extension created by Brian Munz in Qlik Branch (`http://branch.qlik.com/#/project/56728f52d1e497241 ae69781`).

2. In **Web View**, add this extension to the sheet and assign the Keyword field to **Words**.

3. Add the following expression to **Measurement**:

```
=sum([Keyword Relevance])
```

4. In **Color Expression**, paste the expression created by the **Colormix Wizard** in either of the two previous exercises.

As we would expect, the words QlikView and Qlik Sense are common in our word cloud. These words in the context of training is also quite common. The biggest single keyword trend is the word Anniversary. Its relevance in each tweet where it appeared multiplied by the number of times is was retweeted make it the largest word in the cloud. If we want to investigate which tweets are related to Anniversary, we can click on the word.

We also discover that the negative tweets are mistakenly classified by the sentiment analysis tool. The words generic and mixed usually have a negative connotation, but they are neutral words referring to technical subjects in this case. All sentiment analysis tools will occasionally classify words incorrectly and we can use the word cloud to identify these errors.

After all our work to understand our current customers, find potential markets, and analyze our social media presence, we want to figure out the tangible consequences of our work. Let's end this chapter by analyzing sales opportunities.

Sales opportunity analysis

The sales pipeline is the bridge between marketing and sales. Potential customers that are discovered by a market analysis or motivated by a advertising campaign are registered in the CRM system as leads. The sales team then goes through a series of steps to convert the lead into a customer. These steps may include having a first meeting, sending product samples, or sending an initial sales quote.

It is very important to monitor the number of opportunities that we have in the pipeline along with their progress through the steps. An opportunity that doesn't advance consistently through each step is likely to end up as a lost opportunity. It is also important to monitor the potential amount of sales that we currently have in the pipeline. This potential amount not only tells us what we can expect to sell in the immediate future, it also gives us first-hand information about a market's potential.

Let's create a flow chart like the following figure that shows us how each sales opportunity is progressing through the different stages of a sales process. Each line represents a sales opportunity. As it climbs higher, it is advancing to the next step in the sales process.

We can also appreciate the total number of opportunities that are at each stage throughout the month, and how many total opportunities are moving between stages. The lines that come to an end before the final month in the chart are opportunities that are closed.

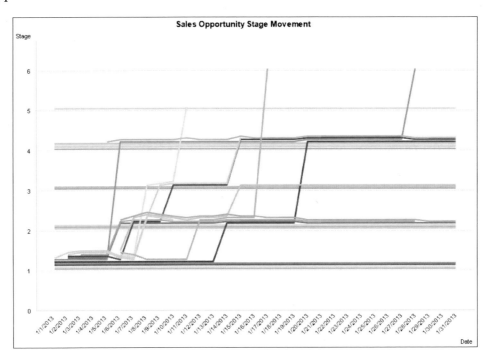

Exercise 4.11

This chart is only possible when we've linked the master calendar with the sales opportunities using `intervalmatch()`, as we did for this data model:

1. Create a line chart with `Date` and `Document ID` as dimensions.

2. Create a metric labeled `Sales Opportunity Stage` with the following expression:

```
dual(
only([Sales Opportunity Stage ID])
,only([Sales Opportunity Stage ID])
+
    aggr(
        rank(
            -only({$<_DocumentType={'Sales Opportunities'}>}
[Document ID])
        ,4,1)
    ,Date,[Sales Opportunity Stage ID],[Document ID])
```

```
/
    max(total
        aggr(
            rank(
                -only({$<_DocumentType={'Sales Opportunities'}>}
    [Document ID])
                ,4,1)
            ,Date,[Sales Opportunity Stage ID],[Document ID])
        )
    *.5
    )
```

3. In the **Axes** tab, enable the option to **Show Grid** in the **Expression Axes** section and set the **Scale** with the following values:

Option	Value
Static Min	1
Static Max	6.75
Static Step	1

The text value of the metric returns the sales opportunity stage, while the number is the sales opportunity stage plus a decimal amount that makes each line stack one on top of the other. The decimal amount is calculated by dividing the rank of the Document ID, which is a sequential number by the total number of documents in each stage during each day.

Summary

As we saw in this chapter, the QlikView marketing perspective is filled with opportunities to visualize both internal and external data sources. We should also take advantage of third-party extensions to expand QlikView's analytical capacity. At the same time, we can find different ways to adjust QlikView's native visualizations to perform more advanced analysis. Let's now take a more detailed look at the company's finances and analyze its inventory, accounts receivable, and accounts payable in the next chapter.

5

Working Capital Perspective

A business's financial health depends heavily on its short-term assets, such as inventory and **Accounts Receivable (A/R)**, along with short-term liabilities, such as **Accounts Payable (A/P)**. If these elements are managed well, then the business will have the cash to invest in finding potential customers, developing new products, and hiring new talent. We refer to these three pivotal financial measurements as working capital.

We can find inventory, A/R, and A/P, as separate line items in the balance sheet that we created for our financial perspective in a previous chapter. However, there is also a series of additional analyses that all three have in common. For example, the analysis of the average number of days that a product is in inventory, a customer takes to pay an invoice, or the business takes to pay a vendor invoice requires the same type of data model and formulation. We can also make this information more actionable if we include it in a product, customer, or vendor stratification. As an example, we will complement the customer stratification that we began to create in our sales perspective.

After we examine what each has in common, we also look at the distinct operational analysis of each measurement that helps us maintain a healthy working capital. For example, a customer aging report can help lower the average number of days a customer takes to pay an invoice. Inventory stock level analysis can also help procurement know when to purchase the correct amount of inventory and lower just the right amount of a product.

In this chapter, we review the following topics while we create our QlikView working capital perspective:

- Working capital data model (snapshots)
- Account rotation and cash-to-cash analysis
- A detailed analysis of working capital
- Inventory stock level analysis and customer aging report
- A more complete customer stratification

Let's get started and look at how we combine these three elements of working capital into one data model.

Working capital data model

The working capital data model can be constructed in a variety of ways. The most important feature of the data model is its ability to accumulate account balances over time. In *Chapter 3*, *Financial Perspective*, we accomplish this by adding an *as-of* calendar. However, we can also create a model that uses periodic snapshots and avoid accumulating individual transactions after every user selection. A periodic snapshot is a recurring event that saves a copy of the data at the end of every day, week, or month.

 Even though we may end up only using monthly snapshots in a QlikView application, it is wise to take a daily snapshot of the data and save it in QVD files in case business requirements change.

In this chapter, we will use a periodic snapshot to measure following events in the data model:

- Month-end inventory balances by item and warehouse over three years
- Day-end inventory balances by item and warehouse over the last the last three months
- Month-end balances of A/R invoices over the last three years
- Month-end balances of A/P invoices over the last three years

Periodic snapshots do not record individual payments or inventory movements, which may be important for some banking or operational analysis. However, such details are not important when we first analyze working capital.

If we've only recently started to create data snapshots, some of the analysis we perform will be deficient as many metrics are calculated over 90-day periods. However, we sometimes have the option to recreate past snapshots using transaction-level data. Even if they are not completely accurate, they are often worth the effort. The decision on whether we wait until we have enough real snapshots or to recreate past snapshots frequently depends on which option takes less time. It also depends on whether the opportunity gained by having them now is greater than the resources spent to recreate the past.

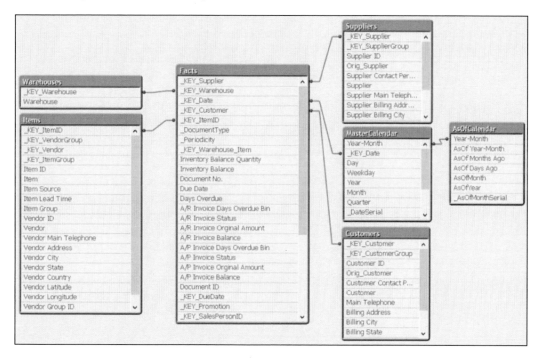

Many of the dimensions that we use to describe these events are the same dimensions that we've used in previous perspectives. We reuse the same tables so that it is easier to maintain the data models and to ensure that everybody in the organization is viewing the same information. Let's take a look at the dimensions and metrics that describe these events:

Dimensions		
7Ws	**Fields**	**Comments**
Who	`Customer`	This is a dimension that we first saw in *Chapter 2, Sales Perspective*.
Who	`Supplier`	This is who provides products or services to the business. This dimension has similar information to that of the `Customer` dimension.
What	`Item`	This is a dimension that we first saw in *Chapter 2, Sales Perspective*.
When	`Month, Year`	These are the same dimensions that we've seen in the previous perspectives. However, instead of recording, for example, the date of an invoice or a payment, it records the date when a snapshot was taken of a customer's outstanding balance.
How	`_Periodicity`	This dimension allows periodic snapshots with different frequencies to be loaded into one data model. For example, we load daily inventory snapshots of the past few months and monthly ones of the past few years. We do this so as to only upload the data that is useful. Otherwise, we risk degrading the QlikView application's performance.
Where	`Warehouse`	This dimension describes where we store goods so that they can easily be distributed to the customers who purchase them. We measure inventory levels by Warehouse.

Metrics		
7Ws	**Fields**	**Comments**
How Many	`Item Lead Time`	This is where we store a predefined time that is needed to receive an item in inventory, which helps procurement know when to purchase or produce a product.
How Many	`A/R Invoice Balance`	This is where we measure the outstanding balance of each customer invoice. The outstanding balance is the original invoice amount minus any corresponding payment or credit memo amount. In the ERP system, we link invoices with their related payments and credit memos through a bookkeeping process called reconciliation.

How Many	A/P Invoice Balance	This is the same concept as A/R Invoice Balance, but it measures the outstanding balance of purchase invoices.
How Many	Inventory Balance Quantity Inventory Balance	This is where we measure both the quantity and monetary value of the business's inventory.

While the calendar dimension is related to every event, every other dimension describes only one event. For example, supplier only describes month-end A/P invoices. It is helpful to understand the relationship between dimensions and metrics in a data model in order to know what type of analysis we can perform. However, we cannot obtain this information explicitly from the QlikView table viewer nor the previous 7Ws table.

Therefore, We use the following table to explain the relationship between metrics and dimensions in a data model. We insert all the metrics in the first column and then create a column for each dimension. The x records where a relationship exists and helps us determine how we can visualize the data:

Dimensions Metrics	Month/ Year	Date	Customer	Supplier	Item	Warehouse
A/R Invoice Balance	X		X			
A/P Invoice Balance	X			X		
Inventory Balance Quantity	X Past three years	X Past three months			X	X

We maintain the relationship as it is likely to exist in the ERP system. For example, payments do not include information about items. This is not always good enough for the visualizations that we want to create. Even though payments don't include item detail, we may want to know the estimated average number of days that a customer pays for a certain item. We examine how to resolve this problem as we develop the analysis and visualizations for the working capital perspective.

Rotation and average days

At a higher level, we analyze each element of working capital using the same methods. The overall objective is to know the average number of days that it takes for an item in stock to be sold, a customer to pay, or a supplier to be paid.

 As a business owner, I want to know how long it takes from the day I pay my supplier to the day the customers pay me so that I can work to free up cash and make investments to grow the company.

We can help free up cash for the business if we reduce the number of days that an item is in a warehouse or the number of days that a customer takes to pay an invoice. Inversely, we want to increase the number of days that we can wait to pay our suppliers without any penalty. Let's start our working capital analysis by calculating the average number of days that an item is in a warehouse. We call this key performance indicator **Days Sales of Inventory (DSI)**.

Days Sales of Inventory

If we store inventory for too long, then it takes up space that could be put to better use or sold. If we store inventory for too few days, then we increase the risk of not being able to satisfy customers' needs. **Days Sales of Inventory (DSI)** tells us the average number of days that we store items in inventory based on our average inventory balance and our cost of sales. The following formula calculates DSI over a one-year period:

*Days Sales of Inventory = (Annual Average Inventory Balance / Annual Cost of Sales) * 365*

Let's create a bar chart that displays total DSI by month. We calculate each month's DSI over a rolling one-year period:

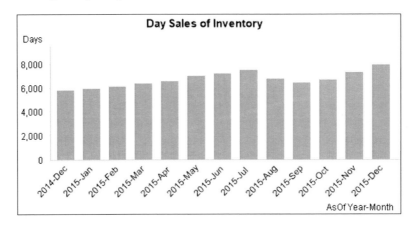

Before beginning the following exercise, we import this chapter's exercise files into the QDF as we did in *Chapter 2, Sales Perspective*.

Exercise 5.1

Let's create a bar chart with the following property options:

Dimensions	
Label	**Value**
AsOf Year-Month	AsOf Year-Month
Expressions	
Label	**Value**

DSI	`avg({$<_Periodicity={'Monthly'}`
	`        ,[AsOf Months Ago]={">0<=12"}>}`
	`    aggr(`
	`        sum({$<_Periodicity={'Monthly'}`
	`                ,[AsOf Months Ago]={">0<=12"}>}`
	`            [Inventory Balance])`
	`        ,[Year-Month],[AsOf Year-Month])`
	`    )`
	`    /`
	`    sum({$<[AsOf Months Ago]={">0<=12"}>} [Cost])`
	`    *`
	`    365`

Similar to the financial perspective, we use the [AsOf Months Ago] field in the set analysis to calculate over twelve rolling months. We first use the aggr() function to sum the inventory balance of each Year-Month and then calculate the average monthly balance. We are careful to include [AsOf Year-Month] in the aggr() function because this function only works properly when it contains all fields used as a chart dimension.

We also make sure to use the same set analysis in the avg() function outside the aggr() as we do in the sum() function within the aggr() function. A function's set analysis only applies to the fields that are directly located within the function. It is never adopted by a parent function or inherited by a nested one. We, therefore, have to repeat it for every function. Feel free to experiment and remove the set analysis from one of the functions to see how the values in the graph change.

An acceptable DSI varies per industry but a result between 60 and 240 days is common. The previous chart shows that the company has too much inventory in relation to its sales. At one end, it needs to stop purchasing or producing goods and, at the other end, it needs to increase sales. Let's now take a look at how well we collect customer payments.

Days Sales Outstanding

Although sales are important, if we don't collect payment for these sales in a reasonable amount of time, then we won't have the cash necessary to keep the business running. **Days Sales Outstanding (DSO)** is a key performance indicator that measures the average number of days it takes a customer to pay an invoice. Its calculation is quite similar to that of DSI:

*Days Sales of Outstanding = (Annual Average A/R Balance / Annual Net Sales) * 365*

Let's now add DSO to the bar chart that we created in the previous exercise.

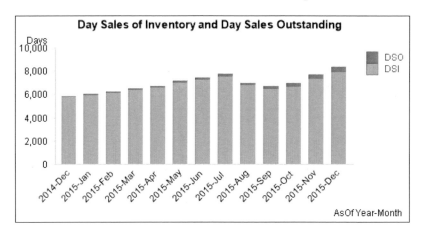

Exercise 5.2

Let's add the following expression to the bar chart from *Exercise 5.1*. We change the bar chart to a stacked bar chart in the **Style** tab:

Expressions	
Label	**Value**

DSO	`avg({$<_Periodicity={'Monthly'}`
	`        ,[AsOf Months Ago]={">0<=12"}>}`
	`    aggr(`
	`        sum({$<_Periodicity={'Monthly'}`
	`                ,[AsOf Months Ago]={">0<=12"}>}`
	`                [A/R Invoice Balance])`
	`        ,[Year-Month],[AsOf Year-Month])`
	`    )`
	`    /`
	`    sum({$<[AsOf Months Ago]={">0<=12"}>} [Net Sales])`
	`    *`
	`    365`

A healthy DSO depends on the business, but we should expect anything between 15 and 90 days. In the previous chart, we started the year with a DSO that wasn't too far from this range, but, as the year progressed, the DSO grew. As DSO is a ratio that is based on sales and A/R balance, this increase could be caused by an increase in the A/R balance, a decrease in sales, or a mixture of the two. Alongside any DSO analysis, we recommend creating auxiliary charts that can show what is causing the DSO to change. This recommendation also applies to DSI and the final working capital element—Days Payable Outstanding.

Days Payable Outstanding

In order to determine whether we have a healthy DSO and DSI, we compare them with the key performance indicator **Days Payable Outstanding (DPO)**. DPO measures the average number of days before we pay our suppliers and has the same structure as the previous two indicators:

*Days Payable of Outstanding = (Annual Average A/P Balance / Annual Cost of Sales) * 365*

Let's now add DPO to the bar chart that we created in the previous exercise.

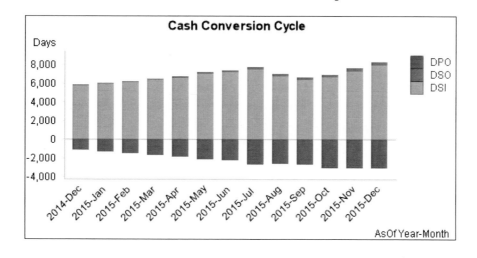

Exercise 5.3

Let's add the following expression to the bar chart from Exercise 5.2:

Expressions	
Label	**Value**

DPO	```-avg({$<_Periodicity={'Monthly'}```
	 ``` ,[AsOf Months Ago]={">0<=12"}>}```
	 ``` aggr(```
	 ``` sum({$<_Periodicity={'Monthly'}```
	 ``` ,[AsOf Months Ago]={">0<=12"}>}```
	 ``` [A/P Invoice Balance])```
	 ``` ,[Year-Month],[AsOf Year-Month])```
	 ```)```
	 ``` /```
	 ``` sum({$<[AsOf Months Ago]={">0<=12"}>} [Cost])```
	 ``` *```
	 ``` 365```

An ideal DPO is greater than the sum of DSO and DSI. Such a situation means that the business's suppliers finance its operations. Regardless of whether this is really possible, we aim to reduce the time it takes to convert cash spent into cash received, which is called the **Cash Conversion Cycle (CCC)**:

Cash Conversion Cycle = DSO + DSI – DPO

We make a slight change to the previous chart so that we can explicitly analyze CCC.

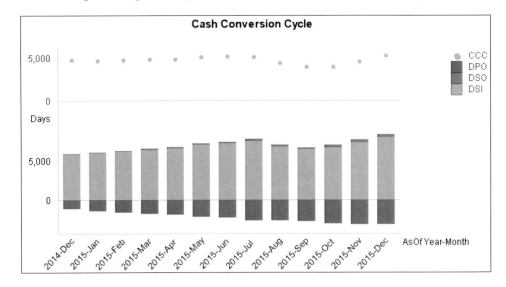

Exercise 5.4

Let's go through the following steps to adjust the bar chart from *Exercise 5.3*:

1. Change the bar chart to a combo chart in the **General** tab.

2. In the **Expressions** tab, add the following expression:

Expressions	
Label	Value
CCC	DSO + DSI – DPO

    Enable only the **Bar** option for all the expressions except CCC, which should only have the **Symbol** option enabled.

3. In the **Axes** tab, select **CCC** in the **Expressions** list and enable **Right (Top)** in the **Position** section. Enable **Split Axis**.

We can now analyze all the working capital elements in a single chart. In the previous chart, we can see how an increase in DPO has been offset by an even greater increase in DSI. In the next section, let's look at how we can break down and analyze each of the working capital elements. We'll do this using DSI as an example.

Working capital breakdown

We complement the previous section's working capital analysis with a closer look at the elements that make up each measure. In the case of DSI, we analyze **Average Inventory Value** and **Annual Cost of Goods Sold (COGS)**. This auxiliary analysis helps us understand whether an increasing DSI is the result of rising inventory levels or decreasing sales. It also helps us detect which product is not rotating frequently enough.

 As a warehouse manager, I want to know which items spend the most time in the warehouse and whether this is because there is too much stock or too few sales. This information will help me reduce the amount of unnecessary stock and free up available cash.

Let's combine the related metrics and have them share the same dimension axis, as in the following visualization:

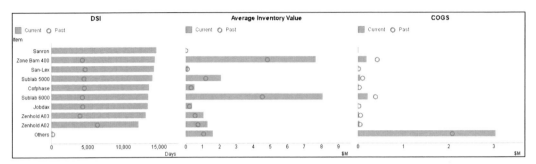

Exercise 5.5

1. Let's create three separate combo charts. We represent the current period with bars and the last period with circles. In each chart, we set the orientation to be horizontal, and move the legend to the top. When we use **Ctrl + Shift** to place the legend on top, we wait until its red outline covers the entire top section so that the labels appear in a row:

Title	DSI
Dimensions	
Labels	**Value**
Item	`Item`
Expressions	
Labels	**Value**

Current	`avg({$<_Periodicity={'Monthly'},[AsOf Months Ago]={">0<=12"}>}`
	`    aggr(`
	`        sum({$<_Periodicity={'Monthly'},[AsOf Months Ago]={">0<=12"}>} [Inventory Balance])`
	`        ,[Year-Month],Item)`
	`    )`
	`    /`
	`    sum({$<[AsOf Months Ago]={">0<=12"}>} [Cost])`
	`*365`

Past	This is the same as the Current DSI but replace `[AsOf Months Ago]={">0<=12"}` with `[AsOf Months Ago]={">12<=24"}`

Title	Average Inventory Value
Dimensions	
Labels	**Value**
Item	`Item`
Expressions	
Labels	**Value**

Current	```avg({$<_Periodicity={'Monthly'},[AsOf Months Ago]={">0<=12"}>}```
	    ```aggr(```
	        ```sum({$<_Periodicity={'Monthly'},[AsOf Months Ago]={">0<=12"}>} [Inventory Balance])```
	        ```, [Year-Month],Item)```
	    ```)```

Past	This is the same as the Current Inventory Value but replace `[AsOf Months Ago]={">0<=12"}` with `[AsOf Months Ago]={">12<=24"}`

Title	COGS
Dimensions	
Labels	**Value**
Item	`Item`
Expressions	
Labels	**Value**
Current	```sum({$<[AsOf Months Ago]={">0<=12"}>} [Cost])```
Past	This is the same as the Current COGS but replace `[AsOf Months Ago]={">0<=12"}` with `[AsOf Months Ago]={">12<=24"}`

    Create a container object and, in the **Presentation** tab, select **Container Type** as **Grid**. Set **Columns** to **3** and **Rows** to **1**.

2. Drag each chart into the container object.

3. In the **Sort** tab of each chart, enable only **Expression** and select **Descending**. Insert the following code into the expression field:

```
avg({$<_Periodicity={'Monthly'},[AsOf Months Ago]={">0<=12"}>}
    aggr(
        sum({$<_Periodicity={'Monthly'},[AsOf Months
```

```
Ago]={">0<=12"}>} [Inventory Balance])
    , [Year-Month] , Item)
)
/
sum({$<[AsOf Months Ago]={">0<=12"}>} [Cost])
*365
```

4. We cannot scroll through the three charts at the same time, so, in the **Dimension Limits** tab of each chart, let's select the option to **Restrict which values are displayed using the first expression**.

5. In the same tab and under the **Show Only** option, we change the value to **First**.

6. In the Presentation tab, disable the option to Suppress Zero-Values.

7. Finally, after verifying that each row of bars corresponds to the same item, let's remove the dimension labels in the second and third charts by deselecting the **Show Legend** option in the **Dimensions** tab.

Instead of using a common scroll bar, we repeatedly click on the bar that represents **Others** in order to scroll through the charts and review more items. When we analyze all three measures in a single view, it becomes clear that the DSI of most of the items is increasing and that this increase is due to both an increase in the inventory value and a decrease in COGS.

After breaking down each working capital element and analyzing its parts, the next step is to analyze more closely the operations that cause these results. Let's continue to explore the inventory data in more detail and compare each product's inventory levels with their corresponding minimum, reorder, and maximum levels.

Inventory stock levels

The business defines each product's minimum, reorder, and maximum stock levels so as to maintain an adequate quantity in inventory. We often calculate these numbers and insert them into an ERP system that automatically generates purchase orders or work orders every time an item reaches the reorder stock limit In QlikView, we can use sales and purchase cycle data to easily calculate each limit and compare it to historical inventory behavior.

We use the following formulas to calculate each stock level:

 As a purchasing team manager, I want to dynamically calculate stock limits so that I can be sure to have just the right amount of stock according to historical sales trends.

*Reorder Stock Level = Max Lead Time * Max Daily Sales*

*Minimum Stock Level = Reorder Stock Level – (Avg Lead Time * Avg Daily Sales)*

*Maximum Stock Level = Reorder Stock Level – (Min Lead Time * Min Daily Sales) + Reorder Quantity*

We use a predefined lead time, or the time needed to restock an item, from the item master data table. We review, how to dynamically calculate the lead time in *Chapter 6, Operations Perspective*. We also assume that the minimum daily sales amount of any item is 0 and that the reorder quantity is equal to the reorder stock level. Given these assumptions the maximum stock level is the reorder stock level multiplied by two.

Like much of the information at a glance. We therefore use the following trellis chart to compare each item's historical inventory behavior with the calculated stock levels.

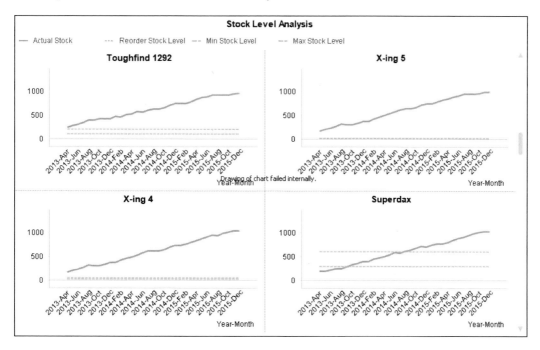

Exercise 5.6

Let's create a line chart with the following dimensions and expressions:

Dimensions	
Labels	**Value**
Item	Item
Year-Month	Year-Month
Expressions	
Labels	**Value**
Actual Stock	`sum({$<_Periodicity={'Monthly'}>} [Inventory Balance Quantity])`

Reorder Stock Level	`max(Total <Item> {$<$(vSetRolling12Modifier)>}`
	`    aggr(`
	`        sum(Quantity)`
	`    ,_KEY_Date, Item)`
	`    )`
	`*`
	`max([Item Lead Time])`

Min Stock Level	`[Reorder Stock Level]`
	`-`
	`sum({$<$(vSetRolling12Modifier)>}`
	`    Total <Item>`
	`Quantity)`
	`/`
	`networkdays(`
	`    addmonths(max(Total _KEY_Date),-12)`
	`    ,max(Total _KEY_Date)`
	`)`
	`*`
	`avg([Item Lead Time])`

Max Stock Level	`2*[Reorder Stock Level]`

In the **Dimensions** tab, click **Trellis...** and tick the **Enable Trellis Chart** option.

8. Set **Number of Columns** to **Fixed** and **2**. Set **Number of Rows** to **Fixed** and **2**.

9. In the **Expressions** tab, change the **Line Style** properties of **Reorder Stock Level**, **Min Stock Level**, and **Max Stock Level** to a thin, dotted line. For example, use `'<S2><W.5>'`.

10. In the **Sort** tab, select the option to sort by **Y-value**.

The set analysis variable in the previous expression is from Rob Wunderlich's QlikView Component's library and allows us to determine the stock levels based on twelve months of sales data. The actual twelve-month period we use depends on the date that we select in QlikView. In the particular case of Min Stock Level, we use the `networkdays()` function to calculate the average daily sales by working days. We also have the option to calculate the maximum and minimum daily sales using more advanced methods. For example, we can experiment with the fractile() function and use 5% or 95% fractiles to remove outliers. We can also use the same t-distribution functions that we used in *Chapter 2, Sales Perspective*, to calculate a more conservative daily sales average.

Finally, let's create a customer aging report that helps us monitor the operations that impact DSO.

Aging report

If we are to lower DSO, we need to make sure that customers pay on time. We monitor collections using a customer aging report. The following report shows the customers' total balances and categorizes it into bins based on the original due date of the each payment. As we're mostly interested in the past due payments, it groups these amounts into thirty-day period bins.

As the collections team manager, I want to quickly recognize which customers are the most delinquent and which have the largest debt so that I can follow up with these customers.

The same report structure can be used to monitor suppliers in order to maintain a healthy DPO:

Customer Aging Report											
A/R Invoice ...	Total			Current		0-30		30-60		60-90		90+
Customer	A/R Balance		A/R Balance		A/R Balance		A/R Balance		A/R Balance		A/R Balance	
Total	7,592,107		219,172		1,075,299		1,058,234		255,534		4,983,868	
Divanoodle	1,265,584		0		312,625		20,062		0		932,897	
Fanoodle	1,039,788		62,843		175,538		225,859		41,544		534,004	
Jaloo	628,561		8,610		0		68,962		0		550,989	
Realcube	962,064		26,481		32,099		87,869		173,867		641,748	
Skipfire	313,829		0		106,996		8,961		0		197,872	
Yakitri	663,913		0		112,345		53,996		0		497,572	
Yozio	1,639,153		15,715		0		592,526		0		1,030,913	
Zoomlounge	1,079,214		105,524		335,696		0		40,123		597,872	

Exercise 5.7

Let's create a pivot table with the following dimensions and expressions:

Dimensions	
Labels	**Value**
Customer	`Customer`
Status	`[A/R Invoice Days Overdue Bin]`
Expressions	
Labels	**Value**
A/R Balance	`sum({$<_Periodicity={'Monthly'}>} [A/R Invoice Balance])`
<space>	`sum({$<_Periodicity={'Monthly'}>} [A/R Invoice Balance])`
<space>	`=''`

1. Select the second expression and select **Linear Gauge** in **Display Options**.

2. Click **Gauge Setting** and define the **Min** in the **Gauge Settings** section as 0 and **Max** as the following expression:

   `sum({$<_Periodicity={'Monthly'}>} [A/R Invoice Balance])`

3. In the **Segments Setup** section, delete **Segment 2** and change the color of **Segment 1** to blue.

4. In the **Indicator** section, select **Mode Fill to Value**.

5. Disable the **Show Scale** option.

6. Enable the **Hide Segment Boundaries** and **Hide Gauge Outlines** options.

7. In the **Sort** tab, select **Status** and only enable **Numeric Value**.

8. In the **Presentation** tab, enable the option to **Show Partial Sums** for both dimensions and enable the option to show **Subtotals on Top**.

9. Pivot the table as shown in the previous figure.

The creation of the `[A/R Invoice Days Overdue Bin]` field in the script makes this report easy to create. In the script, we subtract the invoice due date by the date of the data snapshot and then use several nested if-statements to assign that result to a bin. As this field is relative to each snapshot's date and not today's date, we can analyze the aging report over time. The field is also a `dual()` data type where **Current** is 0, **0-30** is 1, **31-60** is 2, and so on. This feature allows us to sort the field more easily by selecting only Numeric Value option in the **Sort** tab.

How well a customer pays us, or their DSO is an important indicator of how important that customer is to our business. Let's continue the customer stratification exercise that we started in *Chapter 2, Sales Perspective,* and see how we use DSO to evaluate a customer's importance.

Customer stratification

In *Chapter 2, Sales Perspective,* we had the following user story:

 As a sales representative, I want to see who my most important customers are so that I can focus my time and effort on them.

A customer's importance is determined by a mixture of measures. In the sales perspective, we started to determine a customer's importance using a Pareto analysis over sales. The following diagram shows the results of a customer stratification based on sales:

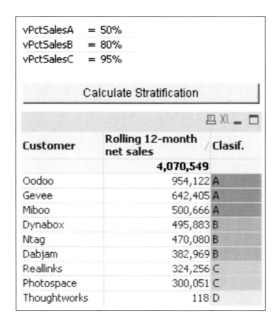

We can use *Pareto analysis* to stratify all measurements whose total is the sum of its parts, such as gross profit and quantity. However, there is another set of customer metrics whose total is an average of its parts. For example, the total company DSO is a weighted average of the DSO of each customer. In this case, we use quartiles to stratify customers.

Finally, once we have more than one measurement that stratifies customers, we look at how to combine them both numerically and visually. Even though we discuss customer stratification, the same principles apply to stratification based on any other dimension, such as item, sales representative, or supplier. The only difference between these is the exact measurements that we use to stratify them.

Stratification by distribution

When the measurement that we want use to stratify customers is based on averages, we use the distribution of the averages to classify them. As we use four letters to stratify customers in the example, we group them by quartiles. Each quartile will contain the same—or nearly the same—number of customers.

Let's create the following chart in the next exercise to see how quartiles group customers by DSO:

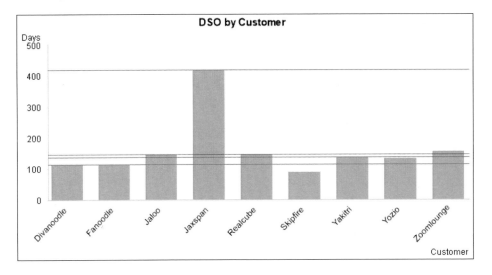

Exercise 5.8

Let's create a bar chart with the following property options:

Dimensions	
Label	Value
Customer	Customer
Expressions	
Label	Value

| DSO | ```
avg({$<_Periodicity={'Monthly'}
        , [AsOf Months Ago]={">0<=12"}>}
    aggr(
        sum({$<_Periodicity={'Monthly'}
                , [AsOf Months
Ago]={">0<=12"}>}
                    [A/R Invoice Balance])
        , [Year-Month], [Customer])
    )
    /
    sum({$<[AsOf Months Ago]={">0<=12"}>} [Net
    Sales])
    *
    365
``` |
|-----|------|

1. In the **Presentation** tab, add the first reference line. This represents the first quartile and uses the following expression:

```
fractile(
    aggr(
        avg({$<_Periodicity={'Monthly'},[AsOf Months
Ago]={">0<=12"}>}
            aggr(
                sum({$<_Periodicity={'Monthly'},[AsOf Months
Ago]={">0<=12"}>} [A/R Invoice Balance])
            , [Year-Month],Customer)
        )
        /
        sum({$<[AsOf Months Ago]={">0<=12"}>} [Net Sales])
        *365
    ,Customer)
,.25)
```

2. Add three more reference lines for the second, third, and fourth quartile. For each quartile, We use the same expression as in the previous step and change the second parameter in the `fractile` function from `.25` to `.5`, `.75`, and `1`, respectively.

We make slight changes to the `aggr()` function in the expression we used to calculate DSO in *Exercise 5.2*. calculated total DSO by year-month, We replace [AsOf Year-Month] with [Customer] as this is the dimension we use this chart. We also go as far as to use a second `aggr()` function to calculate each fractile as the `fractile()` function only works over a set of numbers. This second `aggr()` function creates a list that contains the DSO of every customer for the `fractile()` function.
```

Stratification by distribution divides the customers into nearly equal-sized bins. The bar belongs to the nearest quartile reference line above it. According to the previous chart, **Divanoodle**, **Fanoodle**, and **Skipfire** are in the first quartile. Every other quartile has two customers. As the best customers have a low DSO, we classify customers in the first quartile as A, in the second quartile as B, in the third quartile as C, and in the fourth quartile as D.

Let's add DSO to the customer stratification we started in the sales perspective:

Customer	Rolling 12-month net sales	Sales Class	DSO	DSO Class	Total Weighted	/ Total Class
	4,070,549					
Yozio	954,122	A	404	B	3.6	A
Yakitri	382,969	B	376	A	3.4	B
Divanoodle	642,405	A	414	C	3.2	B
Fanoodle	495,883	B	388	B	3	B
Realcube	500,666	A	522	D	2.8	B
Skipfire	300,051	D	263	A	2.2	C
Zoomlounge	470,080	B	585	D	2.2	C
Jaloo	324,256	C	436	C	2	C
Jaxspan	118	D	420	C	1.4	D

Exercise 5.9

1. Let's create the following variables:

Variable	
Label	Value

vExp_DSOCustomer	avg({$<_
	Periodicity={'Monthly'},[AsOf Months Ago]={">0<=12"}>}
	    aggr(
	        sum({$<_
	Periodicity={'Monthly'},[AsOf Months Ago]={">0<=12"}>} [A/R Invoice Balance])
	        ,[Year-Month],Customer)
	)
	/
	sum({$<[AsOf Months Ago]={">0<=12"}>} [Net Sales])
	*365

vExp_
DSOCustomerStratificationBoundaries
	fractile(Total
	    aggr(
	        $(vExp_DSOCustomer)
	    ,Customer)
	 ,$1)

2. In the working capital perspective, let's create the same customer stratification table that we created in the sales perspective (*Exercise 2.3*).

3. Let's add the following expressions to the previously created customer stratification table:

Expressions	
Label	**Value**
DSO	`$(vExp_DSOCustomer)`

DSO Class	`if($(vExp_DSOCustomer) < $(vExp_DSOCustomerStr`
	`atificationBoundaries(.25)),'A'`
	`    ,if($(vExp_DSOCustomer) < $(vExp_DSOCustom`
	`erStratificationBoundaries(.5)),'B'`
	`        ,if($(vExp_DSOCustomer) < $(vExp_DSOCu`
	`stomerStratificationBoundaries(.75)),'C','D'`
	`)))`

Total Weighted	`match([Sales Class],'D','C','B','A') * .6`
	`+`
	`match([DSO Class],'D','C','B','A') * .4`

Total Class	`pick(round([Total Weighted])`
	`,'D'`
	`,'C'`
	`,'B'`
	`,'A'`
	`)`

4. Change the background color of the DSO Class expression to the following expression:

```
if($(vExp_DSOCustomer) < $(vExp_DSOCustomerStratificationBoundarie
s(.25)),blue(100)
    ,if($(vExp_DSOCustomer) < $(vExp_DSOCustomerStratificationBoun
daries(.5)),blue(75)
        ,if($(vExp_DSOCustomer) < $(vExp_DSOCustomerStratification
Boundaries(.75)),blue(50),blue(25))))
```

5. Change the background color of the Total Class expression to the following expression.

```
pick(round([Total Weighted])
,blue(25)
,blue(50)
,blue(75)
,blue(100)
)
```

We create the `vExp_DSOcustomerStratification` variable with a `$1` parameter so that we can calculate different factiles using only one variable. In general, when we encounter several expression variables whose only difference is a number, we reduce them to one variable and add a parameter.

The `Total Weighted` stratification is calculated by first converting the letters A, B, C, and D of each individually stratified metric into the numbers 1, 2, 3, and 4, respectively. In this example, We use the `match()` function to efficiently turn the letters into numbers. We then multiple each number by a factor that allows us define how important each metric is to the final customer stratification. Other than the fact that the sum of the factors should be equal to one, they are completely arbitrary and depend on the business's strategy. For example, as we want to put more emphasis on the sales stratification, we multiply it by .6 and the DSO stratification by .4.

As the sum of factors is equal to one, the sum of the all the weighted stratifications is between one and four which makes it possible for us to convert it back to a letter format. In this example, we use the `pick()` function in `Total Class` to convert a rounded `Total Weight` back into letters. In this way, we can combine multiple customer stratifications into one. For many business users, such as sale representatives, this can help them more easily determine a customer's importance according to the business's strategy. Finally, we introduce a way to visualize how individual customer measures influence how they are classified.

Visualizing stratification

We can use a native scatterplot to compare two measures used for stratification. For example, we create the following chart using the expressions we use in the customer stratification table. The legend at the top is a group of eight text objects — one for each dot and letter:

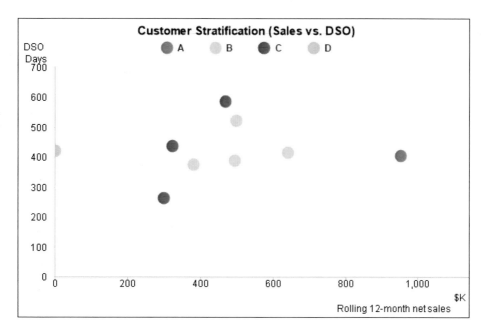

The scatterplot helps us identify whether each classification describes a tight group of closely-related customers or a disparate group of loners. It also helps describe the characteristics of an ideal customer. Although scatterplots appear to be too simple for complex stratifications that use more than two variables, it has the advantage of being easy to read. For most business users, we can add two cyclical expressions to a scatterplot and give them the power to compare any two of a potentially large group of customer stratification metrics. For the more experienced analysts, we can also create a more involved visualization called a scatterplot matrix.

The following figure shows a scatterplot matrix that compares three variables: Sales, DSO, and Gross Profit:

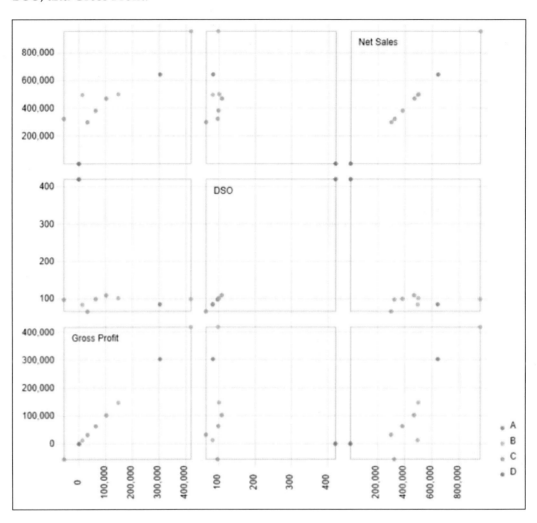

Exercise 5.10

1. Download and install the scatterplot matrix from Qlik Branch (http://branch.qlik.com/#/project/56d99a0a20d00edd11554ea9).

2. Add a third stratification metric based on gross profit. Use the example of the sales stratification in *Chapter 2, Sales Perspective*, in *Exercise 2.3* to create the gross profit stratification that is based on a Pareto.

3. Add the following variables:

Variable	
Label	**Value**
vExp_DSOCustomerStratification	if($(vExp_DSOCustomer) < $(vExp_DSOCustomerStratificationBoundaries(.25)),'A' ,if($(vExp_DSOCustomer) < $(vExp_DSOCustomerStratificationBoundaries(.5)),'B' ,if($(vExp_DSOCustomer) < $(vExp_DSOCustomerStratificationBoundaries(.75)),'C', 'D')))
vExp_SalesCustomerStratification	if(len(only({A_CustomerSales}Customer)) <> 0, 'A', if(len(only({AB_CustomerSales}Customer)) <> 0, 'B', if(len(only({ABC_CustomerSales}Customer)) <> 0, 'C', if(len(only({$}Customer)) <> 0,'D'))))
vExp_GrossProfitCustomerStratification	if(len(only({A_CustomerGrossProfit}Customer)) <> 0, 'A', if(len(only({AB_CustomerGrossProfit}Customer)) <> 0, 'B', if(len(only({ABC_CustomerGrossProfit}Customer)) <> 0, 'C', if(len(only({$}Customer)) <> 0,'D'))))

In the **Web View**, add a **New Sheet Object** called **Scatterplot Matrix**:

Dimensions	
Label	**Value**
Customer	`Customer`

Customer Classification	`=aggr(`
	`  pick(`
	`    round(`
	`      match($(vExp_SalesCustomerStratification),'D',`
	`'C', 'B','A') * .35`
	`      +`
	`      match($(vExp_DSOCustomerStratification),'D','C',`
	`'B','A') * .3`
	`      +`
	`      match($(vExp_GrossProfitCustomerStratification),`
	`'D','C','B','A') * .35`
	`    )`
	`    ,'D'`
	`    ,'C'`
	`    ,'B'`
	`    ,'A'`
	`  )`
	`  ,Customer)`

Expressions	
Label	**Value**
Rolling 12-month net sales	`=sum({$<$(vSetRolling12Modifier),_ActualFlag={1}>}` `[Net Sales])`
DSO	`$(vExp_DSOCustomer)`
Rolling 12-month gross profit	`=sum({$<$(vSetRolling12Modifier),_ActualFlag={1}>}` `[Gross Profit])`

Multivariate analysis leads to complex data visualization. The scatterplot matrix serves as a tool for more advanced analysts who want a rough idea of correlations and clustering between multiple variables at a glance. For example, we can observe that there is a stronger relationship between gross profit and sales than there is between DSO and either of these two metrics.

In the same way we use DSO for customer stratification, we can also use DSI and DPO for product and supplier stratification. This type of analysis helps us understand each working capital element within the context of other measurements. For example, a top-selling customer with a high DSO may be acceptable. However, we might lower the credit available to customers that buy little and have a high DSO.

Summary

We started analyzing the working capital perspective at a high level and then worked our way through different levels of analysis that empowers the whole business to help raise capital for further development. Additionally, a more complete customer stratification helps sales representatives focus on customers that pay in fewer days. We can also develop item and supplier stratification and help the purchasing or production department.

Finally, we empower warehouse, purchasing, and collection teams to do their jobs more effectively with inventory stock levels and aging reports. Let's continue to make them more productive and create an operations perspective.

6
Operations Perspective

Effective business operations use capital in an efficient way to deliver what the business sells. In other words, we have to discover just the right number of resources needed to deliver the best-possible customer service. In this chapter, we use data to avoid late deliveries and slow responses to our customers' needs without bankrupting our business.

We will start this chapter by examining company-wide indicators and then we will work our way through the data to discover opportunities to improve our internal operations. We will expand on historical analysis and add the ability to use statistics to predict future supplier behavior. We will also add accuracy to our predictive analysis with the help of an integrated planning tool that we will use to confirm future demand.

In this chapter, we will review the following topics while we create our QlikView operations perspective:

- Operations data model (accumulating snapshot)
- On-time in-full analysis
- Predicting supplier lead times
- Supplier and on-time delivery correlation analysis
- Planning in QlikView with KliqPlan

Operations data model

Operations involve multiple discrete events that are represented as documents in the ERP system. For example, our customer selling cycle includes a sales quotation, a sales order, a customer delivery, a sales return, a sales invoice, and a sales credit memo. Our supplier purchasing cycle includes a purchase order, a delivery, a return, a purchase invoice, and a purchase credit memo.

Although we can create a transactional fact table that allows us to analyze each discrete event, we are interested in analyzing the relationship between the events more than the events themselves. For example, we want to know how much time it took to deliver a product after receiving its originating purchase order. It would also be insightful to compare the quantity that we delivered with the quantity of the originating purchase order. We would have to work between multiple rows in a transactional fact table to discover this information; and just like a row-based database, we would find it challenging to work between rows in QlikView.

Therefore, we create a table where one instance of the whole operational process is stored in only one row. Each instance is an evolving event that is updated every time it reaches a milestone in the process. For example, in the beginning a row may only contain a sales order. When this sales order becomes a sales delivery, we update this row with data from the sales delivery. We refer to this fact table as an accumulating snapshot.

We measure the following evolving events in our data model:

- Customer selling cycle
- Supplier purchase cycle

We keep the accumulating snapshot table simple by modeling every cycle as a one-way, linear process. In our ERP system, we can begin this process with any discrete event. For example, we may start the selling cycle with a sales quotation, or we could skip this step and start with a sales order. In the script, we assume that a document created from nothing is a new cycle and concatenate a new row to the accumulating snapshot.

When we generate a document from another document, we assume that we are adding on to an existing cycle. We link this new document's data with an existing row that contains the base document's data. For example, if we generate a sales invoice from a customer delivery, we will insert this invoice into the same row as the base delivery document.

Each event contains multiple dates and amounts that correspond to different discrete events in the process. For example, one row can potentially contain the sales order date, the delivery date, and the sales invoice date. As such, accumulating snapshots tend to have more columns and fewer rows than a transactional fact table.

Although we focus on the number of rows in a fact table when we estimate the size of a QlikView application, the number of columns in a fact table is also important to consider. A large number of columns (>50) in a fact table may cause slow response times.

As sales and purchasing cycles have a similar sequence of events, we use the same columns for each cycle. For example, we use a column called [Order Quantity] to hold the quantity of both sales and purchase orders. We differentiate between each order using a field called [Process Type] that holds a text value that is either Sales or Purchasing. Even with this table optimization, the fact table contains almost one hundred columns.

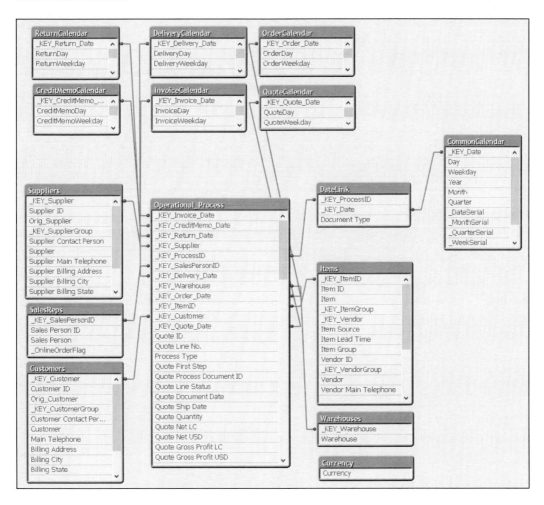

Most of this data model's dimensions are similar to the ones from previous perspectives. The difference is in how it handles dates. Each date has its own master calendar and they all share a common master calendar. We need a bridge table to link this common master calendar to the fact table so that it can handle the multiple date fields that exist in each row. Before we look deeper into this subject in the next section, let's review the 7Ws of our operations data model:

Dimensions		
7Ws	**Fields**	**Comments**
Who	Customer	This is a dimension that we first saw *Chapter 2, Sales Perspective*.
Who	Sales Person	This is a dimension we first saw in *Chapter 2, Sales Perspective*.
Who	Supplier	This is a dimension we first saw in *Chapter 5, Working Capital Perspective*.
What	Item	This is a dimension we first saw in *Chapter 2, Sales Perspective*.
What	[Quote Line Status], [Order Line Status], [Delivery Line Status], [Invoice Line Status]	This is how we keep track of both finished and pending cycles in the accumulating snapshot. The last step of pending cycles has an O as its line status. Otherwise, the line status is C.
When	Month, Year	This is a common set of calendar fields where we store the dates of multiple discrete events.
When	[Quote Due Date], [Order Due Date], [Delivery Due Date], [Invoice Due Date]	This is where we store event-specific due dates.
How	[Quote First Step], [Order First Step], [Delivery First Step], [Invoice First Step]	This indicates with a Yes or No value how the operations cycle was started.
Where	Warehouse	Warehouse is a dimension that we first saw in *Chapter 5, Working Capital Perspective*.

Metrics		
7Ws	**Fields**	**Comments**
How Many	`[Quote Quantity]`, `[Order Quantity]`, `[Delivery Quantity]`, `[Invoice Quantity]`	These are the metrics that we measured in our transactional fact table, which are also in an accumulating snapshot. However, all these metrics are on one row and we begin the name of each metric with the name of the discrete event that it measures.

Handling multiple date fields

When we have multiple date fields on one row, we can't just fit every date into one calendar. At the same time that we handle multiple date fields in one common calendar, we also create a master calendar for each important date. The important dates in this case are when we create a new document in a cycle. We use these dates and the same calendar subroutine that we used in previous perspectives to create a separate calendar for each date field for that date. We use calendars that correspond to certain documents in the analysis that we perform in this perspective:

```
call Qvc.CalendarFromField('_KEY_Quote_Date','QuoteCalendar','Quote');
```

We also create a common calendar that helps the user navigate through the data without having to first think about what calendar to filter. This calendar behaves as shown in the following figure. When we select a process cycle that is identified by `_KEY_ProcessID`, which is equal to `1399`, we notice that it contains multiple dates starting from May 15, 2012, until June 9, 2012. As a result, we can see in the common calendar's Year and Month filters that both May and June 2012 are possible values:

We make this behavior possible by creating a bridge or link table between the fact table and the `CommonCalendar` dimension. This link table is called `DateLink` and it stores the date of each cycle's discrete events in individual rows:

_KEY_ProcessID	_KEY_Date	Document Type
1399	5/15/2012	Order
1399	5/15/2012	Quote
1399	5/20/2012	Delivery
1399	6/9/2012	Invoice

The following code is an example of the script to include the dates of the first two discrete events in the `DateLink` table. The other dates can also be added in the same way:

```
DateLink:
Load
    _KEY_ProcessID,
    [Quote Document Date] as _KEY_Date,
    'Quote' as [Document Type]
Resident Operational_Process
Where not isnull([Quote Document Date]);


Concatenate (DateLink)
Load
    _KEY_ProcessID,
    [Order Document Date] as _KEY_Date,
    'Order' as [Document Type]
Resident Operational_Process
Where not isnull([Order Document Date]);
```

Now that we've reviewed the operations data model and how we handle multiple date fields, let's start to analyze our operational cycles.

On-Time and In-Full

Our objective is to help the teams that are in charge of purchasing, production, and shipping, to deliver on the expectations that the sales and marketing teams have built for our customer. We may sell items based on prices or quality, but our customers expect us to deliver what we sell. The first requirement is that we deliver our products **On-Time and In-Full (OTIF)**.

 As a logistics manager, I want to analyze what percentage of our orders are OTIF so that I can look for opportunities to improve our operations or adjust the expectations built by the sales team.

We are not only concerned about whether the delivery arrives on time but also whether it is completed without any returns. Although, in some cases, early deliveries may be a problem, we will assume that they are not in this case. We calculate OTIF with the following formula:

OTIF = the number of line items shipped on or before promised delivery and complete divided by the total number of line items shipped

When we use the number of line items, we apply an equal weight to all line items, regardless of whether they represent large or small volumes. If we want to place a bias on deliveries that generate more value for the company, we can replace the number of line items with gross profit, sales, or quantity. We calculate OTIF by line item and by total quantity in the following chart:

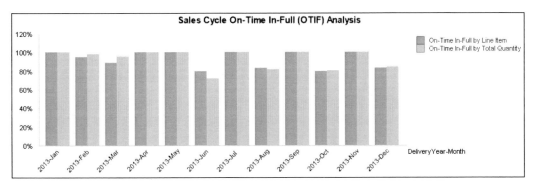

Exercise 6.1

Before beginning the following exercise, we import this chapter's exercise files into the QDF as we did in *Chapter 2, Sales Perspective*. Let's create a bar chart that analyzes OTIF with the following property options in `1.Application\Operations_Perspective_Sandbox.qvw`:

Dimensions	
Label	Value
Delivery Year-Month	DeliveryYear-Month

Expressions	
Label	**Value**
| On-Time In-Full by Line Item | ```
sum({$<[Process Type]={'Sales'},[Delivery First
Step]={'No'}>}
    if([Delivery Document Date]<=[Order Due Date]
        and [Order Quantity]=rangesum([Delivery
Quantity],-[Return Quantity])
        ,1)
)
/
count({$<[Process Type]={'Sales'},[Delivery First
Step]={'No'}>}
    DISTINCT [Delivery Line No.]
)
``` |
| On-Time In-Full by Total Quantity | ```
sum({$<[Process Type]={'Sales'},[Delivery First
Step]={'No'}>}
    if([Delivery Document Date]<=[Order Due Date]
        and [Order Quantity]=rangesum([Delivery
Quantity],-[Return Quantity])
        ,[Delivery Quantity])
)
/
sum({$<[Process Type]={'Sales'},[Delivery First
Step]={'No'}>}
    [Delivery Quantity])
``` |

We use the `Delivery Year-Month` field as a dimension because we specifically want to analyze the deliveries in the month that they were made. In each expression, we use an if-statement within the `sum()` function. For better performance, we can also migrate this logic to the script and create a field in the data model that identifies which line items were OTIF. The conditional expression of the if-statement evaluates whether what we promised in the sales order matches the delivery. Therefore, we filter out delivery documents that start a sales cycle in the set analysis because no promise was ever documented in the ERP system.

An accumulating snapshot tends to contain many null values that represent steps in the cycle that have yet to happen or that never will. In QlikView, binary functions, such as +, -, *, and /, do not work when one of the variables is a null value. For example, the `=8+null()` expression returns a null value instead of eight. On the other hand, the `rangesum()` function treats a null value as if it were zero, so we add we use it to sum `[Delivery Quantity]` and `[Return Quantity]` because they often contain a null value.

We can gather from our OTIF analysis that, for six months in 2013, we delivered 100% of our orders on-time and in-full. The most difficult month in 2013 was June when we delivered 80% of the line items and 72% of the quantity satisfactorily. Assuming that we use a standard unit of measurement for all of our products, this discrepancy between line items and quantity is due to a higher OTIF among lower-quantity deliveries. Let's now analyze how we work through our data to discover opportunities to improve our OTIF.

OTIF breakdown

There are various ways to analyze OTIF in more detail. Just like we did with the DSI calculation in our working capital perspective, we can break up the OTIF calculation into its parts. For example, we can analyze on-time deliveries separately from in full deliveries and also analyze the total absolute number of deliveries per month see its behavior.

We can also analyze the different cycles that support OTIF. For example, we can explore data from the production cycle, the purchasing cycle, or the shipping cycle. As we've added the purchasing cycle to our operations perspective, we can easily analyze our suppliers' OTIF rate in the following chart:

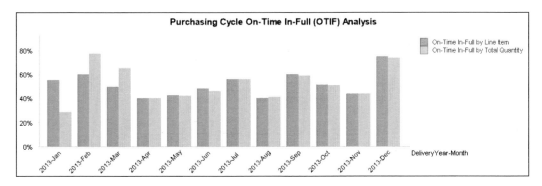

Exercise 6.2

To perform this exercise:

1. Clone the chart that we created in *Exercise 6.1*.

2. Change the code, [Process Type]={'Sales'}, in the metric expressions to [Process Type]={'Purchasing'}.

Finally, we can break down the cycles by their corresponding dimensions, such as supplier, customer, sales person, or item. We notice in the previous chart that our suppliers do not have a high OTIF and we decide to break down the metric by supplier:

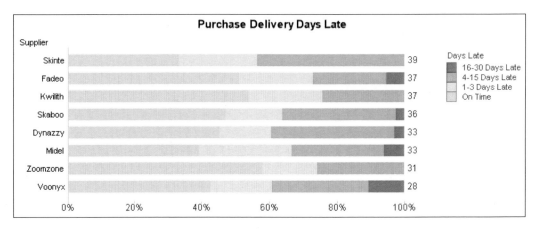

Exercise 6.3

To perform this exercise:

1. We create the following variable so that the code looks cleaner:

Variable	
Label	Value
vSA_PurchaseDelivery_ NotFirstStep	{$<[Process Type]={'Purchasing'} ,[Delivery First Step]={'No'}>}

2. Let's create a bar chart with the following dimensions and metrics options:

Dimensions	
Label	**Value**
Supplier	`Supplier`

Days Late	`=aggr(`
	`        if(only($(vSA_PurchaseDelivery_NotFirstStep)`
	`[Delivery Days Late])<=0, dual('On Time',1)`
	`        ,if(only($(vSA_PurchaseDelivery_NotFirstStep)`
	`[Delivery Days Late])<=3, dual('1-3 Days Late',2)`
	`        ,if(only($(vSA_PurchaseDelivery_NotFirstStep)`
	`[Delivery Days Late])<=15, dual('4-15 Days Late',3)`
	`        ,if(only($(vSA_PurchaseDelivery_NotFirstStep)`
	`[Delivery Days Late])<=30, dual('16-30 Days Late',4)`
	
	`        ,dual('>30 Days Late',5))))))`
	`        ,_KEY_ProcessID)`

Expressions	
Label	**Value**

% of Deliveries	`count($(vSA_PurchaseDelivery_NotFirstStep)`
	`    DISTINCT [Delivery Line No.])`
	`/`
	`count($(vSA_PurchaseDelivery_NotFirstStep)`
	`        Total <Supplier> DISTINCT [Delivery Line No.])`

Number of Deliveries	`count($(vSA_PurchaseDelivery_NotFirstStep)` `        Total <Supplier> DISTINCT [Delivery Line No.])`

3. Change the background color attribute expression for % of deliveries to the following code:

```
=aggr(if(only($(vSA_PurchaseDelivery_NotFirstStep) [Delivery Days
Late])<=0, RGB(171,217,233)
        ,if(only($(vSA_PurchaseDelivery_NotFirstStep) [Delivery Days
Late])<=3, RGB(254,217,142)
        ,if(only($(vSA_PurchaseDelivery_NotFirstStep) [Delivery Days
Late])<=15, RGB(254,153,41)
        ,if(only($(vSA_PurchaseDelivery_NotFirstStep) [Delivery Days
Late])<=30, RGB(217,95,14)
        ,RGB(153,52,4))))),_KEY_ProcessID)
```

4. Select the expression `Number of Deliveries` and, in **Display Options**, disable **Bar** and enable **Values on Data Points**.

5. In the **Sort** tab, sort the `Supplier` by **Expression** in **Descending** order using the following code:

```
count(Total <Supplier> $(vSA_PurchaseDelivery_NotFirstStep)
    DISTINCT [Delivery Line No.])
```

6. Sort `Days Late` using **Numeric Value**.

7. In the **Style** tab, change **Orientation** to horizontal bars and change the **Subtype** to **Stacked**.

We've created the `[Delivery Days Late]` field in the script to make for cleaner code and reduce calculation time. For larger datasets, it may also be necessary to create days late bins in the script instead of using a calculated dimension, as we did in this exercise. Either way, we should create bins using the `dual()` function so that we can easily sort them.

We can use this chart for any step in a cycle that has a due date. We group all on-time instances in one bin and then we divide late instances into bins that represent ranges that are analytically significant. On the other hand, if we simply want to analyze the time that it takes to complete a step, we can use a histogram. Let's take what we've discovered about our suppliers' OTIF and analyze each item's real lead time.

Predicting lead time

Lead time is the time that it takes from the moment that we order an item to the moment that we receive it in inventory. We first saw lead time in our working capital perspective in *Chapter 5, Working Capital Perspective*. In that chapter, we used a predefined lead time to calculate each item's reorder stock level. In this section we look at how to use data to calculate a more accurate lead time. We can also apply these same methods to analyze the time taken to complete any of the steps in a cycle. For example, we can measure how long it takes to generate a customer invoice or convert a quotation into an order.

We begin our analysis by visualizing the average time that it takes from the moment we create a purchase order until we create an inventory delivery receipt. We analyze the trend of average lead times by month.

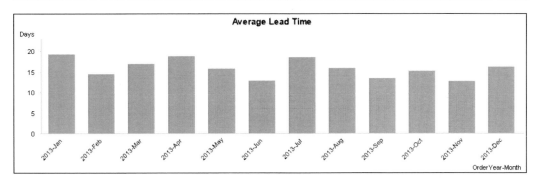

Exercise 6.4

Let's create a bar chart with the following dimensions and metrics options:

Dimensions	
Label	**Value**
OrderYear-Month	`OrderYear-Month`
Expressions	
Label	**Value**
Average Lead Time	`avg({$<[Process Type]={'Purchasing'}>} [Lead Time])`

We create a `[Lead Time]` field in the script that is the difference between `[Delivery Document Date]` and `[Order Document Date]`. The `avg()` function works without the help of *aggr()* because we want the average lead time of each line item, which has the same level of detail as our accumulating snapshot.

If the only statistical measurement that we use is average, then we risk over-simplifying our analysis and failing to define optimal inventory levels. Let's study the time span between a purchase order and its receipt in more detail with a distribution analysis that we first saw in the sales perspective in *Chapter 2, Sales Perspective*:

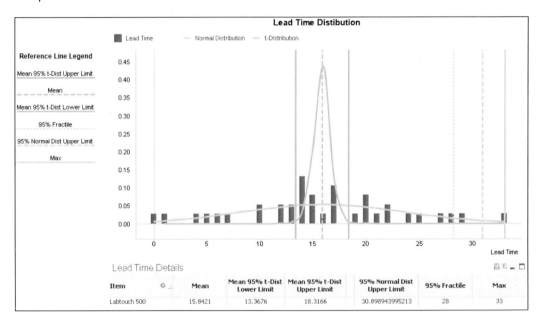

Item		Mean	Mean 95% t-Dist Lower Limit	Mean 95% t-Dist Upper Limit	95% Normal Dist Upper Limit	95% Fractile	Max
Labtouch 500		15.8421	13.3676	18.3166	30.898943995213	28	33

Exercise 6.5

Lead time distribution contains the following three objects:

Let's first create the **Lead Time Details** table:

Dimensions	
Label	**Value**
Item	Item
Expressions	
Label	**Value**
Mean	avg({$<[Process Type]={'Purchasing'}>} [Lead Time])
Mean 95% t-Dist Lower Limit	TTest1_Lower({$<[Process Type]={'Purchasing'}>} [Lead Time], (1-(95)/100)/2)
Mean 95% t-Dist Upper Limit	TTest1_Upper({$<[Process Type]={'Purchasing'}>} [Lead Time], (1-(95)/100)/2)
<empty>	=''

95% Normal Dist Upper Limit	avg({$<[Process Type]={'Purchasing'}>} [Lead Time]) +2*Stdev({$<[Process Type]={'Purchasing'}>} [Lead Time])
97.5% Fractile	Fractile({$<[Process Type]={'Purchasing'}>} [Lead Time],.975)
Max	max({$<[Process Type]={'Purchasing'}>} [Lead Time])

Just as we did in *Chapter 2, Sales Perspective*, we calculate the mean and evaluate its range using a t-distribution. We can use one of these results as the average lead time to calculate our minimum stock level. For example, we can use the upper limit if we want to reduce the risk of any inventory shortage or the lower limit if we want to reduce the risk of purchasing too much stock.

The other set of statistics tells us the maximum lead time that we've recorded and introduces two alternatives that we can use to avoid stocking too many items if the maximum happens to be an outlier. The first alternative, 95% Normal Dist Upper Limit assumes that we have more than thirty lead times in our data sample and that lead times are distributed normally. If this is the case, then we can add the mean and two standard deviations to calculate the upper limit of a 95% confidence level for a standard normal distribution. The result is the lead time that we predict will be larger than 97.5% of past and future lead times.

We can also use fractiles to remove possible outliers. The result of the 97.5% fractile is a number that is larger than 97.5% of past lead times. This fractile works regardless of how lead times is distributed and is easier for the business user to grasp. We can also use it as a test to evaluate whether lead times are normally distributed. If there is a large difference between the 97.5% fractile and the upper limit of the 95% confidence level, then lead times may not be normally distributed.

We may also decide to use the actual maximum lead time even when it is an outlier because the cost of not having an item in stock is greater than the cost of storing too much inventory. Which method we use to determine maximum lead time depends on our strategy and neither is perfect. We should test the accuracy of each and constantly fine tune the calculation according to our findings.

1. Let's create a **Combo Chart** that helps us visualize lead time distribution and the key numbers in our **Lead Time Details** table:

Dimensions	
Label	**Value**
Lead Time	`=ValueLoop($(=min([Lead Time])) ,$(=max([Lead Time])).1)`

Expressions	
Label	**Value**
| Lead Time | ```
sum({$<[Process Type]={'Purchasing'}>}
     if([Lead Time]=
          round(ValueLoop($(=min([Lead Time]))
               ,$(=max([Lead Time]))),.1)),1))
/
count({$<[Process Type]={'Purchasing'}>} [Lead Time])
``` |
| Normal Distribution | ```
NORMDIST(
    ValueLoop($(=min([Lead Time]))
         ,$(=max([Lead Time]))),1)
     ,avg({$<[Process Type]={'Purchasing'}>} [Lead Time])
     ,stdev({$<[Process Type]={'Purchasing'}>} [Lead
Time])
     ,0)
``` |
| t-Distribution | ```
TDIST(
   (fabs(ValueLoop($(=min([Lead Time])),$(=max([Lead
Time]))),.1)
   -avg({$<[Process Type]={'Purchasing'}>} [Lead Time])))
/
   (Stdev({$<[Process Type]={'Purchasing'}>} [Lead Time])
/ sqrt(count({$<[Process Type]={'Purchasing'}>} [Lead
Time])))
   ,count({$<[Process Type]={'Purchasing'}>} [Lead Time])
   ,1)
``` |

2. In the **Axes** tab, enable the **Continuous** option in the **Dimension Axis** section.

3. In the **Presentation** tab, add the six metrics in the **Lead Time Details** table as reference lines along the continuous *x* axis. Make the line style and color the same as the previous figure so that we can create a legend in the next step.

4. Finally, let's add a **Line Chart** that serves as our **Reference Line Legend**:

Dimensions	
Label	**Value**
Lead Time	`=ValueLoop(0,2)`
Expressions	
Label	**Value**
Max	`=dual(if(ValueLoop(0,2)=1,'Max',''),sum(.1))`
| 95% Normal Dist Upper Limit | ```
=dual(if(ValueLoop(0,2)=1
     ,'95% Normal Dist Upper Limit',''),sum(.2))
``` |

97.5% Fractile	=dual(if(ValueLoop(0,2)=1 ,'95% Fractile',''),sum(.3))
Mean 95% t-Dist Lower Limit	=dual(if(ValueLoop(0,2)=1 ,'Mean 95% t-Dist Lower Limit',''),sum(.4))
Mean	=dual(if(ValueLoop(0,2)=1,'Mean',''),sum(.5))
Mean 95% t-Dist Upper Limit	=dual(if(ValueLoop(0,2)=1 ,'Mean 95% t-Dist Upper Limit',''),sum(.6))

5. Modify the **Background Color** and **Line Style** in the following way:

Expression	Background Color	Line Style
Max	RGB(178,223,138)	='<s1>'
95% Normal Dist Upper Limit	RGB(178,223,138)	='<s2>'
97.5% Fractile	RGB(178,223,138)	='<s3>'
Mean 95% t-Dist Lower Limit	RGB(192,192,192)	='<s1>'
Mean	RGB(192,192,192)	='<s2>'
Mean 95% t-Dist Upper Limit	RGB(192,192,192)	='<s1>'

6. In the **Expressions** tab, enable **Values on Data Points** in the **Display Options** section.

7. Disable **Show Legend** in the **Presentation** tab.

8. Disable **Show Legend** in the **Dimensions** tab.

9. Enable **Hide Axis** in the **Axes** tab.

10. Resize and adjust each of the objects as necessary.

As in *Chapter 2, Sales Perspective,* we use the valueloop() function as a dimension to create a continuous X-Axis so that we can visualize the distribution curves. We also use it in the **Reference Line Legend** to create a dummy line with three points. We then use the dual() function in each line's expression to add a text data value in the center point.

We've just used advanced statistical methods to create a more complex model to estimate lead time. Let's now use another statistical method called the Chi-squared test of independence to test whether on-time deliveries depend on the supplier.

Supplier and On-Time delivery correlation

When we want to test whether two numeric metrics are correlated, we use scatterplot charts and R-squared. Similarly, we can also test the correlation between two categorical groups using the Chi-squared test of independence.

In this example, we want to confirm that the supplier is not one of the factors that determines a delivery's timeliness. In order to test this hypothesis, we calculate a value called p, which is the probability that supplier and delivery status are independent. Before analyzing the results of the Chi-squared test of independence, we decide that if p is less than .05, then we will reject the assumption that delivery timeliness does not depend on the supplier. This then implies that there is a relationship between them. We call this point (.05) where we would reject the hypothesis of independence as the critical point. Let's analyze and evaluate whether there is a relationship between these two variables:

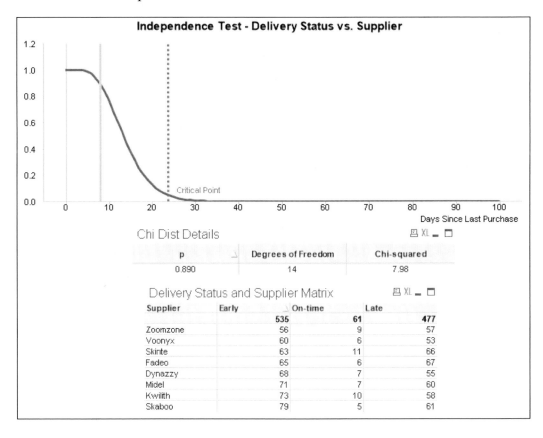

Independence Test - Delivery Status vs. Supplier

Chi Dist Details

p	Degrees of Freedom	Chi-squared
0.890	14	7.98

Delivery Status and Supplier Matrix

Supplier	Early	On-time	Late
	535	61	477
Zoomzone	56	9	57
Voonyx	60	6	53
Skinte	63	11	66
Fadeo	65	6	67
Dynazzy	68	7	55
Midel	71	7	60
Kwilith	73	10	58
Skaboo	79	5	61

Exercise 6.5

Our independence test contains the following three objects:

1. Let's first create the **Delivery Status and Supplier Matrix** pivot table:

Dimensions	
Label	**Value**
Supplier	Supplier
Status	Status
Expressions	
Label	**Value**
Number of Deliveries	`count({$<[Process Type]={'Purchasing'}>} [Delivery ID])`

We notice from the table that there are deliveries that have a null status. Upon further investigation, we find that some deliveries do not have originating orders and therefore no due date to evaluate the timeliness of the delivery.

Aside from that observation, it is hard to use this matrix to detect whether the status depends on the supplier or not. Therefore, we use a statistical method to evaluate the numbers.

2. Let's create the **Chi Dist Details** table that contains the statistical results. This straight table has no dimensions and the following expressions:

Expressions	
Label	**Value**

p	`Chi2Test_p(Supplier,Status`
	`,aggr(count({$<[Process Type]={'Purchasing'}>}`
	`[Delivery ID])`
	`,Status,Supplier))`

Degrees of Freedom	`Chi2Test_df(Supplier,Status`
	`,aggr(count({$<[Process Type]={'Purchasing'}>}`
	`[Delivery ID])`
	`,Status,Supplier))`

Chi-squared	`Chi2Test_Chi2(Supplier,Status`
	`,aggr(count({$<[Process Type]={'Purchasing'}>}`
	`[Delivery ID])`
	`,Status,Supplier))`

The *p* value of .89 is much larger than the critical point of .05, so we don't have enough evidence to reject our assumption that [Delivery Status] and Supplier are independent. If the *p* value were below .05, then that would imply that [Delivery Status] and Supplier are correlated in some way.

We use degrees of freedom and Chi-squared to create and build the distribution curve. We can confirm that our chi-squared of 7.98 is far from the chi-squared that crosses the critical point in the distribution curve in the chart.

3. Let's create a **Line Chart** with the following dimensions and expressions:

Dimensions	
Label	**Value**
Lead Time	=ValueLoop(0,100,1)
Expressions	
Label	**Value**
Chi Distribution	CHIDIST(ValueLoop(0,100,1) ,$(=Chi2Test_df(Supplier,Status ,aggr(count({$<[Process Type]={'Purchasing'}>} [Delivery ID]),Status,Supplier))))

4. In the Axes tab, enable the Continuous option in the Dimension Axis section.

5. Add the following reference lines along the continuous x axis of the chart:

Reference Lines	
Label	**Value**
Chi-squared	=Chi2Test_Chi2(Supplier,Status ,aggr(count({$<[Process Type]={'Purchasing'}>} [Delivery ID]),Status,Supplier))
Critical Point	=CHIINV(.05,$(=Chi2Test_df(Supplier,Status ,aggr(count({$<[Process Type]={'Purchasing'}>} [Delivery ID]),Status,Supplier))))

In a Chi-squared distribution curve, the p value of .89 is actually the area of the curve to the right of Chi-squared value of 7.98. QlikView draws an accumulated distribution curve that indicates the area that corresponds to a particular Chi-squared value. Therefore, we can see that the Chi-squared reference line crosses the accumulated Chi-squared distribution curve where the y value is close to .89. We also note that it is far from the critical point.

We've used advanced statistical methods to perform both relational analysis and predictive analysis. Other than predictive analysis through statistical methods, our business users can also input data into QlikView and help us plan demand.

Planning in QlikView with KliqPlan

Each person in our company is a data source and it is important that they can easily input data that will enrich our analysis. If we combine analysis with planning, then we can be better prepared for the future and support our statistical analysis. In QlikView, business users can simultaneously analyze and input data.

Traditionally, data input in QlikView is limited to what-if scenarios that use variables or input fields. However, when we have a large number of variables, neither of these methods are ideal. A large number of variables is hard to maintain and input fields take up too much RAM. Furthermore, users cannot easily input a large number of values at once and there is a risk they will lose their input that is not directly saved to a database.

Planning tool extensions

As an alternative, we have the option to use an extension that enables us to perform more advanced data input in QlikView. One of these extensions is called KliqPlan (`http://www.ktlabs.com`) and it allows users to input data directly into a relational database from a QlikView application. It can also read the content from a relational database in real time and allow users to reload a QlikView application from their browser.

In order to implement KliqPlan, you should be familiar with SQL and go through its manual to learn all the property options of its extensions. Although these property options are unique to KliqPlan, it reuses QlikView expression logic to dynamically calculate many property options.

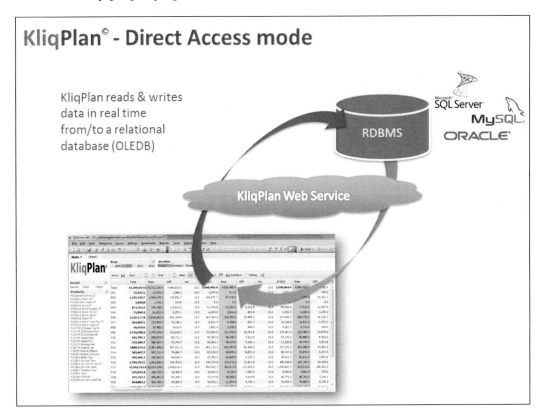

Sales forecasts and purchase planning

If we have a tool like KliqPlan, sales representatives can simultaneously analyze their past sales data and input what they expect to sell over the course of the next month. We can facilitate their planning by using QlikView expressions in a KliqPlan table to propose a future sales amount. For example, we can use a rolling average to predict next month's sales but still allow the sales representatives to adjust it accordingly.

We can then use this information to better plan our purchasing and production activities. We can cross-analyze data from sales representatives with historical data to confirm that it is not exaggerated. We may even experiment with multiple forecast versions as we learn more about our sales process.

It is especially insightful to visualize actual and forecast data side-by-side like in the following figure:

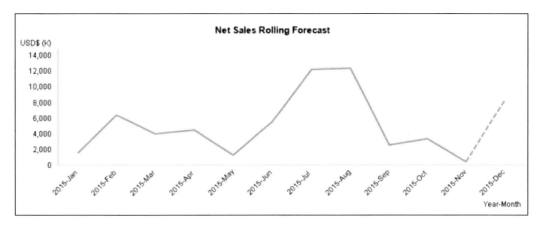

We use `rangesum()` and set analysis to combine actual and forecast data into the same line. Our expression would be similar to the following code:

```
rangesum(
sum({$<_ActualFlag={1},_MonthSerial={'<=$(=max({$<_ActualFlag={1}>}
_MonthSerial))'}>} [Net Sales])
,sum({$<_BudgetFlag={1},_MonthSerial={'>$(=max({$<_ActualFlag={1}>}
_MonthSerial))'}>} [Net Sales])
)
```

We then use the following code for the **Line Style** attribute expression:

```
if(_MonthSerial < max({$<_ActualFlag={1}>} Total _
MonthSerial),'<s1>','<s2>')
```

Along with the use of historical data, new products and customers are an important part of planning. Therefore, KliqPlan includes a component called *KliqTable* that allows users to add new customers and products.

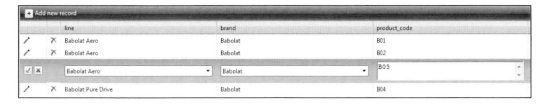

Other applications

KliqPlan is designed as a planning tool, but we can use it for any task that requires us to input data directly in QlikView. We often face analytical tasks that require the user to add information that cannot be found in any other data source. We usually end up using Excel files to input data that is not found anywhere else, but, in some cases, KliqPlan may be the better option, as in the following examples:

Options where KliqPlan is better	Description
Balanced Scorecard	Often, the goals and actual results of some of the indicators do not come from any ERP, CRM, or other formal operational database. For example, we may not have software to manage training and every month somebody has to input the number of employees that are certified QlikView developers. Instead of using Excel a user can input this data directly into Qlikview with KliqPlan.
Formal What-if Scenarios	Before KliqPlan, we used QlikView's native input fields to develop financial what-if scenarios for a customer. They used a series of drivers, such as the daily number of customers and the average amount spent by each customer, to create an estimated profit and loss statement.
	We developed a macro to export the profit and loss statement in XML so that SAP BW could import it into its database. The user then had to wait for QlikView to reload the new information from SAP BW. This functionality can now be developed using KliqPlan.

Summary

This chapter is a great opportunity to improve our internal processes and provide great customer service without bankrupting the company. After we explore the data with basic statistical methods, we should experiment with more predictive and complex analyses that can make our processes more effective.

Our ability to use such methods depends on the people that execute our internal processes. We need talented people to continually innovate how we analyze use data. As such, we will dedicate the next chapter to our human resources perspective.

7
Human Resources

We've created each of our previous perspectives with the objective of becoming a data-driven business. Robert Kaplan and David Norton considered the measurements in the learning and growth of employees as *the infrastructure to enable ambitious objectives in the financial, customer, and internal-business process perspectives.* We need to invest resources in our human capital so that they are capable of using data to help themselves and work at their optimal level. In this chapter, our goal is to learn more about our employees and help them be more effective.

First, we are interested in which factors make our team more productive. We use data from our **Human Resource Management System (HRMS)** to calculate metrics, such as headcount, salary, vacation days, sick days, and turnover by pertinent dimensions, such as job function, functional area, and demographics. Then, we compare these measurements with financial metrics, such as sales and gross profit.

Our organization's success is based on how well we develop our human talent. Therefore, we use additional metrics to measure performance and training. Along with our enterprise perspective, we also empower our employees to measure themselves. We look to achieve mutual success in helping them establish their own goals and measure their own performance with their own personal perspective.

We will cover the following topics as we develop our QlikView human resources perspective:

- HR data model
- Personnel productivity
- Personal behavior analysis

Let's begin by reviewing the HR data model that we will create from our HRMS system.

Human resources data model

The HR data model is a transactional fact table with discrete events. This includes the employee-related events along with a few financial events that help us measure productivity. We record the following events in this model:

- Employee payroll

- Employee absences

- Employee training

- Employee hiring and dismissals

- **General Journal (GJ)** entries related to sales, costs, and expenses

Here is a representation of this model:

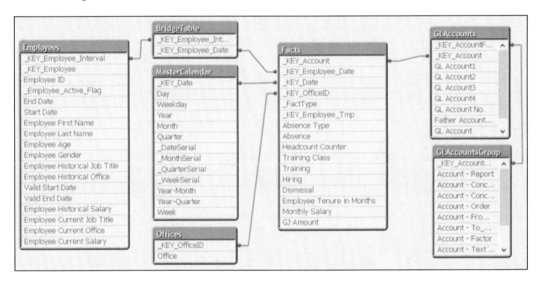

We combine these events into one fact table and use the same type of master calendar as in *Chapter 2, Sales Perspective*. The data model includes a new dimension table called **Employees**. Let's review the 7Ws of our HR data model.

Dimensions		
7Ws	**Fields**	**Comments**
Who	`Employee`	This is the focus of our HR data model. We include various attributes that are related to their role in the company and general demographic information here.
When	`Month, Year`	This is where we include a single master calendar that describes the exact date of an event.
Where	`Office`	We cannot usually measure sales by employee unless they are a sales representative. So, along with describing an employee's geographical location, we also use `Office` so that we can evaluate the productivity of an employee group.
What	`_FactType`	We store the event type of each fact table row in order to determine what event it represents. One row could record an absence, a training day, a hiring, a dismissal, or a paid salary.
What	`GL Account`	This is a dimension that we first saw *Chapter 3, Financial Perspective*.
Why	`Absence Type`	This is where we store why an employee was absent and whether it was due to sickness, vacation, or unexcused.
Metrics		
7Ws	**Fields**	**Comments**
How Many	`[Absence]`, `[Training]`, `[Hiring]`, `[Dismissal]`	Several events, such as vacation, training, hiring, and dismissals, are measurements only because of the fact that they occurred on a given date. Therefore, we create a field that measures the event using the number, 1, and use it as a counter in our analysis.

How Much	[Monthly Salary]	We measure how much each employee earns on a monthly basis. We also define our headcount as the number of employees that receive pay. We create a field called [Headcount Counter], which contains the number 1 every time they are paid.
How Much	[Sales], [Costs], [Expenses]	We measure this in the same way as we did in *Chapter 3, Financial Perspective*.

Slowing changing dimensions attributes

Over time, employees will learn and grow and they will earn promotions or transfer to different departments in the company. Some HRMS systems, such as SAP HR, contain tables that conserve history and tell us when an employee has changed their job position or department. Other systems may just contain an employee's current information and not save any record of their past job positions or departments.

Descriptive information that may change over time is called **Slowly Changing Dimensions (SCD)**. Other examples include reassigning customers to new sales representatives, rearranging customers groups, or rearranging product groups. We need to understand the effect that SCDs can have on our analysis and how business users expect to visualize this data. The following are the most common types of SCD's (Kimball and Ross 2013):

SCD Type	SCD Description
Type 0: Retain Original	This dimension attribute value never changes.
Type 1: Overwrite	This is when we erase history and overwrite the old attribute value with the new one in the dimension table.
Type 2: Add New Row	This is when we conserve history and store the new attribute value in a new row in the dimension table.

Often, users need SCD types 1 and 2 in order to answer all of their questions. For example, we may want to assess each office's current employee knowledge. So, we use SCD Type 1 to analyze the amount of training taken by employees regardless of whether some of this training was taken while assigned to other offices. On the other hand, we may want to analyze which office is investing more in training. In this case, we would need to use SCD Type 2 so that we can take into account where employees were working when they were trained.

Therefore, it is worthwhile to allow advanced users the option to compare both types in one application. We'll store Type 1 dimension attributes in fields that contain the word `"Current"` (for example, *Employee Current Job Title*) and Type 2 dimension attributes in fields that contain the word `"Historical"` (for example, *Employee Historical Job Title*).

We can easily create a SCD Type 1 field by assigning the current HRMS attribute value to the appropriate field in the script. The creation of SCD Type 2 is more complicated. We have to link the value in the `_KEY_Date` field in the `Facts` table to the attribute value's valid date interval defined by the `[Valid Start Date]` and `[Valid End Date]` fields in the `Employees` dimension table. We use the same `intervalmatch()` function that we used in *Chapter 4, Marketing Perspective*, to create the relationship between the `Facts` and `Employees` tables in our HR data model. For more information on how to handle SCD in a QlikView data model, read Henric Cronström's blog post on the subject at `https://community.qlik.com/blogs/qlikviewdesignblog/2013/06/03/slowly-changing-dimensions`.

> If the ERP or HRMS doesn't save the dates that a dimension attribute is valid and overwrites the values, we can use QVDs to conserve an attribute's history. The start and end dates are created in the script after we detect that a change has been made. A quick way to discover attribute value changes is using the hash function described in Barry Harmsen's blog (`http://www.qlikfix.com/2014/03/11/hash-functions-collisions/`).

Personnel productivity

Human Resources costs can represent up to 70 to 80 percent of the total cost of doing business (Lawler and Boudreau 2012). Our first goal is to analyze headcount, payroll, and how much revenue (or profit) we generate per employee and payroll dollar spent.

 As an HR analyst, I want to discover who our most productive teams are so that I can share their practices with the rest of company.

We start our analysis by comparing headcount and payroll. As these amounts use a different scale, we use the left axis of a dot plot chart for headcount and the right axis for payroll. Before beginning the following exercise, we import this chapter's exercise files into the QDF as we did in *Chapter 2, Sales Perspective*.

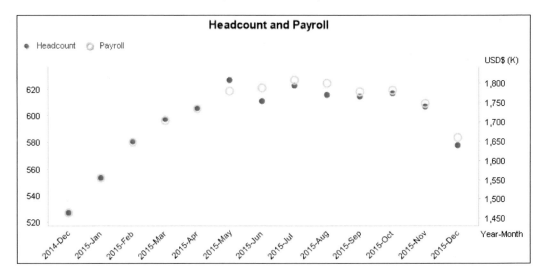

Exercise 7.1

1. In 1.Application\HR_Perspective_Sandbox.qvw, let's create a combo chart that measures headcount and payroll by year-month, as follows:

Dimensions	Details
Label	Value
Year-Month	Year-Month

Expressions	
Label	**Value**
Headcount	`count(distinct [Headcount Counter])`
Payroll	`sum([Monthly Salary])`

2. In the **Expressions** tab, enable only **Symbol** in the **Display Options** section. Define **Headcount** as **Dots** and **Payroll** as **Circles**.

3. In the **Axes** tab, disable the **Forced 0** option for both expressions. Select **Payroll** and enable the **Right (Top)** option in the **Position** section.

4. Adjust the look of the chart accordingly.

When we use a dual axis and remove the **Force the axis to zero** option, QlikView automatically aligns the maximum and minimum values of each metric so that they are at the same height along the Y-axis. We can, therefore, compare the percentage growth of the two metrics. For example, in the **Headcount and Payroll** chart, both **Headcount** and **Payroll** reach their minimum value in December 2014. At the end of 2015, **Payroll** is higher along its axis than **Headcount**, so we can conclude that it grew at a faster rate than **Headcount**. In other words, it implicitly shows an increase in the average payroll per employee.

Also, as we are more interested in the trend of the two metrics than the actual amounts, we can avoid forcing the axis to zero. It is sometimes useful to do this when we are working with a dot plot or a line chart. However, we should be careful to avoid doing the same to bar charts because the length of a bar traditionally represents the total actual value.

Let's apply the same method to compare these two metrics with the company's revenue and determine our personnel's productivity. The first formula compares revenue and headcount:

Revenue per employee = total revenue divided by total headcount

The second formula calculates employee productivity in terms of actual cost:

Employee Productivity = total revenue divided by total payroll

The ideal result of these metrics differ by industry, so we should compare our results with businesses from the same industry. Within our own company, we can also compare the results of different offices or branches. In order to do so, we create a dot plot chart that is similar to the previous example, but use the *Trellis* option so that we can create a series of the same chart by office. Every chart in this series uses the same axis scale so that we can compare the results of different offices as if they were located in only one chart.

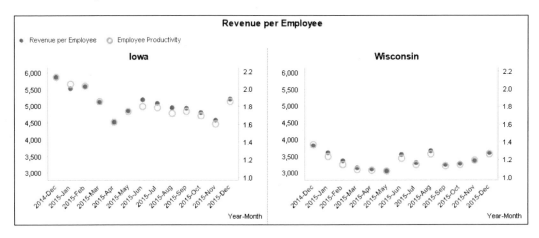

Exercise 7.2

1. Let's create a combo chart that measures headcount and payroll by year-month.

Dimensions	Details
Label	Value
Office	Office
Year-Month	Year-Month
Expressions	
Label	Value

Revenue per Employee	`-sum({$<[Account - Concept]={"Total Revenue"}>}`
	`[GJ Amount])`
	`/`
	`count(distinct [Headcount Counter])`

Employee Productivity	`-sum({$<[Account - Concept]={"Total Revenue"}>}`
	`[GJ Amount])`
	`/`
	`sum([Monthly Salary])`

2. In the **Dimensions** tab, click **Trellis...** and enable the **Enable Trellis Chart** option. Fix the **Number of Columns** to 2 and the **Number of Rows** to 1.

3. In the **Expressions** tab, enable only **Symbol** in the **Display Options** section. Define **Revenue per Employee** as **Dots** and **Employee Productivity** as **Circles**.

4. In the **Axes** tab, disable the **Forced 0** option for both expressions. Select **Payroll** and enable the **Right (Top)** option in the **Position** section.

We can easily see that the office in Iowa is more productive than the one in Wisconsin when the chart uses the same axis scale. Given that the Iowa and Wisconsin offices have equivalent departments and employee functions, the next step is to break down our personnel productivity and analyze why one office may have higher productivity than the other. We begin this process by visualizing our employees' profile and actions.

Personnel productivity breakdown

We begin the analysis of each office's teams by investigating their overall compositions and actions. We have a variety of metrics that may help us understand why one team may perform better than another. The following is a list of common metrics that we can use in our HR perspective:

- Age distribution
- Salary distribution
- Employee-retention rate
- Employee sick and vacation days
- Employee training and performance

Age distribution

Let's begin with our analysis and compare the age distribution between the two offices. Instead of using a histogram, we use a frequency polygon so that we can compare more than one distribution in the same chart.

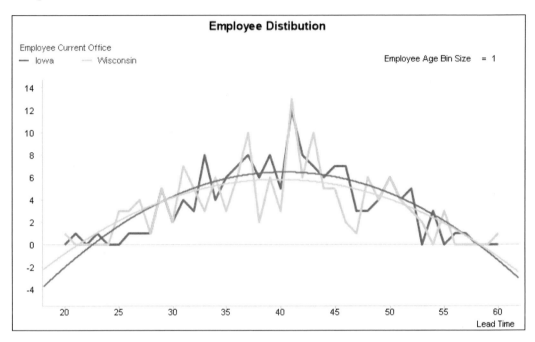

Exercise 7.3

1. Create the following variable:

Variables	Details
Label	Value
vEmployeeAgeBinSize	1

2. Let's create the following line chart:

Dimensions	Details
Label	**Value**

Age	```=ValueLoop(
	        $(=floor(min({$<_Employee_Active_Flag={1}>}
	                [Employee Age]),vEmployeeAgeBinSize))
	                ,$(=floor(max({$<_Employee_Active_
	Flag={1}>}
	                [Employee Age]),vEmployeeAgeBinSize))
	        ,vEmployeeAgeBinSize
	)```

Employee Current Office	Employee Current Office
Expressions	**Details**
Label	**Value**

Number of Employees	```sum({$<_Employee_Active_Flag={1}>}
	        if(floor([Employee Age],vEmployeeAgeBinSize)
	            =ValueLoop(
	                $(=floor(min({$<_Employee_Active_Flag={1}>}
	                [Employee Age]),vEmployeeAgeBinSize))
	                ,$(=floor(max({$<_Employee_Active_Flag={1}>}
	                [Employee Age]),vEmployeeAgeBinSize))
	                ,vEmployeeAgeBinSize
	            )
	        ,1,0)
	)```

3. In the **Expressions** tab, enable the **Polynomial of 2nd degree** option in the **Trendlines** section.

4. In the **Presentation** tab, disable the **Suppress Zero-Values** option.

5. In the **Axes** tab, enable the **Continuous** option.

6. Create an `Input Box` to edit the **vEmployeeAgeBinSize** variable.

Normally, we would use the `class()` function to create a histogram; however, the `class()` function generates bins from existing values. A bin without any corresponding value behaves in the same way that missing or null values behaved in *Chapter 2, Sales Perspective*. Although we are not affected by this behavior when we use a bar chart, we are not so lucky when we work with a line chart. The line jumps from one existing bin directly to another without representing the missing bins as zero.

Therefore, we use the `valueloop()` function rather than the `class()` function because `valueloop()` is a list of numbers that have no relationship with the data. We define the range of `valueloop()` dynamically with the `min()` and `max()` functions and the bin size is determined by the value of the `vEmployeeAgeBinSize` variable. The `floor()` function helps to round down *Employee Age* so that we can assign it to the proper bin. We usually use `floor()` to round down to the nearest one, but we can also use it to round down to the nearest five, ten, or thousand.

Finally, we add a second degree polynomial trend line to get a general idea of the shape of the distributions. As both resemble a normal distribution, this trend line does give us a general idea of the distribution. We can observe that the **Wisconsin** office in general has a greater number of young employees and fewer middle-aged ones. If the distribution does not resemble a normal distribution, we can try using trend lines of different degrees or, more simply, enlarge the bin size. Notice how different the distributions look without the trend lines and with **an Employee Age Bin Size** of **5**:

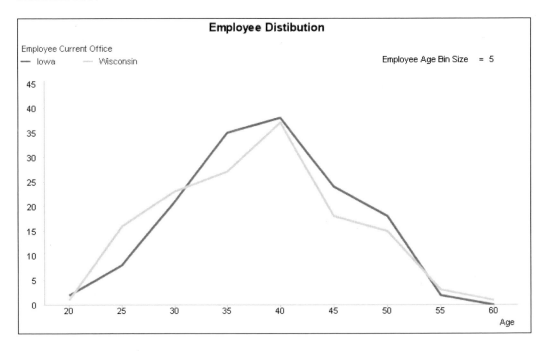

Salary distribution

The next analysis entails comparing how well each office pays their employees. We can analyze salary distribution among various groupings, such as office, job function, age, gender, and performance. In the following exercise, we are going to compare how each office pays each job function. Along with the option to use a frequency polygon trellis chart to compare the **Salary Distribution by Job Function and Office**, we can also use the following box plot chart:

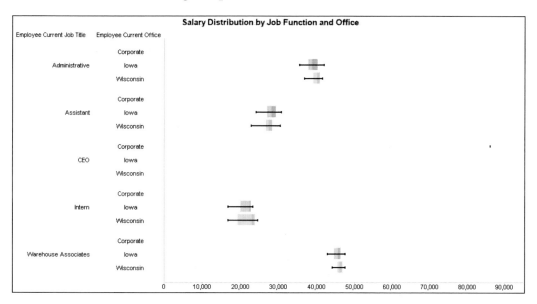

Exercise 7.4

1. Let's create the following combo chart:

Dimensions	Details
Label	Value
Employee Current Job Title	Employee Current Job Title
Employee Current Office	Employee Current Office
Expressions	
Label	Value

| Lower Quartile | ```
Fractile(
        Aggr(only({$<_Employee_Active_Flag={1}>}
                [Employee Current Salary]),[Employee Current
Office],
                [Employee ID],[Employee Current Job Title])
, 0.5)
-
Fractile(
        Aggr(only({$<_Employee_Active_Flag={1}>}
                [Employee Current Salary]),[Employee Current
Office],
                [Employee ID],[Employee Current Job Title])
, 0.25)
``` |
| Upper Quartile | ```
Fractile(
        Aggr(only({$<_Employee_Active_Flag={1}>}
                [Employee Salary]),[Employee Current Office],
                [Employee ID],[Employee Current Job Title])
, 0.75)
-
Fractile(
        Aggr(only({$<_Employee_Active_Flag={1}>}
                [Employee Salary]),[Employee Current Office],
                [Employee ID],[Employee Current Job Title])
, 0.5)
``` |
| Dummy Expression | ```
=0
``` |

2. In the **Expressions** tab, enable the **Bar** option for every expression and the **Has Error Bars** option for **Lower Quartile** in the **Display Options** section.

3. Define the following attribute expression for **Lower Quartile**:

Attribute Expressions	
Label	**Value**
| Background Color | ```
if([Employee Current Office]='Iowa'
        ,ARGB(100,178,171,210)
        ,ARGB(100,253,184,99)
)
``` |
| Bar Offset | ```
Fractile(
        Aggr(only({$<_Employee_Active_Flag={1}>}
                [Employee Current Salary]),[Employee Current
Office],
                [Employee ID],[Employee Current Job Title])
, 0.25)
``` |
```

| Error Below | ```
([Lower Quartile])

-

Min(
      Aggr(only({$<_Employee_Active_Flag={1}>}
            [Employee Current Salary]),[Employee Current
Office],
            [Employee ID],[Employee Current Job Title])
)
``` |
|---|---|
| Error Above | ```
-([Lower Quartile])

+

Max(
      Aggr(only({$<_Employee_Active_Flag={1}>}
            [Employee Current Salary]),[Employee Current
Office],
            [Employee ID],[Employee Current Job Title])
)
``` |

4. Define the following attribute expression for **Upper Quartile**:

Attribute Expressions	
Label	**Value**
| Background Color | ```
if([Employee Current Office]='Iowa'
      ,ARGB(200,178,171,210)
      ,ARGB(200,253,184,99)
)
``` |

5. In the **Error Bars** section of the **Presentation** tab, change **Width** to **Narrow**, **Thickness** to **Medium**, and **Color** to a dark gray.

6. In the **Axes** tab, define the **Static Max** with the following code:

```
Max(
Aggr(only({$<_Employee_Active_Flag={1}>}
[Employee Current Salary]),[Employee Current Office]
,[Employee ID],[Employee Current Job Title])
)*1.1
```

We could create a simple box plot using **Box Plot Wizard** in the file menu, **Tools**; however, in this case, we are limited to using one dimension. As a workaround, we use a combo chart with bars and error bars to create a box plot. As a part of this technique, we have to consider the fact that QlikView will draw the same number of error bars as there are expressions. As we have three distinct values in the Employee Current Office field, we add a third, dummy expression that is not visible because the value is zero. If the second dimension has five distinct values, we create a total of three dummy expressions.
```

Although this trick may seem awkward at first, the chart is not effective when the second dimension has a large number of distinct values. Therefore, we never expect to choose one with more than five or so values and it is not much trouble to create three dummy expressions.

The last adjustment involves the maximum value of the expression axis scale. The maximum that QlikView automatically calculates is unnecessarily large. So, we dynamically calculate the maximum plus a ten percent cushion. This makes it easier to compare the different box plots.

Employee retention rate

As a high-employee turnover can affect a team's productivity, we analyze how many employees leave each month. We also analyze how many people we hire and how our team evolves as they accumulate more years of experience. Along with using histograms, frequency polygons, and box plots to visualize the distribution of experience, we can also show a summarized distribution over time with a stacked bar chart.

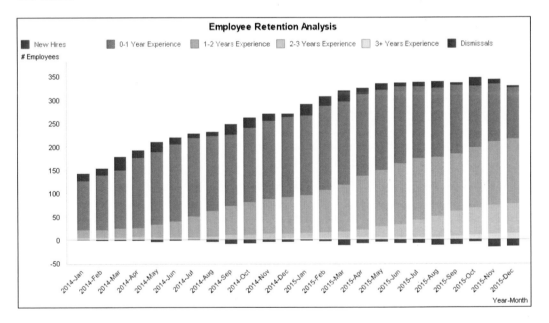

Exercise 7.5

1. Let's create the following bar chart:

Dimensions	
Label	**Value**
Year-Month	Year-Month
Expressions	
Label	**Value**
Dismissals	`-sum(Dismissal)`
3+ Years Experience	`count({$<[Employee Tenure in Months]={">36"}>}` `    distinct [Headcount Counter])`
2-3 Years Experience	`count({$<[Employee Tenure in Months]={">24<=36"}>}` `    distinct [Headcount Counter])`
1-2 Years Experience	`count({$<[Employee Tenure in Months]={">12<=24"}>}` `    distinct [Headcount Counter])`
0-1 Year Experience	`count({$<[Employee Tenure in Months]={">0<=12"}>}` `    distinct [Headcount Counter])`
New Hires	`sum(Hiring)`

2. In the **Style** tab, enable the **Stacked** option in the **Subtype** section.

This chart is simple to create because much of the work is done in the script. We create a new row in the fact table for every dismissal and new hire. The `Dismissal` and `Hiring` fields contain the value, `1`, so that we only have to sum them up to discover the total occurrences of each event. Also, every time we add to the employee payroll event, we calculate how many months have passed since they started working for the company.

Employee vacation and sick days

When our employees take too little vacation and too many sick days, this may indicate an overstressed team who may not be as productive as they could be. We can analyze these events with a bar or line chart, but if we want to visualize them on a daily level, it may be more insightful to use a calendar heat map. This heat map was inspired by Julian Villafuerte's blog post at `https://qlikfreak.wordpress.com/2014/03/09/heat-map/`.

Exercise 7.6

1. Let's create the following pivot table chart:

Dimensions	
Label	**Value**
Month	Month
Week	Week
<empty>	Year
<empty>	`=if(wildmatch(Weekday,'s*','t*')` `    ,left(Weekday,2),left(Weekday,1))`
Expressions	
Label	**Value**

% Absent	`sum({$<[Absence Type]={'Sick Day','Unexcused'}>}`
	`Absence)`
	`/`
	`(count(Total <Month,Year> distinct [Headcount Counter])`
	`*`
	`max(Total <Month,Year> Day))`

2. Pivot this table's dimensions as shown in the following figure:

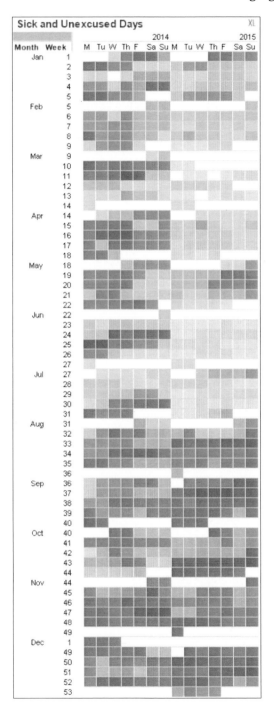

3. In the **Background Color** expression attribute, go through the **Colormix Wizard** found in the **File** menu. Use the same formula in the value expression as we did in the metric expression.

4. Copy the formula generated by **Colormix Wizard** and paste it in the **Text Color** expression attribute.

5. In the **Presentation** tab, disable the **Allow Pivoting** option and enable the **Always Fully Expanded** option. Replace the dashes in **Null Symbol** and **Missing Symbols** with spaces.

6. In the **Style** tab, disable the **Vertical Dimension Cell Borders** option.

7. Open the **Custom Format Cell** dialog window and make all backgrounds and borders white.

Sick days will tend to increase as the team grows; so, instead of basing our heat map on the actual number of sick days, we calculate sick days as a percentage of the total number of employee working days. According to the chart, after a lull in sick days in the beginning of 2015, there seems to have been an increase in the later part of the year. We can also compare the different offices by adding [Employee Current Office] as a dimension and placing it above the Year dimension.

Employee training and performance

Our final break down of employee productivity is to analyze our employee training and the results of this training. We expect employees to have greater success in the company after they are trained; however, sometimes it is inevitable that they leave or transfer to another office. Along with analyzing whether employees stay with the company after training, we also take advantage of the SCD Type 2 in our HR data model to analyze how often employees transfer or earn promotions after their training.

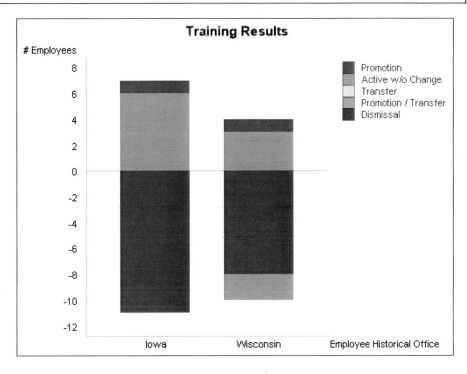

Exercise 7.7

Let's create the following bar chart:

Dimensions	
Label	**Value**
Employee Historical Office	Employee Historical Office
Expressions	
Label	**Value**
Dismissal	`-sum({$<_Employee_Active_Flag={0}>} Training)`

Promotion / Transfer	`-count({$<Training={1},_Employee_Active_Flag={1}>}`
	`distinct`
	`    if([Employee Historical Job Title]`
	`            <> [Employee Current Job Title]`
	`        and [Employee Historical Office]`
	`            <> [Employee Current Office]`
	`, [Employee ID]))`

| Transfer | ```-count({$<Training={1},_Employee_Active_Flag={1}>}
distinct
    if([Employee Historical Job Title]
            = [Employee Current Job Title]
        and [Employee Historical Office]
            <> [Employee Current Office]
, [Employee ID]))``` |
|---|---|
| Active w/o Change | ```sum({$<_Employee_Active_Flag={1}>} Training)
-[Promotion]
+[Promotion / Transfer]
+[Transfer]``` |
| Promotion | ```count({$<Training={1},_Employee_Active_Flag={1}>}
distinct
    if([Employee Historical Job Title]
            <> [Employee Current Job Title]
        and [Employee Historical Office]
            = [Employee Current Office]
, [Employee ID]))``` |

The `Training={1}` set analysis filters the data model, so we only see each employee's historical job title and office at the time he or she was trained. In this data model, we constantly update the current job title and office in every employee record so that we can always compare it with the historical records.

We use an if-statement within the `count()` function in this example in order to highlight how to compare fields of different SCD types. If we are dealing with a large amount of data, then we migrate this if-statement to the script and create a flag in the data model that indicates which dimension attributes have changed. We can then use this flag in the expression's set analysis.

In the chart, we observe that both offices suffer from a large number of dismissals after training employees and employees in the Wisconsin office tend to transfer when they earn a promotion. This example demonstrates why it is important to understand how the data model handles slowly changing dimensions and how we use both SCD Type 1 and SCD Type 2 to create an insightful analysis.

Personal behavior analysis

We collect a huge amount of data about each employee's work habits. Much of this data is located in log files generated when they connect to company servers or work on their own computers. A company that excessively uses this information to evaluate their employee's may be considered intrusive by their employees and the result may be counterproductive.

However, if we train employees in such a way as to form a mutually beneficial relationship, then we can rely on the employees themselves to analyze and improve their own productivity. In this case, the responsibility of the company is to give employees the proper tools to be more effective. One such tool may be RescueTime (https://www.rescuetime.com/), which helps a person keep track of which programs and websites he or she uses throughout the day. It also assigns a productivity score to each activity. For example, facebook.com has the minimum productivity score of -2, while MS Word scores the maximum score of 2, and MS Outlook may have a neutral productivity score of 0. The following chart reveals the productivity of a person's computer activities throughout several days:

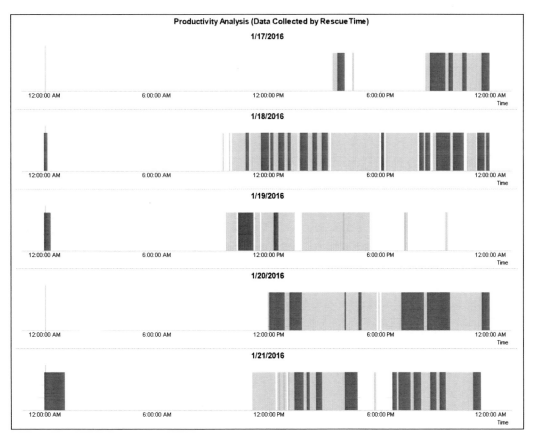

Exercise 7.8

1. Let's create the following bar chart in `1.Application\Personal_ Performance_Analysis.qvw` in the `HR_Perspective` container:

Dimensions	
Label	**Value**
Date	Date
Time	Time
Expressions	
Label	**Value**
<Empty>	=1

2. Place the following code in the **Background Color** expression attribute:

```
=pick(match(round(
      sum([Time Spent (seconds)]*Productivity)
       /sum([Time Spent (seconds)])),-2,-1,0,1,2)
  ,RGB(215,25,28)
  ,RGB(253,174,97)
  ,RGB(255,255,191)
  ,RGB(171,217,233)
  ,RGB(44,123,182)
)
```

3. In the **Axes** tab, enable the **Continuous** option in the **Dimension Axis** section.

4. In the **Dimensions** tab, click **Trellis...** and enable the **Enable Trellis Chart** option with **Number of Columns** set to 1.

In this chart, the colors belong to a typical heat map that uses a diverging color sequence. Red indicates unproductive activity and blue indicates productive activity. The white space in between indicates that no activity was detected.

Summary

This chapter first analyzed the productivity of our personnel. Once we found an opportunity to improve, we explored what may have made one team more productive than the rest. We also proposed the idea that employees can use data that they collect about their own activities to analyze and improve their own personal productivity.

In the same way that we focus on one employee, it is also useful to create reports that focus on one customer, product, supplier, or sales person. Let's take a look at how we can use fact sheets to better execute our day-to-day tasks.

8
Fact Sheets

When sales representatives make customer visits, we want to give them the opportunity to quickly review information about each customer and make every visit as productive as possible. Our proposal to meet this need is to combine the most important measures from several perspectives into one customer fact sheet.

In the same way that we create a customer fact sheet, we can also create a product, an employee, a supplier, or a branch fact sheet. In each fact sheet, we focus on one master data element and include related facts from multiple perspectives. For example, in our customer fact sheet, we include information from our sales, marketing, working capital, and operations perspectives.

Our goal is to discover techniques to best summarize key performance indicators with numbers, spark lines, and bullet charts. We also aim to allow business users to create their own dynamic reports in order to answer any new questions that they may ask.

We will cover the following topics in this chapter as we build a customer fact sheet:

- Consolidated data models
- Agile data visualization design
- Bullet graphs and sparklines
- Customizing the QlikView User Experience

Customer fact sheet consolidated data model

Fact sheet data models combine facts from various perspectives. The customer fact sheet data model combines information from our sales, marketing, working capital, and operations perspectives. However, we don't necessarily include all the facts that are measured in each perspective. In this example, we store the following events in our data model's fact table:

- Sales invoices
- Sales credit memos
- Sales budget
- Sales opportunities
- Sales quotes
- Sales activities like customer meetings and service calls
- Month-end A/R invoice balances
- Customer selling cycle

There are two principal ways to combine all of these events into one data model in QlikView. The first option is to combine all these events into one fact table, while the second option is to create a link table between various fact tables. The link table contains existing key combinations of every fact table, and serves as a bridge between the separate fact tables and a common set of dimensions.

On one hand, the link table creates an additional layer of links in the QlikView data model that often slows the performance of our analysis and data visualization. On the other hand, combining all these separate fact tables into one all-inclusive fact table may drastically increase the application's use of RAM memory if the tables contain a large number of columns.

For this example, we choose to combine all these fact tables into one table. As this consolidated table is directly linked to the dimension tables, it is more likely to have better performance, unless, in the extreme case, it creates an extremely wide fact table with numerous columns. If performance becomes an issue, we test this fact table against the option to create a link table.

According to Qlik, the recent upgrade of QlikView's Associative Data Indexing Engine to the second-generation columnar-based QIX engine in QlikView 12 improves the performance of wide-data tables.

Whether we use one fact table or a link table, we may confront a situation where the data volume is too much to include each detailed transaction. In this case, we only add fields and the level of detail that we know that we are going to use. In our following example, we explore the ideal case of when we can add all customer-related data at the most detailed level.

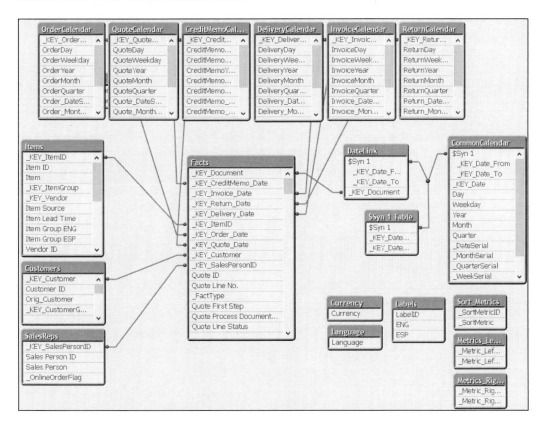

We've already used most of this data model's tables in previous perspectives. We add a few tables called island tables that have no relationship to this data model. These tables store data that helps us create certain elements of our user experience. For example, we are going to allow business users to choose the currency and language of the QlikView application. We also allow business users to choose from a list of metrics and dimensions in order to create their own reports on the fly:

Dimensions		
7Ws	**Fields**	**Comments**
Who	`Customer`	This is the central character in this data model. We first saw `Customer` in in *Chapter 2, Sales Perspective.*
Who	`Sales Person`	This plays a supporting role in our customer fact sheet, but we may later use this as the central focal point of a Sales Person fact sheet. We first saw this field in *Chapter 2, Sales Perspective.*

When	`Month, Year`
	
	`OrderMonth, OrderYear`
	
	`QuoteMonth, QuoteYear`
	
	`DeliveryMonth,`
	`DeliveryYear`
		These make up a common calendar to know when both transactional facts and snapshots took place. Although the calendar also tells us when an event occurred in an accumulating snapshot, we've also loaded the separate calendars of each step. We saw how to handle multiple calendars in *Chapter 6, Operations Perspective.*

What	`Item`	This is another dimension that plays a supporting role in our customer fact sheet, but which also deserves its own fact sheet. We first saw `Item` in *Chapter 2, Sales Perspective.*
What	`_FactType`	This field is used to help us sift through the large number of different facts that we've added to our customer fact sheet.
Metrics		
7Ws	**Fields**	**Comments**

How Much	`[Net Sales LC],`
	`[Net Sales USD],`
	`[Gross Profit LC],`
	`[Gross Profit USD],`
	`Quantity`
		These measure discrete events, such as invoices, credit memos, and sales budget, which use the same fields. We use set analysis with the `_FactType, _ActualFlag,` and `_BudgetFlag` fields to differentiate the amounts if necessary. We use different fields for LC (local currency) and USD (US Dollars) amounts to support multi-currency analysis.

How Much	`[Customer Activity Counter]`	This is an example of how we measure other discrete events that are related to customers, such as activities that we extract from our CRM system.

How Much	[A/R Invoice Balance LC], [A/R Invoice Balance USD]	These fields measure a recurring event that is the A/R balance monthly snapshot. We must take care to never add more than one month's snapshot.
How Much	[Quote Quantity], [Order Quantity], [Delivery Quantity], [Invoice Quantity]	This data model includes the same metrics that were present in the operation perspective's sales process accumulating snapshot.

We have to be careful when performing analysis over a data model that mixes transactional facts with periodic and accumulating snapshots. For example, the pitfalls that we can avoid here are: while we can sum transactional facts over various months or years, we cannot sum periodic snapshots over time. The sum of several months' balances does not serve any analytical purpose. We can prevent any incorrect summation using set analysis to select the latest month's balance even when the user selects more than one month.

In the case of the accumulating snapshot, the challenge is to determine which date we need to use for our analysis. In the customer fact sheet, we expect the user to select a certain period using fields from the common calendar. In an expression that requires that we analyze the average time delivery for a certain month, we use set analysis to clear the common calendar selection and transfer this selection to the corresponding delivery calendar fields.

In addition to the 7Ws table, we create the following table to clarify how each event is recorded in the fact table. The manner in which we've classified most of the facts should be obvious from the way we've used them in their corresponding perspectives. The one event that is not so clearly defined is a sales opportunity. In other data models, we may handle the sales opportunities like a traditional accumulating snapshot that is similar to the sales operations process. However, in *Chapter 4, Marketing Perspective*, we recorded each stage in our sales pipeline as a separate row instead of a separate column. This treatment is similar to that of a slowly changing dimension, but, instead of a dimension, this is a long-lived event.

Even though each stage is stored by row and not by columns, we treat it the same as any other accumulating snapshot. For example, we cannot sum the amounts between different stages; however, we may want to analyze how the amount changes as we progress through the sales pipeline process:

Facts Fact Type	Sales	Sales Budget	Activities	Sales Opportunities	Sales Operational Process	A/R Invoice Balances
Transactional	X	X	X			
Periodic Snapshot						X
Accumulating Snapshot				X	X	

Finally, when we mix several events together, as we did for our working capital perspective, we tend to have a fact table with mixed granularity. We use the following table to visualize at what level of granularity we can analyze each metric:

Dimensions Events	Month/Year	Date	Customer	Sale Person	Item
Sales	X	X	X	X	X
Sales Budget	X	X	X	X	X
Activities	X	X	X	X	
Sales Opportunities	X	X	X	X	
Sales Operational Process	X	X	X	X	X
A/R Invoice Balances	X		X		

In our example data model, the *A/R Invoice Balances* event is the least detailed and cannot be viewed by the *Date*, *Sales Person*, or *Item* filters. Also, we cannot analyze events, such as activities and sales opportunities by Item.

Now that we've reviewed our customer fact sheet data model, let's design how we want to visualize our customer fact sheet.

Customer Fact sheet Agile design

We aim to involve our business users from the beginning of the customer fact sheet design. As a non-technical, collaborative process, we use Agile project tools, such as Post-It notes and a whiteboard to begin the design process. We begin by writing user stories that we think would be important to include in the fact sheet on Post-It notes.

Creating user stories

The user epic we want to solve with our customer fact sheet is as follows:

As a sales representative, I need an easy way visualize all the information related to a customer and its relationship to the business so that I can plan more productive customer calls and meetings.

This user epic then gets broken down into the following user stories that we can eventually translate into a type of data visualization:

- As a sales representative, I need to compare this year's accumulated sales against last year's sales so that I can detect changes to our customers' buying habits

- As a sales representative, I need to compare this year's accumulated sales against the budget so that I can detect whether I'm going to reach the company's objective

- As a sales representative, I need to know of any outstanding payment that is owed to the company so that I can remind the customer and identify the cause

- As a sales representative, I need to know a customer's available credit and payment performance so that I can be prepared if they ask for more credit

- As a sales representative, I need to know a customer's open opportunities and quotations so that I focus on their closing

- As a sales representative, I need to benchmark this customer against others so that I can identify opportunities to negotiate better terms

- As a sales representative, I need to know how well we have delivered our products or services and of any recent service complaints so that I can be prepared to address such issues

- As a sales representative, I need to know how much a customer is expected to purchase so that I can foresee any abnormal behavior

- As a sales representative, I need to know what products I can recommend to a customer so that I can increase sales

- As a sales representative, I need to be able to create my own visualizations so that I can easily answer any ad-lib questions

User story flow

After we've written out the user stories, let's include a shorter version of each of them on a Post-it note and begin to arrange how we want to organize them in a customer fact sheet. Let's group related user stories together before determining what data visualization satisfies their requirements.

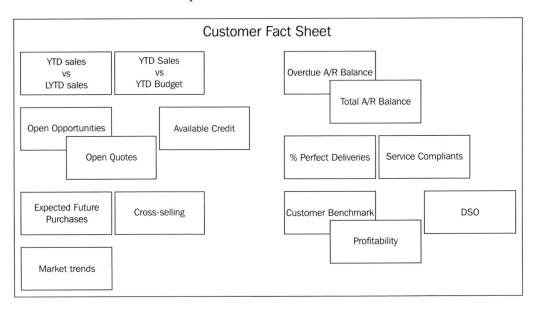

We create a scenario where a sales representative opens the customer fact sheet and reviews the first group of sales-related indicators. They first compare the current status of the YTD sales against last year's sales and the budget. The next information that they review is what is going to fuel the growth in these numbers in the short-term. This data can be found in open sales quotes and opportunities, in addition to the customer's available credit to close these new sales. The final sales indicators predict future sales and make suggestions to sell products that the customer has yet to purchase. We call this last concept *cross-selling* and recommend products based on what similar customers are purchasing.

After reviewing sales, the sales representative reviews post-sales activities that could affect future sales. The first indicator is the customer's A/R Balance and how much of it is overdue. They also analyze how well we as a company have delivered our products and whether there have been any service complaints.

Now that we have a general overview of our customer, we compare it with other customers using the customer stratification method that we've developed as a benchmarking method. We look closely at their profitability and DSO to give us a better idea how we should negotiate pricing and credit terms. Customer stratification also indicates with what priority we should follow up on all the previous indicators.

Converting user stories into visualizations

Once we've logically grouped our user stories and understood how they are interconnected, we convert each element of the story into a visualization. Just like the previous exercise, we design our customer fact sheet in a non-technical and highly collaborative way.

It is quite easy to create an application in QlikView, but it isn't as easy or as inclusive as using Post-it notes and a whiteboard. Although we can begin to design many applications directly in QlikView or develop visualizations in real time in front of the business users, we prefer a non-technical first approach for the following reasons:

- If business users actively participate in an application's design, then they will make it their own at an early stage and avoid asking for frivolous changes later.

- If we design a QlikView application in the presence of the business user, we risk getting hung up by a complex formula or data visualization. Nobody, especially a busy user, likes to wait ten minutes while someone is trying to figure out why their expression doesn't work properly.

- We break the habit of receiving asynchronous feedback about our designs, which can be less productive and create a discouraging 'us against them' attitude.

- We can use this collaborative design as part of our project documentation. A picture of the design may be worth a thousand or more words.

Today's collaborative technology still involves looking at our computer screens more than looking at our peers and, as such, we still do not have the same communication fidelity as a face-to-face activity. While video conference calls and virtual whiteboards may be the best solution for remote teams, it is otherwise better for everyone to gather around a real whiteboard with dry erase markers and Post-it notes.

The following figure shows the layout of our customer fact sheet. As many data-analysis applications use the same set of visualizations, we can save time and paper by breaking down the visual components into smaller, reusable parts. For example, we can reuse the sparklines, bullet charts, tables, monetary numbers, and percentages for other collaborative design exercises.

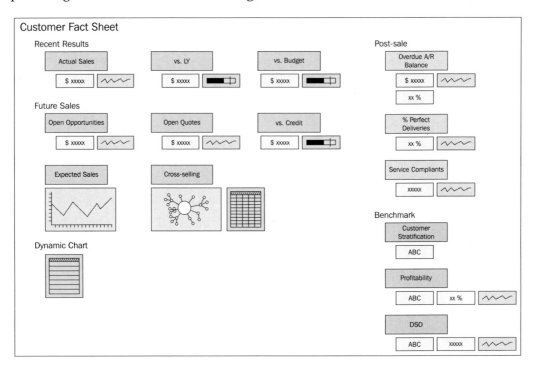

Let's organize our fact sheet in the same way that we broke down the user stories. We start at the upper, left-hand side of the sheet and review the customer's recent sales activity. We propose to use the actual monetary amounts, a *sparkline*, and two bullet charts to show actual sales and compare it with last year's sales and the budget. The next section reveals possible future sales from opportunities and quotes along with these amounts in comparison with the customer's credit limit. We also add a line chart to evaluate expected customer behavior and cross-selling recommendations that may improve sales. We end the main section of the fact sheet with a dynamic chart that the sales representatives can use to do their own visual ad-hoc analysis.

On the upper, right-hand side of the sheet, we include visualizations that fulfill the user story requirements that are related to post-sales activities. We propose using actual and relative numbers along with sparklines to represent the customer's overdue A/R Balance, % perfect deliveries, and the number of service complaints.

Finally, we end the fact sheet by benchmarking our customer using the customer stratification method that we developed in previous perspectives. Along with a general rating, we also include details about profitably and DSO.

This design does a great job of introducing each concept and fulfills the basic requirements of each user story. However, we often cannot fulfill an entire user story requirement with only one visualization.

Going beyond the first visualization

At first glance, the customer fact sheet should pique user curiosity and beg them to investigate each concept in greater detail. We can, of course, create a sheet that is dedicated to each section, but, many times, the user has a quick question that they want answered in one click without changing their context.

Alongside the general layout of the customer fact sheet, we include a second level of more detailed visualizations that users can access with one click. The following figure illustrates how we extend the original design to show how we want to display and visualize the details of several metrics.

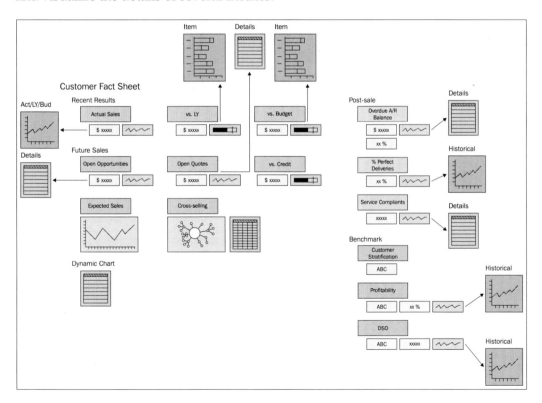

Together with the user, we choose the appropriate visualization for each concept. We also plan to take advantage of *Fast Change* and *Cyclical Dimensions* to make them more dynamic. If a user has more questions that can't be answered will these two levels of visualization, then we can give them the opportunity to navigate to a sheet.

Customer Fact sheet advanced components

Now that we've discussed the business story behind the customer fact sheet, let's review the different visualizations that compose it. We aim to create this perspective in the most precise way possible, so each one of the Post-it notes in our design will be separate objects. The labels and the numbers will be text objects that we align using the design grid tool that we introduced in *Chapter 2, Sales Perspective*.

In the next sections, we will review the following, more advanced components:

- Bullet graphs
- Sparklines

Bullet graph

The bullet chart was invented by Stephen Few to replace the bloated gauge chart in an information dashboard. Its compact design allows us to insert more information into a single view. The following bullet graph definition is from Mr. Few's website (https://www.perceptualedge.com/articles/misc/Bullet_Graph_Design_Spec.pdf) and you can read more about their use in his book *Information Dashboard Design*:

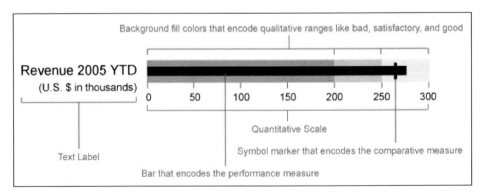

We can find an excellent, easy-to-use bullet graph made by Stefan Walther in Qlik Branch (`http://branch.qlik.com/#/project/56728f52d1e497241ae6980a`). There are also a few means to create a bullet graph using native QlikView objects. Let's explore one way that uses a single object. Before beginning the exercise, let's import this chapter's exercise files into the QDF as we did in *Chapter 2, Sales Perspective*. The following bullet chart compares actual sales YTD against the budget YTD:

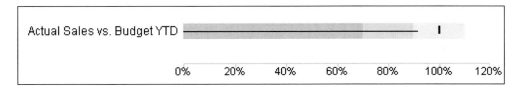

Exercise 8.1

In `1.Application\CustomerFactSheet_Sandbox.qvw`, let's create the following combo chart:

Dimensions	
Label	**Value**
<Empty>	='Actual Sales vs. Budget YTD'
Expressions	
Label	**Value**
0-70%	.7 * 1
70-90%	.2 * 1
90-110%	.2 * 1

1. In the **Expressions** tab, define each expression as a **Bar** in the **Display Options** section. Select the first expression and enable the **Has Error Bars** option in the **Display Options** section.

2. Define the following attribute expressions for **0-70%**:

Attribute Expressions	
Label	**Value**
Error Above	(-.7 * 1) + 1
Error Below	(.7 * 1) - 1

The **Error Below** formula can be confusing because the result is subtracted from the top of the bar in order to calculate the beginning of the error line. For example, if **Error Below** were .1, then the error line would start .1 below the top of the bar and, if it were -.1, then the line would start .1 above the top of the bar. Therefore, we first add the bar expression (.7) and then subtract 1 so that the result (-.3) will cause the error line to begin .3 above the bar. The **Error Above** calculation results in .3 so the error line also ends .3 above the bar. When the **Error Below** and **Error Above** are the same, then a line is drawn across the width of the bar.

3. In the **Style** tab, enable the **Stacked** option in the **Subtype** section and select the horizontal bars in the **Orientation** section.

4. In the **Presentation** tab, change the **Width** and **Thickness** to **Medium** in the **Error Bars** section.

The next series of steps involves a trick to create a **Stock** expression. Stephen Redmond explained how to add a *Stock* expression in his book, *QlikView for Developers Cookbook*. Before we begin, click **OK** to close the **Chart Properties** window and open it again.

1. In the **Expressions** tab, add a new expression and enter 0 into the **Edit Expression** window. Disable the **Line** option and enable the **Stock** option in the **Display Options** section.

2. Click **OK** to close the **Chart Properties** window and open it again.

3. Define the following attribute expressions for a new stock expression:

Attribute Expressions	
Label	**Value**

Stock High	`sum({$<$(vSetYTDModifier),_ActualFlag={1}>}`
	`        [Net Sales USD])`
	`/`
	`sum({$<$(vSetYTDModifier),_BudgetFlag={1}>}`
	`        [Net Sales USD])`

Stock Low	0

The only fault in this native, one-object bullet graph is the inability to change the width of the line that encodes the performance measurements. We increase the chart's readability by organizing the chart's **Color** tab so that the qualitative ranges are very light and the stock line is black.

The advantage of a one-object bullet graph is that we can easily modify it into a series of bullet graphs that are based on absolute values. The following chart allows us to compare how our sales are performing against the budget in both relative and absolute terms by item. We can easily create this by using the result of the previous exercise.

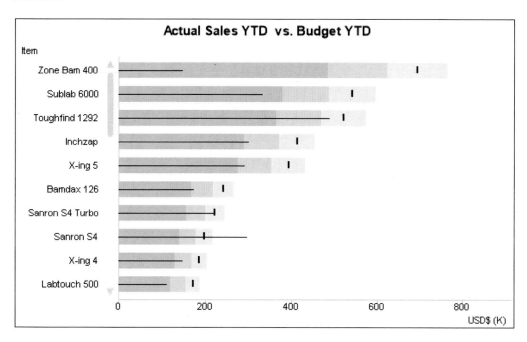

Exercise 8.2

The following exercise tells you how to recreate the chart using the result of the previous exercise:

1. Clone the chart from the previous exercise and replace the calculated dimension with Item.

2. Replace 1 in every expression, including the **Error Below** and **Error Above** attribute expressions, with the following code:

```
sum({$<$(vSetYTDModifier),_BudgetFlag={1}>}
    [Net Sales USD])
```

3. Change the Stock High attribute expression to the following expression:

```
sum({$<$(vSetYTDModifier),_ActualFlag={1}>}
        [Net Sales USD])
```

We now have an excellent alternative to using an extension or overlaying two charts when we create a bullet graph in QlikView. We place the single bullet graphs in the customer fact sheet and open the more detailed ones when the user clicks on that performance indicator. Next, let's review how to create sparklines for our fact sheet.

Sparklines

Sparklines are small, high-resolution graphs that allow users to understand the general trend of a performance indicator. A sparkline can be a line, a bar, or a win/loss chart, and they are drawn without any axes. We can easily create sparklines in a QlikView table using the **Mini Chart Representation** in the **Display Options** section. However, we may occasionally want to create a sparkline from a more customizable QlikView chart object.

In the following sparkline, we can review the percentage of deliveries that were OTIF over the last twelve months. Along with observing the performance indicator's trend, we can also appreciate how often the percentage of perfect deliveries fell below two different ranges. The top, dark-colored range is our preferred target, while the next light-colored range is our minimally acceptable range. Any point below these ranges is unacceptable.

Exercise 8.3

Let's create the following combo chart:

Dimensions	
Label	Value
Delivery Year-Month	DeliveryYear-Month
Expressions	
Label	Value

OTIF	`sum({$<$(vSetRolling12Modifier)`
	`,_FactType={'Sales Process'}`
	`,[Delivery First Step]={'No'}>}`
	`if([Delivery Document Date]<=[Order Due Date]`
	`and [Order Quantity]`
	`=rangesum([Delivery Quantity]`
	`,-[Return Quantity])`
	`,1)`
	`)`
	`/`
	`count({$<$(vSetRolling12Modifier)`
	`,_FactType={'Sales Process'}`
	`,[Delivery First Step]={'No'}>}`
	`DISTINCT [Delivery Line No.])`
	`-1`

90-100%	`-.1`
80-90%	`-.1`

1. In the **Expressions** tab, define **OTIF** as line and the other two expressions as a **Bar** in the **Display Options** section.

2. Insert `'<w.5>'` into the **Line Style** attribute expression for **OTIF**.

3. In the **Style** tab, enable the **Stacked** option in the **Subtype**.

4. In the **Presentation** tab, set the **Bar Distance** and **Cluster Distance** to 0 in the **Bar Settings** section.

5. In the **Presentation** tab, disable the **Suppress Zero-Values** option.

6. In the **Axes** tab, select the expression **OTIF** and disable the option, **Forced 0**.

7. Finally adjust the colors and hide all elements other than the lines and the background created by the bars.

We may also add context to the primary sparkline by adding a second sparkline within the same two-dimensional space. We must be careful to give users more data without distracting their attention from the main information. We do this by making the second line lighter and transparent so that it will never overlap the first. In the following example, we compare this year's actual sales with last year's sales in the same sparkline:

Customizing the QlikView User Experience

Much of the QlikView **User Experience (UX)** is customizable. For example, we can develop ways to guide users through a well-defined series of reports or give them the power to create their own reports. We can also allow them to change the interface's language or the currency. In this section, we will create the following UX components:

- Quick access to supplementary information
- Dynamic data visualization
- Regional settings

Quick access to supplementary information

When users notice something interesting in concise visualizations such as numbers, sparklines, and bullet graphs, they often want to take a glance at the details that compose it. For example, in our customer fact sheet, we want to quickly analyze the detail behind the high-level comparison between actual and budget sales. During the design stage we chose to open a detailed comparison by item when the user clicks on **vs. Budget**, as shown in the following figure:

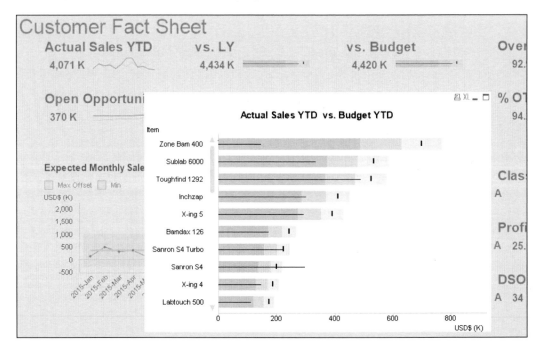

Exercise 8.4

Let's create the following variable:

Variable	
Label	**Value**
vCustomerFactSheetPopUp	None

1. Adjust the position of the detailed bullet graph that we created in exercise 8.2.

2. In the **Layout** tab of the chart's properties, enable **Custom** in the **Layer** section and set it to 3.

3. Also in the **Layout** tab, enable the **Conditional** option in the **Show** section and enter the following code in the expression field:

    `=vCustomerFactSheetPopUp='BudgetDetail'`

4. Create an empty text object that spans the whole fact sheet.

5. In the **General** tab of the text object change the background color to a transparent gray.

6. In the **Layout** tab, enable **Custom** in the **Layer** section and set it to 2.

7. Also in the **Layout** tab, enable the **Conditional** option in the **Show** section and enter the following code in the expression field:

    `=vCustomerFactSheetPopUp<>'None'`

8. In the **Actions** tab, create a **Set Variable** action with the following values:

Action	
Label	**Value**
Variable	vCustomerFactSheetPopUp
Value	None

9. Create a text object that contains the following text:

    `Vs. Budget`

10. In the **Actions** tab, create a **Set Variable** action with the following values:

Action	
Label	**Value**
Variable	vCustomerFactSheetPopUp
Value	BudgetDetail

If everything works correctly, then the detailed bullet graph will appear in front of a transparent, gray background. When we want to close the detail and go back to the general view of our customer fact sheet, we click on the grayed-out background. We could also create a **Close** button, but it is now common UX practice to close a pop-up window by clicking anywhere else on the screen.

As only one pop-up window will appear at any one time, we use one variable to determine which popup is displayed. One variable is obviously easier to maintain than having one for each corresponding popup. However, if we want to give the users the ability to open as many detailed charts as they like, then we would have to create a control variable for each popup.

Dynamic data visualization

It is relatively easy to create a dynamic straight table or pivot table in QlikView and we can find examples in various demos to imitate. However, it can be a challenge to create a simple way for users to make their own attractive graphic charts in a server environment. Qlik Sense is the ultimate tool for users who want to create their own charts and stories, but we can also give users the power to build insightful, ad-hoc data visualization in QlikView. The following chart was created using a few variables that users can readily modify in a server environment:

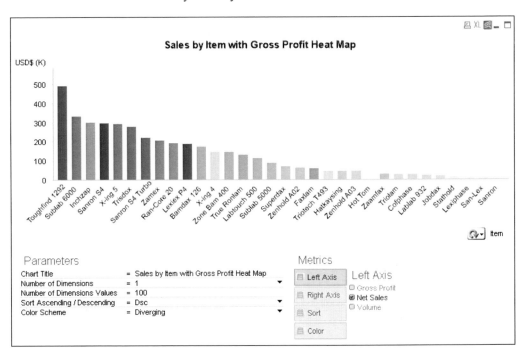

Exercise 8.5

Let's create the following variables:

Variables	
Label	**Value**
vNumDimensions	1
vChartTitle	Please add the chart's title here.
vSortMetric	=pick(match('|' & GetFieldSelections (_SortMetric,'|') & '|' , '|Net Sales|' , '|Gross Profit|' , '|Volume|') ,'sum({$<_ActualFlag={1}>} [Net Sales USD])' ,'sum({$<_ActualFlag={1}>} [Gross Profit USD])' ,'sum({$<_ActualFlag={1}>} [Quantity])')
vColorMetric	=pick(match('|' & GetFieldSelections (_ColorMetric,'|') & '|' , '|Net Sales|' , '|Gross Profit|' , '|Volume|') ,'sum({$<_ActualFlag={1}>} [Net Sales USD])' ,'sum({$<_ActualFlag={1}>} [Gross Profit USD])' ,'sum({$<_ActualFlag={1}>} [Quantity])')
vAscDsc	Dsc
vAscDscNum	=if(vAscDsc='Asc',1,-1)
vColorScheme	Diverging
vNumDimensionValues	10

1. Add vChartTitle, vNumDimensions, vNumDimensionValues, vAscDsc, and vColorScheme to an Input Box.

2. In the **Constraints** tab, set the **Input Constraints** for vNumDimensions, vAscDsc, and vColorScheme to **Predefined Values Only** and disable the **Enable Edit Expression Dialog** option. For the same variables, select the **Value List** as **Predefined Values in Drop-down** and enable **Listed Values** in the **Predefined Values section**. The list values should be the following for each variable:

Variables	
Label	**Listed Values**
vNumDimensions	`0;1;2;3`
vAscDsc	`Asc;Dsc`
vColorScheme	`Diverging;Sequential`

3. Create four list boxes for the _Metric_LeftAxis, _Metric_RightAxis, _ColorMetric, and _SortMetric fields and insert them in a container.

4. Create a bar chart with the following dimensions and metrics:

Dimensions	
Label	**Value**

Dimension 1	A cyclical dimension with the following fields:
	
	`Billing State`
	`Customer`
	`Item`
	`Sales Person`
	`Year`
	`Month`

Dimension 2	A cyclical dimension with the same fields as Dimension 1
Dimension 3	A cyclical dimension with the same fields as Dimension 2
Expressions	
Label	**Value**
Net Sales	`sum({$<_ActualFlag={1}>} [Net Sales USD])`
Gross Profit	`sum({$<_ActualFlag={1}>} [Gross Profit USD])`
Volume	`sum({$<_ActualFlag={1}>} Quantity)`

5. In the **General** tab, enable all the **Fast Type Change** options except **Gauge Chart**.

6. In the **Dimensions** tab, tick the **Enable Conditional** option for all dimensions and place the following values for each of them:

Dimensions	
Label	**Value**
Dimension 1	vNumDimensions>=1
Dimension 2	vNumDimensions>=2
Dimension 3	vNumDimensions=3

7. In the **Expressions** tab, tick the **Conditional** option for all expressions and place the following values for each of them:

Expressions	
Label	**Value**
Net Sales	SubStringCount('|' & GetFieldSelections(_Metric_LeftAxis,'|') & '|' , '|Net Sales|')
Gross Profit	SubStringCount('|' & GetFieldSelections(_Metric_LeftAxis,'|') & '|' , '|Gross Profit|')
Volume	SubStringCount('|' & GetFieldSelections(_Metric_LeftAxis,'|') & '|' , '|Volume|')

8. In the **Background Color** attribute expression run the **Color Mix Wizard** twice using the expression, $(vColorMetric). In the first run-through select a sequential color scheme from light blue (247, 251, 255) to dark blue (8, 48, 107). In the second run-through select a diverging color scheme from dark red (178, 24, 43) to dark blue (33, 102, 172) passing through a light gray (247, 247, 247) at 0. Place the resulting color mix functions into the following if-statement:

```
if(vColorScheme = 'Diverging'
,ColorMix2 (…)
,ColorMix1 (…)
)
```

Use the same code for the background color of every expression.

9. Copy and paste a duplicate of each expression so that there is a total of six expressions. In the duplicate expression replace _Metric_LeftAxis in the **Conditional** expression with _Metric_RightAxis.

10. In the **Sort** tab, tick the **Override Group Sort Order** option and then tick the **Expression** option and insert the following code in the expression field:

```
=$(vSortMetric)*vAscDscNum
```

Repeat the same steps for every dimension.

11. In the **Presentation** tab, tick the **Enable X-Axis Scrollbar** option and insert the following code in the expression field:

```
=vNumDimensionValues
```

12. In the **Axes** tab, select the duplicate copy of each expression and enable **Right (Top)** in the **Position** section:

13. In the **Numbers** tab, adjust each expression's number format and symbols, appropriately:

The user now has a way to create custom visualizations using only a few variables. We can continue to create more variables to control the property options defined by an expression field or preconfigure certain properties that can only be modified in the properties windows. However, the result of the previous exercise allows users to create the best possible charts using the fewest variables.

The cyclical dimensions are also more user friendly as they are located next to their axis or legend. We create three of them because graphs may use a maximum of three dimensions. Each should be sorted each dimension alphabetically or numerically by default, but we can easily select an expression by which to sort them in either ascending or descending order. We've also added a variable to limit the number of dimension values as there are often more than those that can fit in a graph at one time.

The metrics are divided by left and right axis as it is common practice to visualize two metrics that do not share the same scale. We also include the ability to add a heat map to the custom visualization to make them more insightful. The heat map can either be sequential, if the metric can only be positive, or it can be diverging if the metric can also be negative.

Although it seems like we use few variables in comparison to the hundreds that exist in the chart properties windows, the users can create a wide variety of different visualizations. Users who want the ability to create even more personalized charts should start working with Qlik Sense, which we will review in *Chapter 11, Mastering Qlik Sense Data Visualization*.

Regional settings

Currency, language, date formats, commas, and decimals can change depending on the region and users often become more engaged in the data discovery process when the effort has been made to respect their regional preferences. Some options, such as currency, are best left to the user to select, while others, such as date formats, should be automatic.

Currency

Contrary to what we may think, the currency used to analyze data does not depend on a user's country. Although some analysis may be done using the local currency, it is common to analyze data using one of the reserve currencies, such as the US dollar or the Euro. For this reason, we often add a currency filter to the user interface.

The values of the currency field correspond to the names given to the monetary amount fields in the data model, such as [Net Sales LC] and [Net Sales USD]. In this way, we can easily make our application multicurrency using the following code:

```
sum({$<_ActualFlag={1}>} [Net Sales $(=Currency)])
```

Language

In a similar way to how we make our application multicurrency, we also make it multilingual. We create a table with one field called Language that contains values that correspond to the field names in another table that contain the texts belonging to each language:

LabelID	ENG	ESP
Sales	Sales	Ventas

Then, in every multilingual label, we use the following code to calculate a label. We use a descriptive ID, like `Sales`, for our labels so that we can identify expressions and objects without having to manually look up numerical IDs in a table:

```
=only({$<LabelID={'Sales'}>} $(=Language))
```

Along with the labels, we also choose which descriptive field to use for list boxes and dimensions. For example, we have two fields in our `Customer` table that describes customer groups. `[Customer Group ENG]` contains English descriptions and `[Customer Group ESP]` contains Spanish descriptions. We use the following code as an expression in our list box or as a calculated dimension:

```
=[Customer Group $(=Language)]
```

Although we give the user the option to select any language, the application should open in the user's preferred language. One way to do this is to distribute a copy of the QlikView file with

the language prefiltered by the QlikView Publisher. Another way is to use section access to reduce a field that we use to select the preferred language upon opening the QlikView document.

Date and number formats

Date and number formats depend on the country and it should be automatically selected when opening the QlikView document. We use a set of variables that return the preferred formats based on a user's region along with the formatting functions, `num()` and `date()` in order to dynamically format the data.

We can define a user's region using Section Access. The following code is an example of how the dynamically formatted expressions will look:

```
date([Date],$(vRegional_DateFormat))
num(sum(Quantity),$(vRegional_NumberFormat_FixedDecimal)
    ,$(vRegional_Decimal),$(vRegional_Thousand))
```

Customer Fact sheet n QlikView

In the following figure, we bring together text objects, bullet graphs, sparklines, and the dynamic chart to create the customer fact sheet that we designed using Post-it notes and a whiteboard:

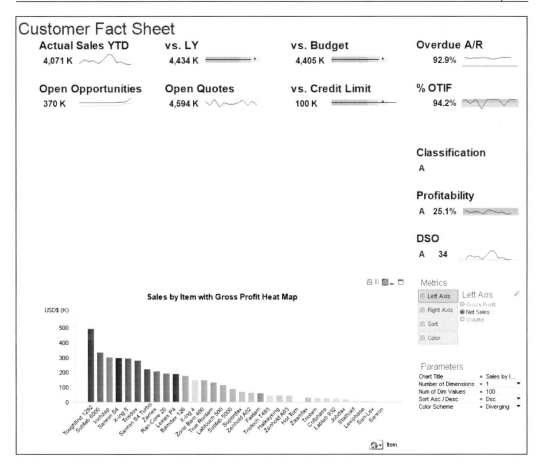

Create the pending expected sales chart in the next chapter and review the cross-selling chart extensions in *Chapter 11, Mastering Qlik Sense Data Visualization.*

Summary

Like the customer fact sheet, we can also create item, project, sales representative, or supplier fact sheets. In the next chapter, we will use many of the same visualizations to build a dashboard based on the balanced scorecard methodology. We will also use a more formal design process to help us organize our business strategy and reveal the results of our initiatives.

9
Balanced Scorecard

Over the course of this book, we learned how to analyze business data through various perspectives. We started with the sales perspective and then went on to develop visualizations for financial, marketing, working capital, operations, and human resources perspectives. Then we brought several perspectives together in a fact sheet that analyzed a customer through a sales representative's point of view.

Our next step is to unite the most pertinent perspectives and analyze the business as a whole from a business owner's point of view. This result is often referred to as the company's information dashboard. Stephen Few was the first person to investigate the real purpose of the information dashboard in his book, *Information Dashboard Design,* and he defines dashboards as follows:

> *A dashboard is a visual display of the most important information needed to achieve one or more objectives, consolidated and arranged on a single screen so the information can be monitored at a glance.*

We often design an information dashboard using the same freestyle process that we applied to create our customer fact sheet. However, we can also use a more disciplined approach such as a **Balanced Scorecard (BSC)** to unite the business's various perspectives into one consolidated viewpoint. This popular method was first developed by Robert S. Kaplan and David P. Norton to both drive and manage company strategy.

In this chapter, we will create an information dashboard that is based on the Balanced Scorecard method. We will cover the following topics in this chapter:

- The Balanced Scorecard method
- The Balanced Scorecard data model
- The Balanced Scorecard information dashboard design
- Additional QlikView UX customization
- Measuring process change with an XmR chart

The Balanced Scorecard method

The BSC method focuses on the following four perspectives:

- Financial
- Customer
- Internal business process
- Learning and growth

In each perspective, an organization should define a series of objectives, measurements, targets, and initiatives that help align its activities with its vision and strategy.

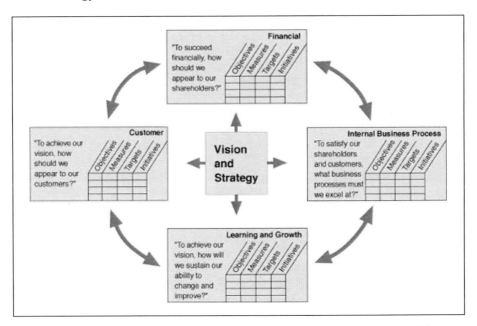

Source: Robert S. Kaplan and David P. Norton, "Using the Balanced Scorecard as a Strategic Management System," Harvard Business Review (January-February 1996):76

The financial perspective is the traditional way to measure an organization, but these measurements tend to tell us more about past events rather than future ones. In other words, the financial perspective uses lagging rather than leading performance indicators. For example, in the financial perspective, sales revenue is a lagging performance indicator that measures the results of a business's past efforts to market, sell, and deliver its products and services. The BSC method helps us to drive and foresee future sales revenue by using leading performance indicators, or we need to use performance drivers, that measure new customer acquisition, customer satisfaction, new product development, and employee retention.

An organization's performance indicators depend on its strategy to accomplish what it envisions as a successful business. The BSC method teaches us how to create a **Strategy Map** through the financial, customer, internal business process, and learning and growth perspectives. This Strategy Map communicates a series of objectives and the cause-and-effect relationships between them.

In our example, our vision of success is to increase the size of our business; therefore, our principal financial objective is to increase revenue. Our strategy to accomplish this is to increase customer retention and customer product mix. We've created the following Strategy Map that breaks down the strategy into objectives that are based on the four BSC perspectives:

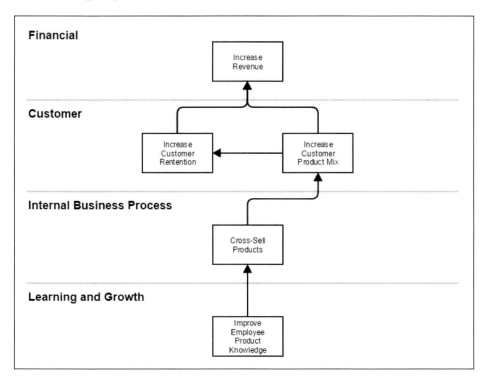

In the following sections, we will review what performance indicators we will use to measure the success of our objectives in each perspective.

The financial perspective

Our financial objective is to increase revenue, so our first financial performance indicator will be revenue growth. We define growth based on **Year-over-Year (YOY)** monthly and **Year-to-Date (YTD)** growth. We look at growth in terms of monetary amounts and percentages, as both ways can be insightful. Also, given that our strategy involves customer product mix and customer retention, we decide to detail revenue growth by product line and to measure the percentage of revenue that comes from existing customers.

Strategic objective	Strategic measurement
Increase Revenue	• YOY revenue growth • YOY revenue growth of existing customer by product line • Percentage revenue from existing customers

The next step is to review how to measure the customer objectives that are part of our strategy to increase revenue.

The customer perspective

Our customer objectives are to increase customer retention and customer product mix. We measure our customer retention using the customer churn rate or the percentage of customers lost. We are not a business that sells products through a subscription, so we consider a customer as lost if they haven't purchased anything in the last twelve months.

We measure customer product mix by evaluating the average number of product lines that a customer purchases during a given period of time. The exact time period that we use often depends on the type of industry our customers belong to and their buying rhythm. In order to simplify this example, we will use the same time period as we do for the customer churn rate; that is, twelve months. In more complex scenarios, we can use analysis techniques, such as a t-test, to evaluate each customer's purchasing rhythm like we did in *Chapter 2, Sales Perspective*.

We use YOY comparisons on a monthly and YTD basis for both indicators, which is consistent with the financial indicators:

Strategic objective	Strategic measurement
Increase customer retention	YOY change in customer churn rate.
Increase customer product mix	YOY change in average product lines purchased by the customer.

The next step is to review how to measure the internal business process objectives that we will use to drive an increase in customer retention and customer product mix.

The internal business process perspective

In a similar way to how supermarkets grew by providing one place to purchase many products, our plan is to promote cross-selling in order to increase customer product mix and customer retention. Cross-selling is simply the act of selling an additional product or service to a customer. However, it can be a powerful way to increase customer satisfaction and retention.

In the customer perspective, we measure the result of our efforts to increase cross-selling using the indicator *average product lines per customer*. However, in this perspective, we aim to use an indicator that focuses on the sales representatives' efforts to promote cross-selling independent of customer actions.

When we first explained lagging indicators, we referred to financial indicators as lagging and every other indicator as leading. In reality, the terms leading and lagging are relative. Therefore, a measurement such as average product lines per customer can be a leading indicator for future revenue growth, but it can also be a lagging indicator of increased cross-selling. We use another measurement such as the number of cross-selling quotations as the leading indicator of average product lines per customer and a confirmation of sales representatives' efforts to promote cross-selling.

Strategic objective	Strategic measurement
Increase cross-selling	YOY changes in the number of sales quotations with products lines not purchased by customers.

The next step is to review the learning and growth objectives that will enable sales representatives' to be able to promote cross-selling.

The learning and growth perspective

Human talent is often what determines the overall success of our strategies. The investment in employees' knowledge and growth is what drives all the objectives in every other perspective. In our example, we are going to give sales representatives product knowledge training and tools that suggest cross-selling opportunities that they may, otherwise, not recognize.

We measure an increase in product knowledge by evaluating the number of employees that attend each training session this year as compared to the last year. We also evaluate the effectiveness of the training and their behavior outside the classroom by analyzing their usage of the cross-selling analysis tool:

Strategic objective	Strategic measurement
Increase product knowledge	YOY change in number of employees who attended product knowledge training sessions.
	Average number of days that the sales representatives use the cross-selling analysis tool.

Now that we've defined the strategic measurements that we are going to use to evaluate the strategic objectives in our BSC, we will review the necessary data model and its supporting information dashboard.

The Balanced Scorecard consolidated data model

Similarly to the fact sheet data model, the BSC data model combines facts from various perspectives. In accordance with the strategic measures that we defined in the previous section, the BSC data model combines information from our sales, marketing, and human resources perspectives. To be specific, we store the following events in our data model's fact table:

- Sales invoices
- Sales credit memos
- Sales quotes
- Employee training
- Employee QlikView usage

The last event is related to the personal behavior analysis that we performed in the human resources perspective in *Chapter 7, Human Resources*. However, instead of using a data log from `RescueTime`, we will use QlikView's own session and audit logs to evaluate how employees' use QlikView's applications.

It is also common to add events from the financial, working capital, and operations perspectives. In this example, as we are only measuring revenue in the financial perspective of the BSC, we use the more detailed sales perspective to calculate revenue growth. As this model has the potential to become quite large, we leave the other perspectives out until a new strategic measurement requires their inclusion.

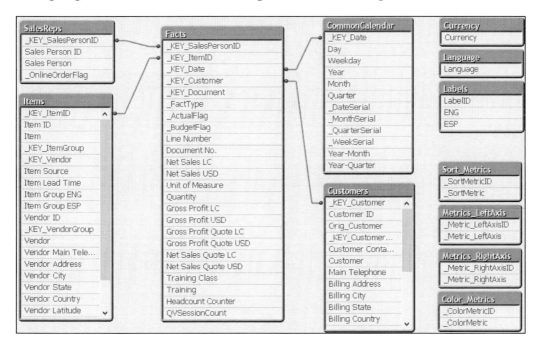

Unlike the customer fact table data model, this one only contains discrete events; therefore, it is far simpler. We only use one calendar table that describes the exact date when each event occurs. The rest of the dimension tables include descriptive information about sales representatives, items, and customers.

As company information dashboards may be used to communicate strategy to the whole company and also to external stakeholders, we include the same regional settings island tables. We also include the option to create dynamic visualizations as we did in the customer fact table. Let's sum up our data model using the 7Ws table:

Dimensions		
7Ws	**Fields**	**Comments**
Who	`Customer`	We first saw `Customer` *Chapter 2, Sales Perspective.*
Who	`Sales Person`	We first saw `Sales Person` in *Chapter 2, Sales Perspective.*
When	`Month, Year`	We use only one common calendar, as all events are discrete. In the case that we have to manage accumulating snapshots and periodic snapshots in one data model, we use the customer fact table data model as an example.
What	`Item`	We first saw `Item` in *Chapter 2, Sales Perspective.*
What	`_FactType`	Like the customer fact sheet data model, we use this field to help us distinguish between the different events in a single fact table.
Metrics		
7Ws	**Fields**	**Comments**
How Much	`[Net Sales LC]`, `[Net Sales USD]`, `[Net Sales Quotes LC]`, `[Net Sales Quotes USD]`,	Although the sales quotation and sales invoice share many of the same concepts, we've elected to create a separate set of fields for each document. While this risks creating an extremely wide table, it makes for simpler metric expressions that don't necessarily require set analysis.
How Much	`[Headcount Counter]`	We count the number of employees that have been in training with this field.
How Much	`[QV Session Counter]`	We count the number of times an employee has used QlikView with this field.

When we create a data model containing multiple perspectives, we take care to only add data that is necessary to calculate the required measurements. This is ultimately the best way to optimize the QlikView data model. Column-wise, we remove fields that are not used as a dimension, expression, or filter. Row-wise, we filter data that is not pertinent to the analysis. For example, we eliminate many of the fields that we created for our sales perspective, such as [Gross Sales USD] and [Cost USD]. We also reduce the number of rows in the fact table by only including QlikView sessions that pertain to cross-selling analysis.

In the following table, we confirm that all the facts are transactional and that they describe events that take place at a discrete moment in time:

Facts Fact type	Sales invoices	Sales credit memos	Sales quotations	Employee training	Employee QlikView usage
Transactional	X	X	X	X	X

We also describe how each event is related to each dimension table. In our example data model, the facts that represent employee training and QlikView usage cannot be analyzed by customer or item:

Dimensions Events	Month/Year	Date	Customer	Sales Rep	Item
Sales Invoices	X	X	X	X	X
Sales Credit Memos	X	X	X	X	X
Sales Quotations	X	X	X	X	X
Employee Training	X	X		X	
Employee QlikView Usage	X	X		X	

Now that we've reviewed our BSC data model, let's continue to design how we want to visualize a company's information dashboard based on the BSC method.

The Balanced Scorecard information dashboard design

Information dashboards that display BSC-related measures are often designed to replicate the strategy map or the cause-and-effect relationships between each measure. Just as we took a more disciplined approach to combine various perspectives, we will also reflect on a set of formal design rules called the Gestalt principles of perceptual organization to design the information dashboard.

The Gestalt principles of perceptual organization

Molded by human evolution, we are biased in the way that we visually perceive our environment. For example, how do we recognize the form of a tree, based on individual leaves and branches? We recognize the shape of a tree by grouping leaves that are close together, are of similar color and shape, or even by how the leaves are connected to the branches.

In the early twentieth century, a group of researchers called *Gestalt* (the German word for *form* or *shape*) psychologists began to study how we were able to unite individual perceptual inputs into complete objects. The following figure is a nonexhaustive list of visual occurrences that we use to perceive groups of individual elements called the Gestalt principles of perceptual organization:

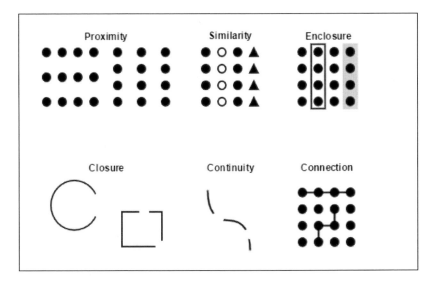

As in the natural world, we use these same principles to organize how we perceive artificial constructs. For example, even though the following sentence is readable, it is less efficient if we don't use proximity to group letters into words:

ThisisatestoftheGestaltprincipleofproximity.

In the same way that we group letters into words with one space, words into sentences with a period, and sentences into paragraphs with a new line, we can also spatially organize the objects of an information dashboard. As it is based on the BSC method, we want to group individual elements into measurements, perspectives, and cause-effect relationships. Along with proximity, we will review the other common principles that we can use to create these three groups.

Proximity

When we work with proximity in an information dashboard, we focus on how white space divides the visual elements on the screen. We often use white space to group information because this does not add any potentially distracting nondata ink. For example, in the following whiteboard design, we use proximity to group nineteen individual visual elements into three groups that represent the three strategic measurements (*YOY Revenue Growth*, *YOY Revenue Growth by Product Line*, and *% Revenue Existing Customers*) in our financial perspective:

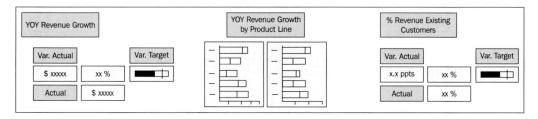

The decision to use proximity to group each measurement leaves us with a greater opportunity to use less obtrusive methods to organize perspectives and relationships. For example, if we were to use the Gestalt principles of closure and and draw a line between each measurement, then we may have to draw a thicker, darker, and more distracting line to separate each perspective. Instead, we are now able to assemble perspectives in subtler ways.

Enclosure

A more explicit way to group elements is to enclose them with a line or a background color. We often use enclosure when we cannot use proximity to group items. For example, when we want to display large amounts of data on a single screen and there is not sufficient white space to separate each visual element, we can use enclosure. In the following whiteboard design, we use a line to draw a box around each perspective:

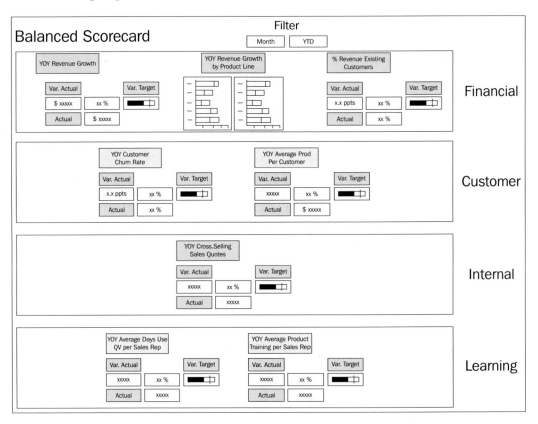

Enclosure is a stronger grouping method than proximity, and we should use it with care so that we do not to interrupt the flow of information in a dashboard. Let's take a look at how we can use the next Gestalt principle, closure, to make enclosure subtler and reduce its nondata ink.

Closure

We don't need a shape to be entirely discovered in order to perceive what form it takes. In the previous whiteboard design, if we draw a single line between each perspective, we still perceive the rectangular enclosures that group each one:

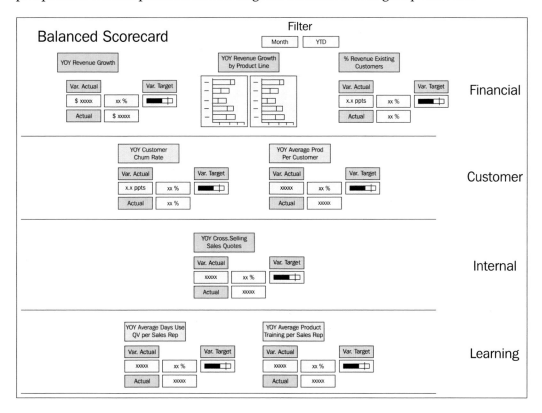

We have now created a subtler way to group different perspectives. An even subtler way would be to replace the lines with the names of each perspective in a very large font size. Sometimes, a simple outdented heading, such as "Balanced Scorecard" in the previous whiteboard design, is enough to perceive an enclosure. However, we elect to use a line so that we avoid overlapping headings with the lines that we will use in the following section to connect related measurements.

Connection

In the previous sections, we used proximity to group measurements, and we used enclosure and closure to group perspectives. In the following sections, we'll use connection, continuity, and similarity to assemble the cause-and-effect relationships. Connection groups elements together more powerfully than proximity but less than enclosure. In the following whiteboard design, we link cause-and-effect measurements in accordance with our strategy map:

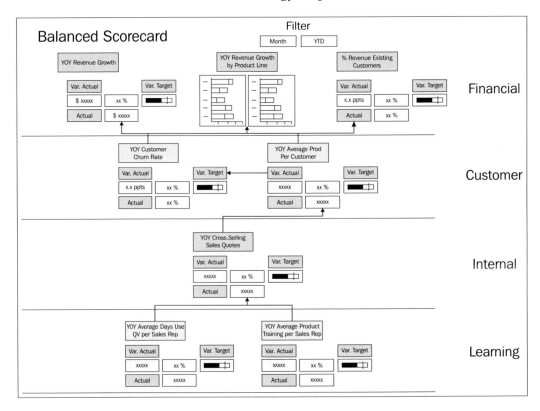

Even though we've now grouped the cause-and-effect measurements, we've also created possible confusion between these new lines and the ones that group each perspective. When we confront conflicting elements, we are often inclined to differentiate them by making one stronger and more explicit than the other. However, for example, if we were to make the lines dividing the perspectives thicker so as to differentiate them from the others, then we risk stealing attention away from what should be the most important element in the dashboard: the data. Let's see how we can use continuity to make sure that our grouping techniques complement rather than supplant the data.

Continuity

Similarly to closure, we don't have to see a complete line in order to perceive one. We can use the Gestalt principle of continuity to create a subtler, dashed line that connects the related measures in the following whiteboard design:

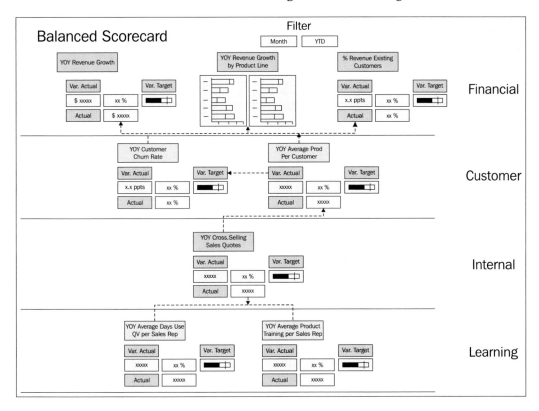

Continuity can also work in a more subtle way when we align objects in the dashboard. For example, the grouping of each perspective is reinforced by the fact that the measurements are vertically aligned. We may also notice that the measurements found in the customer and learning perspectives are also horizontally aligned even though they have no direct relationship. We've aligned them so that the dashboard is symmetric and aesthetically pleasing. In this case, the lines that we've added to enclose each perspective and separate the measurements help lower the risk that they will be interpreted as a meaningful group. We will now review the last Gestalt principle that will help us to further distinguish between the lines that we use to enclose the perspectives and the ones that connect related measurements.

Similarity

Finally, we interpret elements that are alike as part of the same group. Visual likeness can be determined by the elements' color, shape, and size. For example, in the whiteboard design, we've used the principle of similarity to group elements that are alike but dispersed throughout the dashboard. In the previous figure, we can decipher individual bullet charts as neon green and calculated numbers as pale yellow and efficiently identify them during an extremely dynamic agile design exercise.

In the actual dashboard, we use the similarity principle to reaffirm the distinction between the two sets of lines that we use to define two distinct groupings. In the final version of our design that we've migrated to QlikView in the following figure, we use black lines to divide the perspectives and light gray lines to group the cause-and-effect relationships.

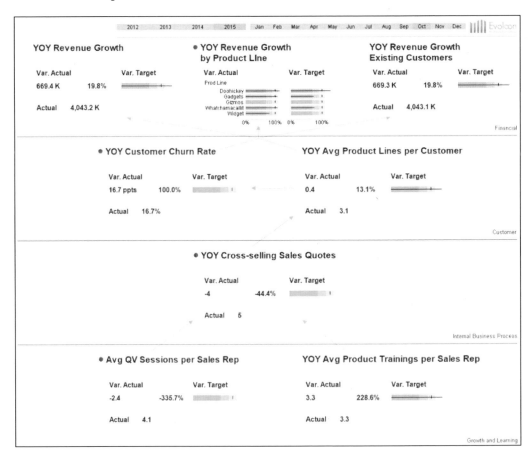

In the same way that we used the continuity principle, we use similarity to differentiate groups by making one subtler rather than making one more explicit. If we were to use a different hue to group the cause-and-effect relationships, then we risk stealing unnecessary attention away from the actual measurements again. In the previous figure, we can appreciate how well the eight BCS measurements stand out at first glance. Then, upon further exploration, we can see how they are first grouped by their perspective and then by their cause-and-effect relationship.

The Gestalt principles of perceptual organization are an important set of rules that help us make user-interface design less an art and more a science. However, they still leave us with plenty of leeway to create unique, aesthetic interfaces. In the next section, we will review how to incorporate a filter pane without changing our original information dashboard design.

Creating the filter pane bubble

The idea that an information dashboard should fit on a single screen is often a design challenge. In QlikView, it is common practice to place the filters to the left and at the top of the screen, where they may take up twenty percent or more of the available screen. Although QlikView list boxes are themselves informative objects that tell us what data is both related and unrelated to the current selection, they aren't always the most important objects on the screen.

This is especially the case with information dashboards, whose principal goal is to provide information that can be monitored at a glance and not necessarily dynamic analysis. However, it would also be a shame to use QlikView to create a fixed information dashboard, so let's allow the user to make data selections in an information dashboard in a way that doesn't take up so much space.

Exercise 9.1

Before beginning the exercise, let's import this chapter's exercise files into the QDF as we did in *Chapter 2*, *Sales Perspective*. To create a filter pane bubble, let's do the following steps in `1.Application\BalancedScorecard_Sandbox.qvw`:

1. First, let's add the following text object to the top, right-hand side corner of the screen. In this case, we've used explicit enclosure to make it stand out more than just simple text:

2. Next, let's place list boxes for the `[Sales Person]`, `[Customer Group ENG]`, and `[Item Group ENG]` fields in a single object container.

3. Then, let's place the container that we created in a previous step, a current selections object, and a search object in the grid container object. The container should look like the following figure after we align it with the **Other Selections** text object and assign it to the **Top** layer in the **Layout** tab:

4. Create a variable called `vToggleFilterPane` and define the grid container's **Conditional Show** expression as `=vToggleFilterPane`.

5. Create a **Set Variable** action in the **Other Selections** text object with `vToggleFilterPane` as the **Variable** and the following code as the **Value**:

```
=if(vToggleFilterPane = 1, 0, 1)
```

6. Finally, let's use the following code to define the background color of the **Other Selections** text object. We only change the color to green if we make a selection in a field that is neither **Year** nor **Month**, as their selected values are evident in their respective list boxes:

```
if(
  len(
    purgechar(
      replace(
        replace(
          GetCurrentSelections('|')
          , 'Year: '&GetFieldSelections(Year),''
        )
        , 'Month: '&GetFieldSelections(Month),''
      )
      ,'|'
    )
  )
  ,LightGreen()
  ,RGB(232,232,232)
)
```

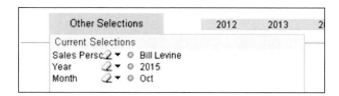

We intentionally use QlikView's native selection color for the background of the **Other Selections** text object. As they review the information dashboard, this helps remind the user of their selection, just like any list box. They can then quickly click **Other Selections** to edit or remove their selection. If they remove their selection, then **Other Selections** turns gray. It would also be reasonable for this to turn white. Although, we've reused QlikView's native color scheme, we may need to create a quick tutorial to help the user understand the application's unique interface.

Creating an interactive tutorial

There are a series of features that users expect to be the same in every application, such as the selection color scheme, bookmarks, cyclical dimensions, fast-type changes, and the ability to export to Excel. However, besides these powerful, generic features, every QlikView application is singular; each has its own data, data model, charts, filters, buttons, and actions. Therefore, if we expect users to get the most out of our applications, then it is often necessary to walk them through the application.

If the application serves one or two users, then the most effective way to show them the application is to give them a short personal tour. However, if we are dealing with an application that has more than a hundred users or has users that are prone to change, then we may want to create more efficient training material. Along with recorded videos lessons, we should also think about something more interactive that forces the user to start playing with the application.

Exercise 9.2

Let's embed a tutorial into our information dashboard and create its first steps in the following exercise:

1. Create variables called `vToggleTutorial` and `vTutorialStepNumber`.

2. Add a text object that uses the following information icon and place it in the upper, right-hand side corner:

   `C:\Qlik\SourceData\1201.Balanced_Scorecard\9.Misc\3.Images\Info_Icon.png`

3. Create a **Set Variable** action in the information icon's text object with `vToggleTutorial` as the **Variable** and the following code as the **Value**:

   `=if(vToggleTutorial = 1, 0, 1)`

4. Create another **Set Variable** action in the information icon with `vTutorialStepNumber` as the **Variable** and with 1 as the **Value**.

5. Let's add *Step 1* and create a text object as it appears in the next figure with this background image and assign it to the **Top** layer in the **Layout** tab, as follows:

```
C:\Qlik\SourceData\1201.Balanced_Scorecard\9.Misc\3.Images\
Bubble_Without_Arrow.png
```

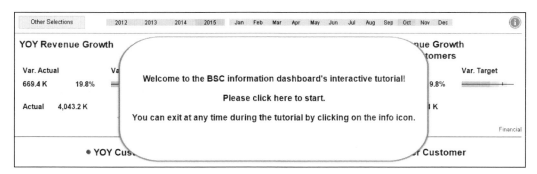

6. Define the text object's **Conditional Show** expression as the following code:

```
=vToggleTutorial and vTutorialStepNumber=1
```

7. In the text object, create a **Set Variable** action with `vTutorialStepNumber` as the **Variable** and 2 as the **Value**.

8. Let's add *Step 2* and create a text object as it appears in the next figure with this background image and assign it to the **Top** layer in the **Layout** tab, as follows:

```
C:\Qlik\SourceData\1201.Balanced_Scorecard\9.Misc\3.Images\
Bubble_UpperCenter_Arrow.png
```

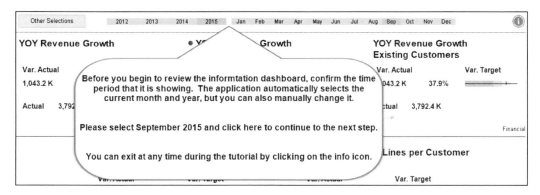

9. Define the text object's **Conditional Show** expression as the following code:

    ```
    =vToggleTutorial and vTutorialStepNumber=2
    ```

10. In the text object, create a **Set Variable** action with `vTutorialStepNumber` as the **Variable** and the following code as the **Value**:

    ```
    =if(only(Year)=2015 and only(Month) = 9, 3, 2)
    ```

11. Let's add *Step 3* and create a text object as it appears in the next figure with this background image and assign it to the **Top** layer in the **Layout** tab, as follows:

    ```
    C:\Qlik\SourceData\1201.Balanced_Scorecard\9.Misc\3.Images\
    Bubble_UpperLeft_Arrow.png
    ```

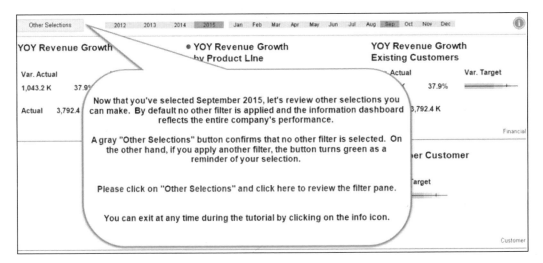

12. Define the text object's **Conditional Show** expression as the following code:

    ```
    =vToggleTutorial and vTutorialStepNumber=3
    ```

13. In the text object, create a **Set Variable** action with `vTutorialStepNumber` as the **Variable** and the following code as the **Value**:

    ```
    =if(vToggleFilterPane, 4, 3)
    ```

We stop the exercise at this point as we create all other steps in the same following way:

*   Describe to the user what they are seeing from their perspective
*   Give the user an action to perform before going on to the next step

The next steps in the interactive tutorial will help the user make a selection in the filter pane and understand that not all the measurements can be filtered by customer or item. It will then describe the measurements and any additional functionality that they may have, such as the detailed pop-ups that we saw in the customer fact sheet, or a link to another sheet or document.

We use the **Set Variable** action in each text object to validate the user's actions and proceed to the next step. We can easily validate user selections and the values in variables, which is what we use to create most custom QlikView UX. We can even validate some native functionality, such as changing a cyclical dimension, with the `GetCurrentField()` function or changing sheets with the `GetActiveSheetID()` function. However, other native functionality, such as exporting to Excel or creating a bookmark cannot be validated through chart functions, so we can only describe their functionality in the tutorial.

In all the other cases, the best practice is to create an interactive tutorial that offers users the chance to learn and remind themselves over and over again through active participation. Just like when somebody shows us how to get somewhere by car and we tend to learn more when we are the driver and not the passenger, we put the user in the driver's seat as we show them how to explore data.

Measuring success with XmR charts

The BSC information dashboards helps us monitor the success or failure of the company's initiatives to reach its objectives and we define this success by creating a target for each measurement. In the dashboard, we've added a series of alerts in the form of dots that only appear when the measurement is below target. For simplicity, we've defined all the targets to be ten percent YOY growth.

> The dots are created using `chr(9679)`.
> You can get Unicode geometric shapes at `http://www.alanwood.net/unicode/geometric_shapes.html`.

Along with reaching our targets, we also should analyze the effect on the sales process using statistical process control. Like all measures, monthly sales naturally fluctuates beyond our control. Therefore, how do we differentiate between variations that are natural and those that are caused by a change in the sales process?

In his book, *Understanding Variation: The Key to Managing Chaos,* Donald Wheeler recommends using the *XmR chart.* The *X* stands for average and the *mR* for moving ranges. It is often used to analyze whether a process is under control or whether process improvement initiatives are successfully reducing process variability. For example, if we were to manufacture bolts, we would notice that each bolt's exact diameter would vary. Some variation is fine as long as the bolt still fits its corresponding screw. However, if the bolts' diameters vary so much so that many have to be scraped and remade, then we confront a costly problem. It is, therefore, important that we monitor the manufacturing process to determine whether its variation is under control. Stephen Redmond includes a recipe to create an XmR chart in QlikView in his book, *QlikView for Developers Cookbook.*

In the previous context, we assumed that a variation is unwanted and that the XmR charts help us eliminate it. However, we can also use it when we want the results of a process to vary. For example, we don't want our sales process to be a controlled process with a predictable result month-in, month-out; but rather, we hope for variation that indicates that our monthly sales average is increasing. We use the XmR chart to eliminate the noise of natural variation and confirm whether this is really happening.

The usage of the XmR chart in this context has been mastered by the *Performance Measure Specialist,* Stacey Barr (staceybarr.com). Her book, *Practical Performance Measurement: Using the PuMP Blueprint for Fast, Easy and Engaging KPIs,* helps companies adopt better performance measurement techniques, such as this version of the XmR chart.

The following chart shows the actual sales and its average, or central line, within a range where sales could naturally vary, or the natural process limit. Unlike rolling averages, the central line only changes under certain conditions. In the chart that results from the following exercise, we change the central line and the range under the following conditions:

- If a value is outside of the natural process limit
- If eight consecutive points lie either above or below the central line (we recalculate the central line and the process limit beginning with the point from which the streak began)
- If ten out of twelve points lie either above or below the central line (we recalculate the central line and the process limit beginning with the point from which the streak began)

  The target that we include in the XmR chart is for the central line to reach. In this way, we can be sure that we've reached it due to real process improvement and not because of natural variation. The target is represented by a single dot in the chart:

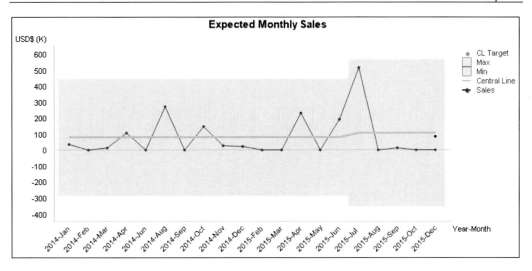

Exercise 9.3

To create an XmR chart, do the following:

1.   Let's create the following variables:

Variables	
Label	**Value**

vPointsGreaterThanCL	`if($1=1`
	`,Above([Central Line]) >`
	`    Below(Sales,0)`
	`,RangeSum(Above([Central Line]) >`
	`    Below(Sales,$(=$1-1))`
	`    ,$(`
	`        $(=if($1=1`
	`        ,'=0'`
	`        ,'vPointsGreaterThanCL($(=$1-1))'`
	`        )`
	`        )`
	`    )`
	`    )`
	`)`

Variables	
Label	**Value**

vPointsLessThanCL	`if($1=1`
	`,Above([Central Line]) <`
	`  Below(Sales,0)`
	`,RangeSum(Above([Central Line]) <`
	`  Below(Sales,$(=$1-1))`
	`  ,$(`
	`    $(=if($1=1`
	`    ,'=0'`
	`    ,'vPointsGreaterThanCL($(=$1-1))'`
	`    )`
	`   )`
	`  )`
	`  )`
	`)`

These variables count the number of points above or below the central line within a given set of points. In QlikView, a conditional expression that is true is equal to -1. So, instead of using `if(Above([Central Line])` `> Below(Sales,0),1,0)`, we just use `Above([Central Line]) >` `Below(Sales,0)` and take care of the negative sign later in the chart.

These variables also use a parameter so that we can count the number of points above or below the central line out of the next six, ten, twenty, or fifty points, and we will be able to use the same variable. We also want to avoid calling the variable for each individual point, like in the following code:

```
-sum($(vPointGreaterThanCL(1)) + $(vPointGreaterThanCL(2))
+ $(vPointGreaterThanCL(3)) + $(vPointGreaterThanCL(4)))
```

Therefore, we make the variable recursive so that we can arrive at the same result as the previous code with only one call:

```
-sum($(vPointsGreaterThanCL(4)))
```

This one call will start by evaluating the point four rows down and then call itself to evaluate the point three rows down. It will continue this process until it reaches the current row.

As a final note, we have to be careful to also make the dollar-sign expansion in the recursive function recursive or else it will get stuck in an infinite loop of dollar-sign expansions and cause QlikView and, possibly, the computer to lock-up.

2. Next, let's create the following combo chart:

Dimensions	
Label	**Value**
Year-Month	Year-Month
Expressions	
Label	**Value**
Sales	`sum({$<_ActualFlag={1}>} [Net Sales USD])`
| Central Line | ```
//if one of the conditions is met then recalculate CL
//check first row
if(RowNo()=1
    ,RangeAvg(Below(Sales,0,count(Total distinct {$<
_ActualFlag={1}>} [Year-Month])))
    ,if(
//check if value outside process limit
    (Sales>above([True Max]) or Sales<above(Min))
        or
//check if next 8 values above or below CL
    ((RangeMax(Above([Central Line])
        ,Below(Sales,0,8))=Above([Central Line])
        or RangeMin(Above([Central Line])
        ,Below(Sales,0,8))=Above([Central Line]))
        and
        count(Total distinct {$<_ActualFlag={1}>}
            [Year-Month])-RowNo()+1 >= 8)
        or
//check if next 10 of 12 values above or below CL
        (-1*$(vPointsGreaterThanCL(12))>=10
            or -1*$(vPointsLessThanCL(12))>=10)
        ,RangeAvg(Below(Sales,0,count(Total distinct {$<
_ActualFlag={1}>} [Year-Month])-RowNo()+1))

//if none of the conditions are met then use previous
//CL
    ,Above([Central Line])
    ))
``` |
| Min | `=[Central Line] - 2.66 * [Moving Range Average]` |
| Max | `=[True Max] - IF(Min<0,0,Min)` |
```

| CL Target | ```
if(RowNo()=1
    ,RangeAvg(Below(Sales,0,count(Total distinct
        {$<_ActualFlag={1}>} [Year-Month]))))*1.1
    ,Above([CL Target])
)
``` |
|---|---|
| True Max | `=[Central Line] + 2.66 *  [Moving Range Average]` |
| Moving Range Average | ```
//if one of the conditions is met then recalculate MR
//check first row
if(RowNo()=1
//check first row
    ,RangeAvg(Below([Moving Range]
        ,0,count(Total distinct
            {$<_ActualFlag={1}>} [Year-Month])))
    ,if(
//check if value outside process limit
    (Sales>above([True Max]) or Sales<above(Min))
        or
//check if next 8 values above or below CL
    ((RangeMax(Above([Central Line])
            ,Below(Sales,0,8))=Above([Central Line])
        or RangeMin(Above([Central Line])
            ,Below(Sales,0,8))=Above([Central Line]))
        and count(Total distinct
        {$<_ActualFlag={1}>}
            [Year-Month])-RowNo()+1 >= 8)
        or
//check if next 10 of 12 values above or below CL
    (-1*$(vPointsGreaterThanCL(12))>=10
        or -1*$(vPointsLessThanCL(12))>=10)
        ,RangeAvg(Below([Moving Range],0,count(Total
            distinct {$<_ActualFlag={1}>}
            [Year-Month])-RowNo()+1))

//if none of the conditions are met then use previous
//CL
    ,above([Moving Range Average])
))
``` |
| Moving Range | `fabs(Above(Sales)-Sales)` |

3. In the **Expressions** tab, define **Sales** as **Line** and **Symbol**, **Central Line** as **Line**, **Min** as **Bar**, **Max** as **Bar**, and **CL Target** as **Symbol** in the **Display Options** section. For the rest of this expression, deselect all the **Display Options** and enable the **Invisible** option.

4. Define the **Background Color** attribute expressions for **Min** as the following code:

```
IF(Min<0,ARGB(100,158,202,225),White())
```

5. Define the **Background Color** attribute expressions for **Max** as the following code:

```
ARGB(100,158,202,225)
```

6. Define the **Background Color** attribute expressions for **CL Target** as the following code:

```
if(
  max(Total [Year-Month]) =
     only([Year-Month])
,black(),black(0))
```

7. In the **Style** tab, enable the **Stacked** option in the **Subtype** section.

8. In the **Presentation** tab, set the **Bar Distance** and **Cluster Distance** to 0 in the **Bar Settings** section.

9. In the **Colors** tab, enable the colors accordingly.

The expressions for **Moving Range Average** and **Moving Range** are invisible, but they help us make cleaner calculations of the natural process limits, **Min** and **Max**. We could also have assigned the expressions to variables and used a dollar-sign expansion. However, we elect to use invisible expressions because they are visual when we export the chart to Excel; therefore, they make the chart easier to debug if we detect any anomaly.

Also, as we use stacked bars to draw the natural process limit's blue background, **Max** only calculates the distance between **Min** and itself. If **Min** is positive, then **Max** will not be equal to the actual maximum process limit. So, we use an invisible expression called **True Max** to evaluate whether any value is beyond the limit. Also, if **Min** is positive, it's background color is white so that only the area between the minimum and maximum limits is blue.

In **Moving Range Average** and **Central Line**, we check the three conditions that indicate the process has changed. If it has changed, then we recalculate these two variables from the point when a streak begins, so we have to be forward looking using the below() function. Also, when we do the recalculation, we do it over all the values from this point onward in the chart. We determine the exact number of values after this point using the following code as the third parameter in the below() function:

```
count(Total distinct {$<_ActualFlag={1}>} [Year-Month])-RowNo()+1)
```

If we were to use a different dimension other than [Year-Month], we would replace it here.

Finally, the explanation for why we use the constant value, 2.66, to calculate the **Min** and **True Max**, and the conditions that indicate a process change can be found in *Understanding Variation: The Key to Managing Chaos, Donald Wheeler*. We can also find a XmR chart recipe in Stephen Redmond's *QlikView for Developers Cookbook* and get a different perspective on how to create one in QlikView. Also, a more detailed explanation about the design and purpose of this chart can be found in Stacey Barr's *Practical Performance Measurement: Using the PuMP Blueprint for Fast, Easy and Engaging KPIs*.

> We incorporate this chart into the customer fact sheet as the expected sales chart. It also serves to align the company's BSC revenue target with the targets for each customer.

Summary

The Balanced Scorecard, the Gestalt principles, and the XmR charts are excellent opportunities to formalize and elevate our level of mastery in QlikView. Like these methods of performance measurement, visualization, and analysis, there are others and there will be more in the future. The XmR chart is the last and most advanced QlikView chart that we will create in this book and it serves as a final example of how far we can go beyond the basics.

Now, it is time for you to go beyond the content of this book and use QlikView in even more advanced and insightful ways. In the next chapter, we will review how to troubleshoot the unknown issues you may encounter in order to help you continue to experiment and lead QlikView into uncharted realms.

10
Troubleshooting Analysis

A paradox development is that we often spend more time troubleshooting QlikView applications than we do developing them. Such is the case that if nobody complains about an incorrect calculation or missing data, then they probably aren't using what we've created. When we become aware of a potential problem, we also tend to invest more time understanding and searching for the anomaly than we do fixing it. Even though this is time well spent when we encounter an issue for the first time, we should avoid repeating the same investigation every time the same issue reoccurs.

In this chapter, we are going to review several common anomalies that occur when we perform data analysis and visualization in QlikView. We document their possible causes and solutions as we would in a knowledge base that we create to help save time when we come across the same issues in the future. Let's cover the following topics to improve our QlikView troubleshooting skills:

- Troubleshooting preparation and resources
- Reporting issues
- Common data model issues
- Common expression issues

Troubleshooting preparation and resources

First, let's go over the general approach that we take when troubleshooting in QlikView and what resources are available to make it easier.

Positive mindset

If we want to create successful QlikView applications, then we have to be prepared to maintain them for many years to come or transfer our knowledge to another person. In reality, we never completely finish great QlikView applications and we continuously transform them when new business questions arise. The troubleshooting, maintenance, corrections, and adjustments that we perform after the initial development is also an excellent opportunity to learn from our mistakes. We also learn what is truly important to business users and constantly improve the quality and value of our work. Therefore, we're better off being positive about post-development work because in the absence of all this feedback, it is hard to master QlikView.

General debugging skills

In addition to a positive mindset, we must possess the basic ability to debug problems. In his book, *Debug It!: Find, Repair, and Prevent Bugs in Your Code (Pragmatic Programmers)*, Paul Butcher proposes the following iterative steps to debug any code:

- Reproduce
- Diagnose
- Fix
- Reflect

These steps also apply to us when we troubleshoot issues in QlikView. Let's take a look at how each applies to QlikView in the following sections.

Reproduce

The first step to debugging any issue is to reproduce it. This allows us to diagnose the anomaly more easily and then confirm that it has been fixed. If we cannot reproduce the issue, then our only recourse is to run a general review of all the components involved and see whether anything stands out as a possible cause. If we don't discover any potential problem, then we could also decide to enable any logging that could help us learn more about the anomaly if it occurs again.

If we can reproduce the issue on our own computer or directly on the server, then it is probable that the issue originates from the QlikView Server, the QlikView document, or the data. Otherwise, if we are only able to recreate the anomaly on the user's own computer, then the problem is usually caused by the network or something in the user's own computer.

For example, QlikView will occasionally not update values that have been cached by the user's web browser. Even though the business user is looking at the same QlikView document with the same selections as those on other computers, they will see different numbers. In this case, we can fix this issue by clearing the user's web browser cache.

Diagnose

Once we reproduce the anomaly, we begin to explore its cause by dividing the problem into smaller parts and independently testing each one. In general, a QlikView document can be broken down into the following parts:

- Script
- Data model
- Expression
- Variable
- Action
- Macro
- Object

In addition to the parts that compose a QlikView document, we also explore the following elements that directly affect it:

- Data
- QlikView Server components
- User's actions

Each of these parts can be recursively divided into smaller and smaller parts. For example, we start by testing an expression and then isolate the problem to its set analysis. We then break this set analysis down into smaller parts and experiment with each set modifier until we find the one that causes the issue.

Also, we often go between various elements in search of the issue's root cause. For example, if we've isolated the issue with an expression to one of its set modifiers but we don't find anything wrong with it, then we look at the set modifier field in the data model. After reviewing the data model, we may need to review the script and, eventually, the source data to find the root cause.

Fix

If we know how to fix an issue's root cause, then we can solve the problem right away. Otherwise, we experiment with possible solutions that we find using the resources that we have available or through our own invention.

We must be careful and take into account that fixing one issue may cause another to appear. Therefore, when we solve our initial problem, we should quickly test anything that may be affected by this fix. We should also define a short list of key tests that we run regardless of whether or not we think that they were affected by the fix. These tests confirm the accuracy and functionality of the most important measurements and charts, along with confirming that the application can successfully reload data.

Reflect

Along with documenting the issue's cause and solution, we reflect on whether the same error could exist in other parts of the application. We also consider whether the same issue may affect other existing QlikView applications or even ones currently being developed. If it does, we analyze if and when to fix them.

We also contemplate on how we can reduce the probability that the same issue will recur. If the mistake is ours, then we should learn from it as soon as we fix it. The issue could also have been caused by some misunderstanding or miscommunication between ourselves and another party. In this case, we work together to find the solution to this issue and continue to work closely to avoid similar ones in the future. In more complex environments, we may also decide to implement tools or processes that help us quickly detect or even prevent future issues.

Resources

There are a number of resources that are available to help us during the whole troubleshooting process, especially when we cannot diagnose or fix the issue. We explore the most popular resources in the next section.

QlikView Help

QlikView Help is filled with examples of both chart and script functions as well as detailed explanations of almost every QlikView property option. This is often the first resource to go to when we have a question about how QlikView works. The sections about set analysis and incremental loads using QVDs are exceptionally well explained.

Local knowledge base

Every QlikView application is unique and we should not just depend on a general QlikView knowledge base to fix our problems. Therefore, we need an efficient way to explore development-related documentation along with past issues and their solutions.

The software that we choose for this job depends on our business's culture. One option is to use a note-taking app, such as Microsoft OneNote (`https://www.onenote.com/`) or Evernote (`https://evernote.com/`) and have the team share a notebook. We can also use a more minimalist notepad approach, such as GitHub Gist (`https://gist.github.com/`). We may also use a wiki, such as Atlassian Confluence (`https://www.atlassian.com/software/confluence`), or a social platform, such as Jive (`https://www.jivesoftware.com/`), which is the same tool that the Qlik Community uses.

Qlik Community

Qlik Community (`https://community.qlik.com/`) is one of Qlik's greatest assets. Developers from various partners, customers, and even Qlik are readily available to help anyone who has a question about QlikView or Qlik Sense. It is also a great repository filled with QlikView tools, templates, and how-to documentation. Let's keep in mind the following tips when we use Qlik Community:

- Search for a solution before asking a question. We rarely ask something that has never been asked before. Our exact data, script, or expression will be different. However, if we diagnose our issue well enough, then we should be able to find a solution to the same problem regardless of the exact example used in the Qlik Community discussion.

- If we don't find an existing solution, then we create a new discussion with a brief explanation of our issue along with a QlikView application that demonstrates the problem. If we can't upload an application, then we should upload one or more of the following artifacts:
    - A screenshot of the issue
    - The current script
    - The current expression code
    - Sample data
    - Our expected results

    An example application or any of these artifacts is far easier to understand than a thousand-word explanation.

- If somebody helps us, then we should mark their answer as either helpful or correct so that they earn points for their contribution. Qlik Community runs on gamification and earning points is like making money. Let's help keep it this way and spend the extra minute that it takes to "pay" those who help us.

- We must avoid the expectation that somebody else will do our work for us. Some so-called QlikView developers create discussions to find people who will develop a report that they themselves are paid to develop. This is an incorrect use of Qlik Community.

- We can't always expect to find answers to our questions in Qlik Community, especially if the issue is related to QlikView Server. We should escalate such issues with Qlik Support.

Qlik Support

If QlikView isn't working as documented in QlikView Help or the issue is related to QlikView Server, then Qlik Support is the best resource to use. Let's keep in mind the following tips when we use Qlik Support:

- Let's not overinflate an issue's priority. If the issue concerns something cosmetic, such as a chart's color, then do not classify it as urgent. Nothing is more annoying or starts a support case on the wrong foot as an overstated priority.

- We can expect the support team to ask us for all sorts of logs, files, and screenshots to help them troubleshoot the issue. Some of the things that they ask us to do or send will appear to be superfluous. However, keep in mind that they are tasked with trying to understand and debug hundreds of issues on remote computers. As this is not any easy job, they do tend to ask for as much information as possible.

- Let's not take advantage of the distance to act overly rude or aggressive. Similar to road rage, technical support rage can be counter-productive. We should promptly and politely answer their inquiries and remain calm.

Reporting issues

An issue that is well-documented is half solved. The fastest, most effective way to report an issue in a QlikView application is to take a screenshot of the anomaly using an image and video screen capture tool like TechSmith's Snagit (`http://www.techsmith.com/snagit.html`). Along with taking an accurate screenshot, it also allows us to easily add annotations that clearly communicate the problem.

In addition to capturing a screenshot, we can also make our troubleshooting process more efficient if we report the anomaly directly into an issue tracking system. BugHerd (`https://www.bugherd.com`) is a bug capturing tool that we can use to track issues or integrate it with other issue trackers, such as Jira or Zendesk. When we capture an issue in BugHerd, it takes an automatic screenshot, records information about the user's system environment, and allows the user to add any additional comment or file.

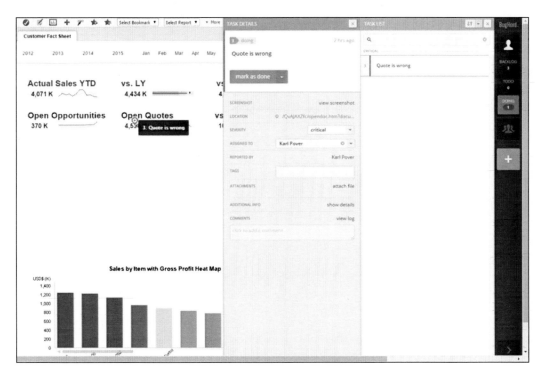

We can create a **BugHerd** project with the hostname, `http://QlikViewServerName/QvAJAXZfc` and use BugHerd's Google Chrome extension in a QlikView Server environment. In case we don't use Google Chrome or we want to report issues directly in the QlikView Desktop WebView, we can use Ralf Becher's BugHerd QlikView document extension (`https://github.com/ralfbecher/QlikView_Extension_BugHerd`). This extension doesn't take an automatic screenshot, but we can easily attach one to the issue.

 In order for the extension to work properly, you may have to add `https://www.bugherd.com` to the list of **Trusted Sites** in the **Security** tab found in **Internet Options**.

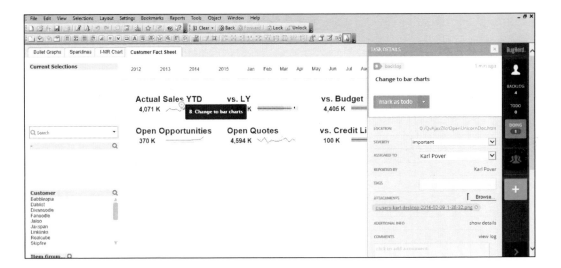

Once we report an issue, we can keep track of its status in a BugHerd project or in one of several issue-tracking tools that integrates with it. The BugHerd project uses the following Kanban board to organize issues:

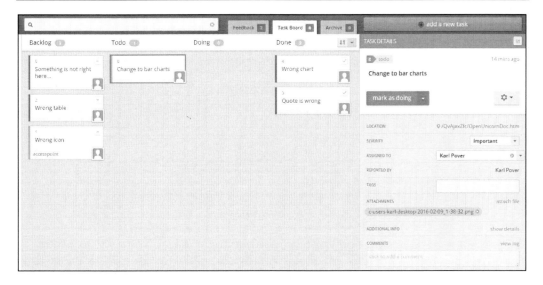

Now that we've reported several issues with help from BugHerd and Snagit, let's review various issues that we commonly encounter in our QlikView applications.

Common QlikView application issues

Along with issues that concern expressions or object properties, we also tend to discover issues related to the data, load script, or model at the moment we create visualizations. Let's review the common issues based on their source in the following sections.

Common QlikView data model issues

We always have to be prepared to review previous steps in the development process when we are diagnosing and fixing a data visualization issue.

All expression values are exactly the same

The following screenshot is an example of what happens when the field that we use as a dimension has no relationship with the field(s) that we use in an expression:

Sales	日 XL _ □
Customer	**Sales**
	16,007,472
Avamba	16,007,472
Dabjam	16,007,472
Divanoodle	16,007,472
Dynabox	16,007,472
Gevee	16,007,472
Miboo	16,007,472

This issue is especially common when we are making quick adjustments to a data model and delete a key field or rename it in only one table, thus breaking an existing link. Another reason may also be that we mistakenly add a field from a legitimate island table to a chart.

When we notice the issue illustrated in the previous chart, our first action should be to look at the data model and confirm whether the tables are linked. If they are in fact not linked, then we fix this error by linking the tables in the script. If they shouldn't be linked, we change either the chart's dimension or expression to contain fields that are related to each other.

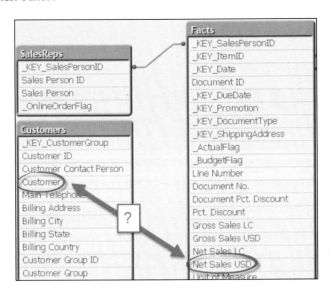

The expression total is not equal to the sum of the rows

When business users export QlikView charts to Excel, they may occasionally report that the sum of the rows in Excel does not match the total in QlikView. For example, the total in the QlikView chart in the following screenshot does not equal the sum of the rows:

Sales	
Item Group	**Sales**
	16,007,472
Doohickey	1,650,772
Gadgets	2,105,677
Gizmos	483,694
Whatchamacallit	11,248,499
Widget	1,363,206

We can confirm this discrepancy when we export the table to Excel and calculate the sum of the rows.

Item Group	**Sales**
Doohickey	1,650,772
Gadgets	2,105,677
Gizmos	483,694
Whatchamacallit	11,248,499
Widget	1,363,206
	16,851,846

A common (and incorrect) fix to this error is to change the way that the chart calculates the total. If we change **Total Mode** to **Sum of Rows**, we will fix the problem in this particular chart, but we are most likely ignoring an underlying problem with the data model. We should always use **Expression Total** as **Total Mode**:

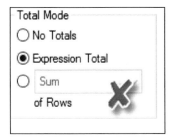

The sum of the rows doesn't equal the expression total because the chart uses fields whose tables have a many-to-many relationship. For example, in the case of the previous example, the error is caused by an item that is assigned to two different item groups. Therefore, two rows in the **Items** table are linked to the same multiple rows in the **Facts** table.

Sales		🖳 XL _ ☐
Item Group	**Item** ○	**Sales**
		844,374
Whatchamacallit	Barndax 126	844,374
Widget	Barndax 126	844,374

If the item is supposed to be in two groups, then we may need to add a business rule to prorate the amount between the two groups. For example, we could prorate the total sales amount so that 40% is assigned to Widgets and 60% to Whatchamacallits. However, in most cases, this issue is caused by poor data quality or an error in the load script.

Duplicate values in a list box

List boxes always show a list of unique values. However, as in the following list box, we sometimes come across ones that appear to contain repeat values. Before we start proclaiming that we've found a bug in QlikView, let's review how QlikView handles data types.

We rarely have to worry about data types in QlikView. For example, we don't declare fields to be a varchar, nvarchar, int, double, or text data type like we do in SQL. In QlikView, the only thing that we have to remember is that every field value is a dual data type or, in other words, it has two values: a string, and a number.

The string value is the one that is displayed in a list box and it's possible that the same string represents different numbers. Even if the numbers have the same string, the list box will not group them into one entry. We force the list box to show the number values that are paired with each string using the following options in the **Number** tab of the list box's property dialog window.

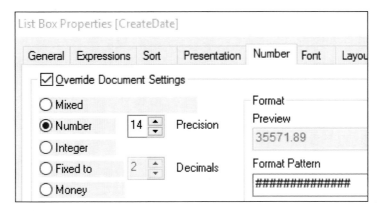

 We maximize the precision of the number in order to avoid scientific notation (e) from appearing when the number is too big or too small.

We can now confirm that the dates represent distinct numbers. We expect the number, 41639, to correspond to the string, 12/31/2013. However, the fractional part of each number is different because it represents a particular time during the day.

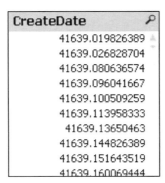

The source of this issue is in the load script and this is where we should fix it. In this case, the `Date()` function, which manipulates the string part of a field value, is used to format a field value that contains a timestamp. Although the string part of the values is formatted as expected, the number part of the value remains the same. If we want to convert a timestamp into a date, then we first need to convert the number part from a decimal into an integer using the `Floor()` function and then format the string using the `Date()` function. For example, we use the following code in the load script to fix our example:

```
...
Date(Floor(CreateDate),'MM/DD/YYYY') as CreateDate,
...
```

Data doesn't match user expectation

Business users often report that the numbers in QlikView don't match their expectations or their own manual reporting. Given QlikView is where they visualize data, this is going to be where they detect numerous data-related issues even if the problem originates in the data source.

When business users report data discrepancies in a stable QlikView application, our first step should be to follow the data's lineage to its source. If the source is correct, then we break down the problem into the different steps of the same path that the data follows until it reaches the user—extraction, transform, model, and visualization.

Along with creating a well-designed folder structure for our QlikView applications, there are a couple of tools that can help us understand the exact path that data takes from its source until its visualization. The first tool is QlikView Governance Dashboard, which you can download from Qlik Market (`https://market.qlik.com/qlikview-governance-dashboard.html`).

QlikView Governance Dashboard offers a complete overview of a QlikView deployment. Once we've entered in the necessary information in the **Configuration** tab and then reloaded the application, we can review data lineage in the **Lineage** tab:

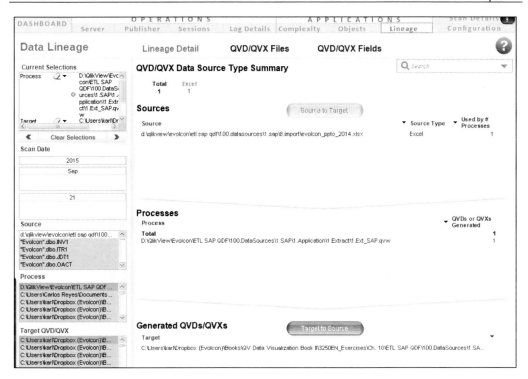

In the **Lineage** tab, we can select a source table in the **Sources** table and take a look at which QlikView files use this table in the **Processes** table. We can also review whether it is used to create a QVD in the **Generated QVDs/QVXs** table. In the same way that we navigate from the source table to its target, we can also begin our analysis by selecting a target table in **Generated QVDs/QVXs** and investigating which process generates it from which possible sources.

The second tool is the `DataLineage` subroutine in **QlikView Components** (QVC) (`https://github.com/RobWunderlich/Qlikview-Components`). In the same way that we used a QVC subroutine to create a master calendar, we first include the QVC library in the load script of the QlikView application whose data lineage we want to analyze:

```
$(Include=..\qvc_runtime\qvc.qvs)
```

Then, we call the `DataLineage` subroutine:

```
CALL Qvc.DataLineage;
```

Finally, we call the `Cleanup` subroutine to clean up any global variables:

```
CALL Qvc.Cleanup;
```

Once we reload the application, we can create the following table that details the application's data lineage:

Target	Source	Creator	Conection String	Load Statement
	c:\users\rob\documents\github\qlikview-components\examples\qvd\customermaster.qvd	C:\Qlikview-NoBackup\Lineage\Loaders\Transform.qvw		
	c:\users\rob\documents\github\qlikview-components\examples\qvd\datafile.csv			
This QVW	c:\users\rob\documents\github\qlikview-components\examples\qvd\dimemployee.qvd	C:\Qlikview-NoBackup\Lineage\Loaders\DBTest.qvw		
	INLINE			
	RESIDENT Qvc.LineageInfo			
c:\users\rob\documents\github\qlikview-components\examples\qvd\customermaster.qvd	C:\Qlikview-NoBackup\Lineage\QVD\DimAccount.qvd	C:\Qlikview-NoBackup\Lineage\Loaders\Transform.qvw		
	C:\Qlikview-NoBackup\Lineage\QVD\DimCustomer.qvd	C:\Qlikview-NoBackup\Lineage\Loaders\Transform.qvw		
c:\users\rob\documents\github\qlikview-components\examples\qvd\dimemployee.qvd	AdventureWorksDW2008R2.dbo.DimAccount	C:\Qlikview-NoBackup\Lineage\Loaders\DBTest.qvw	Provider=SQLOLEDB.1;Integrated Security=SSPI;Persist Security Info=False;Data Sou..	SQL SELECT * FROM AdventureWorksDW2008R2.dbo.DimAccount
	AdventureWorksDW2008R2.dbo.DimCustomer	C:\Qlikview-NoBackup\Lineage\Loaders\DBTest.qvw	Provider=SQLOLEDB.1;Integrated Security=SSPI;Persist Security Info=False;Data Sou..	SQL SELECT TOP 200 * FROM AdventureWorksDW2008R2.dbo.DimCustomer
	AdventureWorksDW2008R2.dbo.DimEmployee	C:\Qlikview-NoBackup\Lineage\Loaders\DBTest.qvw	Provider=SQLOLEDB.1;Integrated Security=SSPI;Persist Security Info=False;Data Sou..	SQL SELECT TOP 25 * FROM AdventureWorksDW2008R2.dbo.DimEmployee

These two tools can help us discover data lineage at the table level. Once we understand it at this level, we analyze it at the field level by reviewing the load scripts of each QlikView application involved in the process.

Once we have an idea of the data lineage, we walk through the following steps to diagnose the issue:

1. Confirm that the source QVDs are being updated properly.

2. Review the data in the QVDs at the extraction level and confirm that it shows the same values as the data source.

3. Review the data in the QVDs at the transform level and confirm that it shows the values we expect. The majority of data issues caused by QlikView will be found at this stage.

4. Review the raw data in the data model and confirm that it shows the values that we expect.

5. Test the visualization that shows the incorrect result in the QlikView application. If the result is calculated by a complex expression or a calculated dimension, then we begin to test it without any set analysis or conditional statements. We then add, bit by bit, the components that were left out and confirm that we see the values that we expect after each change.

Hopefully, we will find the cause of the issue in the first few steps and fix the problem quickly. If not, then at least by the time we get to the visualization, we can be confident that the problem is there.

 In many cases, we can review QVD data more efficiently by opening it in EasyQlik QViewer (`http://easyqlik.com/`) rather than by creating a temporary Qlikview application to load it.

Common QlikView expression issues

Complex analysis can make for complex expressions and potential issues. Let's review the common issues caused by erroneous expressions.

The expression does not calculate every row

The following table shows the total sales and average monthly sales by customer and item group. However, common sense tells us that if a customer has an amount in **Total Sales**, then there should also be an amount listed in **Monthly Sales Avg** and not a null value. It also seems strange that the **Monthly Sales Avg** values that do appear are larger than the **Total Sales** amounts on the same row.

Total Sales			🖫 XL ▬ ☐
Customer	**Item Group**	**Total Sales**	**Monthly Sales Avg**
		16,007,472	1,627,689
Dabjam	Doohickey	81,409	-
Dabjam	Gadgets	315,073	-
Dabjam	Whatchamacallit	1,014,710	1,698,327
Dabjam	Widget	236,594	-
Dynabox	Doohickey	354,863	-
Dynabox	Gadgets	479,882	-
Dynabox	Whatchamacallit	1,418,850	-
Dynabox	Widget	165,172	-
Gevee	Doohickey	287,672	-

In the **Monthly Sales Avg** column, we used the following code with an `aggr()` function to calculate the average monthly sales of each customer and item group:

```
avg(aggr(sum(Amount),Month))
```

However, the dimensions in the `aggr()` function should always include the same fields that are defined as the chart's dimensions. If we change the expression to include `Customer` and `[Item Group]` as parameters to the `aggr()` function, then we get a table with the correct numbers.

```
avg(aggr(sum(Amount),Month,Customer,[Item Group]))
```

Total Sales			凸 XL ▬ ◻
Customer	Item Group	Total Sales	Monthly Sales Avg
		16,007,472	119,517
Dabjam	Doohickey	81,409	81,409
Dabjam	Gadgets	315,073	157,536
Dabjam	Whatchamacallit	1,014,710	101,471
Dabjam	Widget	236,594	78,865
Dynabox	Doohickey	354,863	118,288
Dynabox	Gadgets	479,882	159,961
Dynabox	Whatchamacallit	1,418,850	118,238
Dynabox	Widget	165,172	55,057
Gevee	Doohickey	287,672	95,891

The amounts in the table are not accumulating

Set analysis is a powerful tool, but it is not a panacea for every analytical need. The following table is an example of a chart that cannot be created using set analysis:

Sales - Rolling Accumulation										凸 XL ▬ ◻
Month		Jan		Feb		Mar		Apr		May
Customer	Monthly Sales	Accumulated Sales	Monthly Sales	Accumulated Sales	Monthly Sales	Accumulated Sales	Monthly Sales	Accumulated Sales	Monthly Sales	Accumulated Sales
Thoughtworks	-	-	-	-	-	-	-	-	-	-
Reallinks	9,190	9,190	69,779	78,969	224,949	303,918	141,925	445,843	78,232	524,075
Photospace			83,157	83,157	62,452	145,609	0	145,609	100,039	245,648
Oodoo	73,838	73,838	0	73,838	32,097	105,934	447,278	553,212	0	553,212
Ntag	23,260	23,260	217,224	240,484	57,654	298,138	0	298,138	20,411	318,549
Miboo	-	-	206,563	206,563	22,000	228,563	69,198	297,761	77,856	375,617
Gevee	-	-	635,424	635,424	114,700	750,124	399,328	1,149,452	157,690	1,307,143
Dynabox	22,082	22,082	277,233	299,315	215,190	514,506	157,272	671,778	36,382	708,160
Dabjam	66,857	66,857	0	66,857	20,149	87,006	318,495	405,501	0	405,501

The false belief that set analysis may be the way to create this chart is born from its ability to create the following chart that contains the same monthly and accumulated sales columns:

Customer	Monthly Sales	Accumulated Sales
Reallinks	224,949	303,918
Photospace	62,452	145,609
Oodoo	32,097	105,934
Ntag	57,654	298,138
Miboo	22,000	228,563
Gevee	114,700	750,124
Dynabox	215,190	514,506
Dabjam	20,149	87,006

(Month selector: Jan, Feb, Mar, Apr, May, Jun, Jul, Aug, Sep, Oct, Nov, Dec — Title: Monthy and Accumulated Sales)

In this chart, we used the following code to calculate **Accumulated Sales**:

```
sum({$<Month={"<=$(=max(Month))"}>} [Net Sales])
```

When we use a chart dimension in the set modifier of an expression, we have to understand that this expression can only calculate over the data that corresponds to the dimension value in that row , or in the case of a pivot table, that column. For example, the following chart uses the previous expression in a table with Month as a chart dimension and we can see what happens when we select **March**, as follows:

Sales - Rolling Accumulation (Incorrect)

Month		Jan		Feb		Mar	
Customer		Monthly Sales	Accumulated Sales	Monthly Sales	Accumulated Sales	Monthly Sales	Accumulated Sales
Reallinks		0	9,190	0	69,779	224,949	224,949
Photospace	-	-		0	83,157	62,452	62,452
Oodoo		0	73,838	-		32,097	32,097
Ntag		0	23,260	0	217,224	57,654	57,654
Miboo	-	-		0	206,563	22,000	22,000
Gevee	-	-		0	635,424	114,700	114,700
Dynabox		0	22,082	0	277,233	215,190	215,190
Dabjam		0	66,857	-		20,149	20,149

(Month selector: Jan, Feb, Mar, Apr, May, Jun, Jul, Aug, Sep, Oct, Nov, Dec)

Accumulated Sales does not accumulate because set analysis is not an inter-row function or, in other words, it does not see data outside the data slice defined by the dimension values. Even if we use the `Total` keyword to allow the previous expression to calculate overall data, we still don't get the result that we expect because the maximum `Month` in the set modifier (**March**) is the same for every value in the `Month` chart dimension:

Month		Sales - Rolling Accumulation (Incorrect)						🗷 XL _ ☐
		Month ○		Jan		Feb		Mar
		Customer	Monthly Sales	Accumulated Sales	Monthly Sales	Accumulated Sales	Monthly Sales	Accumulated Sales
Jan Feb Mar Apr May Jun Jul Aug Sep Oct Nov Dec		Reallinks	0	303,918	0	303,918	224,949	303,918
		Photospace	0	145,609	0	145,609	62,452	145,609
		Oodoo	0	105,934	0	105,934	32,097	105,934
		Ntag	0	298,138	0	298,138	57,654	298,138
		Miboo	0	228,563	0	228,563	22,000	228,563
		Gevee	0	750,124	0	750,124	114,700	750,124
		Dynabox	0	514,506	0	514,506	215,190	514,506
		Dabjam	0	87,006	0	87,006	20,149	87,006

The solution in order to create the table at the beginning of this section is to use inter-row functions, such as `above()` or `below()`, in combination with range functions, such as `rangesum()`. We use the following code for **Accumulated Sales**:

```
rangesum(before(sum([Net Sales]),0,ColumnNo(Total)+1))
```

We can also use the **Accumulation** section in the **Expressions** tab if we use a straight table and only one dimension, or we can use a more robust solution such as the **As Of Calendar** we used in *Chapter 3, Financial Perspective*.

Summary

There will always be new issues to investigate and resolve and we have a whole host of resources available to help us troubleshoot them. However, as we resolve more issues and become more experienced, the most important resource will be our own local knowledge base. If we haven't started one yet, then we can start one with the short list of common issues that we reviewed in this chapter.

In the next and final chapter, we will take a look at Qlik Sense, which in some ways allows us to build on the experience that we've gained by working with QlikView. However, in others ways, it challenges us to forget what we know and learn something new.

11
Mastering Qlik Sense Data Visualization

In 2014, Qlik released the first version of its next-generation data visualization and discovery tool, Qlik Sense. Once thought to be a revamped QlikView, it has instead turned out to be part of something larger. Let's take a quick look at what Qlik Sense means to QlikView developers, especially in the area of data visualization.

Let's review the following topics as we devise a plan to master Qlik Sense data visualization:

- Qlik Sense and what it means for QlikView developers
- Qlik Sense visualization extension examples for cross-selling
- Plans and resources to master Qlik Sense data visualization

Qlik Sense and QlikView developers

In short, Qlik Sense is an application to help nontechnical users perform data visualization, analysis, and storytelling, within a governed environment. In this self-service BI tool, users can create simple data models and metric calculations without writing, or even seeing, one line of code. Also, Qlik Sense automatically generates cleaner, more intuitive visualizations without the need to memorize a myriad of property options.

As each new version is released, more and more features will be added to simplify tasks that were once only possible through coding. However, there will still be the need to code the more advanced data models and metric calculations. For example, users with technical aptitude will still be needed to facilitate the advanced analysis that we've seen in this book.

How we develop the load script and chart expressions remains largely unchanged between Qlik Sense and QlikView. Therefore, many data visualization tips and tricks that depend on manipulating the script, a calculated dimension, or a measure expression will work in both tools. On the other hand, Qlik Sense's chart objects have been built anew from the ground up, and they have no direct relationship to the ones in QlikView. Therefore, any tips or tricks that involve a particular chart property option in QlikView will most likely not work in Qlik Sense.

Even though Qlik Sense's chart objects currently offer fewer customizable properties than QlikView's, we can expect more property options to be added with each new version. However, as Qlik Sense's design intent is to be one that nontechnical users can easily manipulate, it would be unlikely that its property dialogs will reach QlikView's complexity or flexibility. Therefore, if we limit ourselves to employ only what is natively available in Qlik Sense, we will fail take full advantage of the opportunities that it offers.

For this reason, it is important that we change how we approach Qlik Sense. There won't be many opportunities to resolve our challenges by playing with an object's property options. So, the primary solution to most of our problems will be to develop a new, or edit an existing *visualization extension*. If we are not familiar with JavaScript, HTML5, and CSS, then we will need to invest time to learn these web programming skills. Such investment is more worthwhile when we see how it can also create opportunities to use Qlik-supported data analytics outside of Qlik Sense.

Qlik Sense is, in fact, only an example of what one could build on top of the **Qlik Analytics Platform (QAP)**, a developer platform that gives us the opportunity to use Qlik's associative data model to address any data analytics need. We can use QAP to embed custom data analytics into existing applications or create our own personalized analytical tools. For example, we can embed data analytics in our customer or supplier portals, our ERP, or our CRM.

Although we can also create extensions in QlikView, we can never make them as powerful as native chart objects. However, QAP gives us access to the same APIs that Qlik uses to develop Qlik Sense, so visualization extensions can be just as robust. In the following section, let's take a look at an example of how we can use a visual extension to help sales representatives discover cross-selling opportunities.

Visualization extension examples for cross-selling

As part of our balanced scorecard in *Chapter 9, Balanced Scorecard*, we purposed giving sales representatives a tool that allowed them to analyze cross-selling opportunities. We've decided to deliver this tool using Qlik Sense for the following two reasons:

- Nontechnical users, such as sales representatives, can create their own analysis
- Developers can create more powerful visualization extensions to help sales representatives discover cross-selling opportunities

The following three Qlik Sense data visualizations were created by Ralf Becher (`http://irregular-bi.tumblr.com/`). The first chart is a table that contains a numerical interpretation of how different items or item sets are related. It was created using a data mining algorithm called Apriori (`https://en.wikipedia.org/wiki/Apriori_algorithm`), which is used to discover associations between items or item sets and is a popular method to perform basket analysis.

Although we can use native QlikView and Qlik Sense to analyze individual associations, a visualization extension using the **Apriori algorithm** offers a more robust solution to discover the statistical correlation of every possible association. Similarly to how we use R-squared along with a scatterplot to understand correlations, we use confidence, support, and lift to understand association rules.

The first row in the table in the next figure evaluates the association rule, "If **Toughfind 1292** and **True Ronlam** are purchased, then **Stathold** is purchased by the same customer." According to this table, **Toughfind 1292**, **True Ronlam**, and **Stathold** are purchased by 22.2% of all customers (**Support**). Also, if a customer purchases **Toughfind 1292**, **True Ronlam**, they are 100% likely to purchase **Stathold** (**Confidence**).

The final column, called **Lift**, takes **Confidence** and divides it by the overall probability that a customer purchases **Stathold**. For example, if **Stathold** was purchased by 50% of all customers, then **Lift** would be 2.00 (100%/50%). This would imply that there is a relationship between purchasing **Stathold**, given that a customer purchases **Toughfind 1292**, and **True Ronlam**. In short, a **Lift** greater than 1.00 implies an association between the item sets, and the greater the lift, the stronger the relationship. In the case of **Toughfind 1292**, **True Ronlam**, and **Stathold**, a lift of 4.5 indicates a strong association:

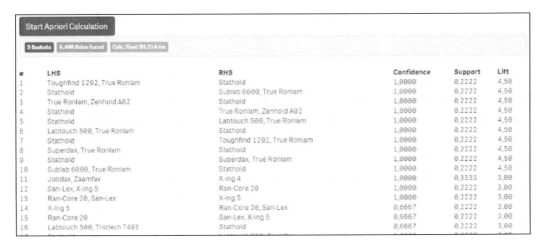

The table in the previous figure alone is powerful, but there are also a couple of visualizations that we can use to detect any customer purchase behavior that would otherwise be difficult to discover. We can also use them to give us a general overview of the data. Again, we use extensions to visualize this complex dataset that would otherwise be laborious, if not impossible, to create through native objects.

The first chart is a network chart that connects customer nodes to the product nodes that they purchase. Along with the *Gestalt principle* of connection to perceive the general connectivity between products and customers, we also use the principle of proximity to detect clusters that may indicate stronger relationships. For example, the remoteness of the customer **Wordtune** indicates how little their purchasing behavior has in common with that of other customers:

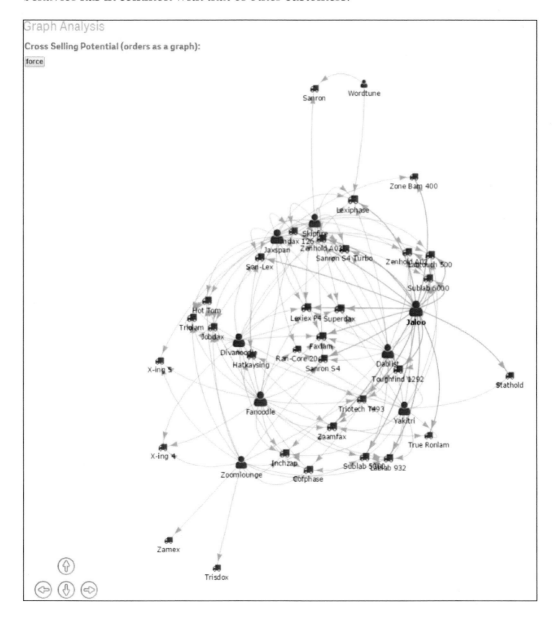

Another example is the cluster of product nodes that comprises the products, **Hot Tom**, **Triolam**, and **Jobdax**, that indicates a strong relationship between them. Upon further investigation, we confirm that all three products are purchased by the same customers. We can find cross-selling opportunities by zooming in on these product clusters to see which customers have yet to purchase one of the related products. We could also do the inverse and zoom in on related customer clusters and look for products which have not been purchased by every related customer.

We could also make cross-selling recommendations based on the length of the path between customer and product nodes. For example, Customer A's path to *Product Y* is three nodes long if *Customer A* purchases the same *Product X* as *Customer B*, who, in turn, also purchases Product Y. Therefore, we may have an opportunity to sell Product Y to Customer A:

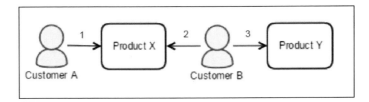

In order to create a list of opportunities based on path distance, we calculate the shortest path between customer and product nodes using the *Dijkstra algorithm* (https://en.wikipedia.org/wiki/Dijkstra's_algorithm) and define the maximum path length that we will interpret as an opportunity. As a longer path implies a weaker relationship between a product and its potential buyer, we create our recommendations using paths of three or fewer nodes. Using the path shown in the previous figure as an example, we will see both Product Y (3-node path) and Product X (1-node path) being recommended for sale to Customer A.

Finally, we visualize these cross-selling recommendations using a Sankey chart that is similar to the one we use in the marketing perspective in *Chapter 4, Marketing Perspective*. In the chart, we can visualize the general extent of the cross-selling opportunities through the connections between customer and product. We can also perceive the number of opportunities per customer and per product through the size of the bar that represents them. For example, the outlier, **Wordtune**, has the most cross-selling recommendations. On the other hand, there are few opportunities to cross-sell the **Zamex** and **Trisdox** products:

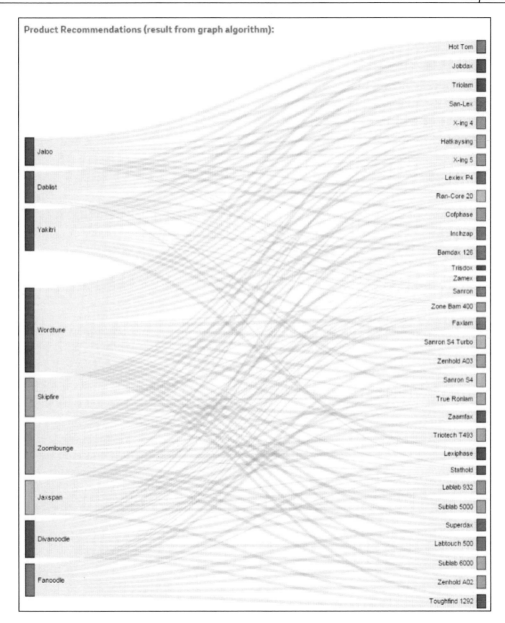

Product Recommendations (result from graph algorithm):

The Qlik Sense visualization extensions that Ralf Becher created are an example of what we can expect from those who want to also become masters in Qlik Sense data visualization. For those of us who have mastered QlikView and are excited to meet this new challenge, let's go over the top-ten list of things that will be important to us during the next year as we learn to master Qlik Sense.

Plan to master Qlik Sense data visualization

For those of us who are QlikView developers with little or no web development experience, developing visualization extensions can seem like a daunting task. However, if we've mastered QlikView's load script and chart expressions and we've learned how to effectively use data visualization and analysis to solve numerous business problems, then this is the most obvious next step forward into growth. Let's review our top-ten list of activities and resources that we need to consider to make this next step successful:

1. Take care of the fundamentals and learn HTML5, CSS, and JavaScript.

    If you have no web development experience or it's been a while since you've actively used HTML, CSS or JavaScript, then brush up on the fundamentals using the free tutorials available at `http://www.w3schools.com/`. If you want something with even more structure, you can also try `http://www.asmarterwaytolearn.com/`.

2. Go through Qlik Sense developer's help documentation and create your first extensions.

    Qlik's online help documentation contains a simple tutorial that will help you get familiar with the development environment called the Dev Hub, and the available APIs, as you create your first extension. As of Qlik Sense 2.2, you can find documentation to create visualization extensions, and the tutorial at `https://help.qlik.com/en-US/sense-developer/2.2/Content/extend.htm`. Make sure that you are looking at the latest version of the documentation by selecting the most current version in the top section of the page. You can also find a similar tutorial by Stefan Walther at GitHub (`https://github.com/stefanwalther/qliksense-extension-tutorial`).

3. Get updated information and insight from the Qlik-related blogs.

    Review the Qlik Branch blog (`http://branch.qlik.com/`) and search for `extensions` at `http://www.askqv.com/` to get the latest news about how to use extensions.

4. Get live advice from the experts.

    There is nothing like live advice from an expert to make sure that you are on the right path. Ralf Becher, who created the extensions used in this chapter, gives online classes on the subject through Q-On Training Center at `http://www.q-on.bi/`.

5. Learn to use a data visualization JavaScript library.

   Keep it simple and learn to use the most popular open source data visualization JavaScript library D3 (`https://d3js.org/`). Along with online examples and documentation, you can also find plenty of books on the subject.

6. Find a visualization to develop and just get started.

   Again, keep it simple and choose a D3 chart that looks fun, and then get started developing it. Even if it's an animated chart that ends up being useless in the end, pick something that will motivate you to show it off.

7. Fail fast and look for answers in the work done by others.

   Although it is important that you try to do it yourself first, when you do get stuck, don't hesitate to look over the example extensions found in `C:\Users\<username>\Documents\Qlik\Examples\Extensions`, or the extensions created by fellow developers in Qlik Branch (`http://branch.qlik.com/`).

8. Contribute to the Qlik Branch.

   Now that you've created the first extension on your own, it's time to give back to the community. As you now know what kind of work is out there in the Qlik Branch (`http://branch.qlik.com/`), choose your next extension based on what you think would be useful to others and upload it. As well as helping others enrich their data visualization, they help you by testing your extension in different environments and giving you feedback.

9. Take the time to learn what will make you better (sharpen the saw).

   Once you have mastered the fundamentals and become a contributor to Qlik Branch, go back to learn anything that you feel would make your development better, such as jQuery, Angular JS, other data visualization JavaScript libraries, or even a predicative analysis JavaScript library.

10. Create an extension to solve a real business need.

    Find a data analysis need that you cannot directly resolve using Qlik Sense and develop a solution using an extension. This could be a user requirement for a visualization that cannot be created using native chart objects, or a data mining example, such as basket analysis. Once you have a customer that demands certain functionality and you are challenged to deliver a solution, you will quickly become a proficient Qlik Sense developer.

Summary

Just as Qlik invested time and resources to rebuild a new, deeper foundation, we also need to take the time to sharpen the saw and become more capable developers. We need to learn web development skills in order to extend Qlik Sense's ability to provide self-service analytics, and make insightful data analysis and visualization ubiquitous using the Qlik Analytics Platform.

Amid all these new developments, QlikView will persist to address the needs of organizations which require analytical applications with a personalized UX. As such, it will continue to be the backbone analytics tools for many customers, and as such, we need to continue to push the limits of what is possible in QlikView. In this book, we've seen examples of how far we can take QlikView within various business perspectives, and by no means is this an exhaustive list of what is possible. Its real intention is to give you the confidence to think outside the box and find the best solution to the user stories that you encounter. When you do, I look forward to learning from you, the QlikView master.

Index

A

Accounts Payable (A/P) 101
Accounts Receivable (A/R) 101
agile development
  about 10, 11
  minimum viable product (MVP) 11
  user story 11
AlchemyAPI
  URL 93
Annual Cost of Goods Sold (COGS) 111
Apriori
  URL 261
AsOfCalendar 53
Atlassian Confluence
  URL 243
Average Inventory Value 111

B

Balanced Scorecard (BSC) Method
  about 209-212
  Business process perspective 213
  consolidated data model 214-217
  customer perspective 212
  financial perspective 212
  growth perspective 214
  internal perspective 213
  learning perspective 214
Balanced Scorecard (BSC) Method,
    dashboard design
  about 218
  Gestalt principles of perceptual
    organization 218, 219

balance sheet 66-70
BugHerd
  URL 245, 246
BugHerd QlikView document extension
  URL 246
bullet graph
  about 192-196
  URL 192
Business Intelligence (BI) 2

C

capital breakdown
  working 111-114
capital data model
  working 102-105
Cash Conversion Cycle (CCC) 110
cash flow statement 70-73
census data
  URL 78
Chi-squared test of independence 147
cross-selling
  visualization extension examples 261-265
CSS
  tutorials, URL 266
Customer Fact sheet
  Agile design 186
  data model, consolidated 182-186
  in QlikView 206
Customer Fact sheet, advanced components
  about 192
  bullet graph 192-196
  sparklines 196, 197

Customer Fact sheet, Agile design
  about 186
  first visualization 192
  user stories, converting into
      visualizations 189-191
  user stories, creating 187
  user story, flow 188, 189
customer profiling
  about 79
  market size analysis 86-89
  parallel coordinates 79-84
  sales opportunity analysis 97-99
  Sankey 84-86
  social media analysis 92-97
Customer Relationship Management (CRM)
      system 75
customer stratification
  by distribution 120-124
  visualizing 125-128

D

dashboard 209
data exploration 2
data model
  about 132
  marketing 76-78
data model, financial perspective
  about 48-51
  AsOfCalendar 53, 54
  balance sheet 66-70
  cash flow statement 70-73
  custom format cell 61-66
  financial report metadata 51-53
  income statement 54-61
data model issues, QlikView
  about 247
  data, requirements 252-255
  expression total 249, 250
  expression values, similarity 248
  list box, duplicate values 250-252
data model, sales perspective
  about 18-21
  case 26
  customer churn 36-41
  data, cleansing 26

  dates and time 27
  dimension value, missing 22, 23
  exercise 31-36
  fact value, missing 24, 25
  master calendar 28-30
  null values 22
  pareto analysis 30, 31
  standardization 26
  unwanted characters 27
data teams and roles
  about 4
  data governance team 8-10
  data research and development
      (R & D) team 5-8
data visualization 2-4
Days Payable Outstanding (DPO) 110
Days Sales of Inventory (DSI) 106, 107
Days Sales Outstanding (DSO) 108-111
Dijkstra algorithm
  URL 264

E

Enterprise Resource Planning (ERP) 17
Evernote
  URL 243
expression issues, QlikView
  about 255
  row calculation, issues 255, 256
  table, amounts 256-258
extensions
  URL 266
Extraction, Transform, and Load (ETL) 14
Extreme Programming (XP) 10

F

filter pane bubble
  creating 225-227

G

GeoQlik
  URL 87
Gestalt principles of perceptual
      organization
  about 218, 219

closure 221
connection 222
continuity 223
enclosure 220
proximity 219
similarity 224, 225
GitHub
URL 266
GitHub Gist
URL 243
governance 44, 46
graphic design
and data visualization 1

H

hash function
URL 159
HTML
tutorials, URL 266
**Human Resource Management Systems
(HRMS) 155**
Human resources data model
about 156-158
dimensions attributes, changing
slowly 158, 159

I

Idevio
URL 87
income statement 55-61
interactive tutorial
creating 228-231
inventory stock levels 115-117
issues
reporting 245, 246

J

JavaScript
tutorials, URL 266
JavaScript library D3
URL 267

K

KliqPlan
about 151
other applications 154
sales forecasts and purchase planning 152
tool extensions, planning 151
URL 151
KliqTable component 153

M

market size analysis 86-92
Microsoft OneNote
URL 243
Minimally Viable Products (MVPs) 3, 11-14

N

**North American Industry Classification
System (NAICS) 78**

O

Online Analytical Processing (OLAP) 2
On-Time and In Full (OTIF)
about 136, 137
bar chart, creating 137, 138
breakdown 139-142
lead time, predicting 142-146
supplier and On-Time delivery,
correlation 149, 150
operations data model
about 131-134
multiple date fields, handling 135, 136

P

parallel coordinates
about 80-84
URL 79
personal behavior analysis 176, 178
personnel productivity, breakdown
about 163
age distribution 164-166

employee retention rate 170, 171
employee training and
        performance 174-176
employee vacation and sick days 172-174
salary distribution 167-170
Point of Sales (PoS) software 17

Q

Qlik Analytics Platform (QAP) 260
Qlik Branch
  URL 126
Qlik Branch blog
  URL 266
Qlik Community 243
QlikMaps
  URL 87
Qlik Market
  URL 93
Qlik Sense
  developers 259, 260
Qlik Sense 2.2
  URL 266
Qlik Sense data visualization
  mastering 266, 267
  URL 261
Qlik Support 244
QlikView
  Customer Fact sheet 206
  developers 259, 260
QlikView application issues
  about 247
  data model issues 247
  expression issues 255
QlikView Components
  URL 28
QlikView Deployment Framework (QDF)
  about 14, 15
  URL 14, 15
QlikView extensions
  and cycle plot 42-44
QlikView Help 242
QlikView User Experience (UX)
  customizing 198
  dynamic data visualization 200-204

regional settings 205
supplementary information,
        quick access 198-200
Q-On Training Center
  URL 266
QVSource
  URL 27

R

regional settings
  about 205
  date and number formats 206
  language 205
report
  aging 117, 118
rotation and average days 106

S

sales opportunity analysis 97-99
Sankey
  about 84-86
  extension, URL 85
Slowly Changing Dimensions (SCD)
        attributes 158
social media analysis 92-97
sparklines 196, 197
Strategy Map 211

T

troubleshooting
  debugging skills, general 240
  diagnose 241
  issue, fixing 242
  local knowledge base 243
  preparing for 239, 240
  Qlik Community 243
  Qlik Support 244
  QlikView Help 242
  reflect 242
  reproduce 240
  resources 242

U

Unicode geometric shapes
  URL 231

W

Word Cloud extension
  URL 96

X

XmR charts
  about 231, 232
  creating 233-236

Y

Year-over-Year (YOY) growth 212
Year-to-Date (YTD) growth 212